# THE NEW FOLGER LIBRARY SHAKESPEARE

Designed to make Shakespeare's great plays available to all readers, the New Folger Library edition of Shakespeare's plays provides accurate texts in modern spelling and punctuation, as well as scene-by-scene action summaries, full explanatory notes, many pictures clarifying Shakespeare's language, and notes recording all significant departures from the early printed versions. Each play is prefaced by a brief introduction, by a guide to reading Shakespeare's language, and by accounts of his life and theater. Each play is followed by an annotated list of further readings and by a "Modern Perspective" written by an expert on that particular play.

Barbara A. Mowat was Director of Research *emerita* at the Folger Shakespeare Library, Consulting Editor of *Shakespeare Quarterly,* and author of *The Dramaturgy of Shakespeare's Romances* and of essays on Shakespeare's plays and their editing.

Paul Werstine is Professor of English at the Graduate School and at King's University College at Western University. He is a general editor of the New Variorum Shakespeare and author of *Early Modern Playhouse Manuscripts and the Editing of Shakespeare* and of many papers and articles on the printing and editing of Shakespeare's plays.

# The Folger Shakespeare Library

The Folger Shakespeare Library in Washington, D.C., a privately funded research library dedicated to Shakespeare and the civilization of early modern Europe, was founded in 1932 by Henry Clay and Emily Jordan Folger, and incorporated as part of Amherst College in Amherst, Massachusetts, one of the nation's oldest liberal arts colleges, from which Henry Folger had graduated in 1879. In addition to its role as the world's preeminent Shakespeare collection and its emergence as a leading center for Renaissance studies, the Folger Shakespeare Library offers a wide array of cultural and educational programs and services for the general public.

EDITORS

BARBARA A. MOWAT
*Former Director of Research emerita*
*Folger Shakespeare Library*

PAUL WERSTINE
*Professor of English*
*King's University College*
*at Western University, Canada*

Folger SHAKESPEARE LIBRARY

*The History of*

# Henry IV

*Part 1*

By
## WILLIAM SHAKESPEARE

EDITED BY BARBARA A. MOWAT
AND PAUL WERSTINE

Simon & Schuster Paperbacks
NEW YORK  LONDON  TORONTO  SYDNEY  NEW DELHI

Simon & Schuster
1230 Avenue of the Americas
New York, NY 10020

Copyright © 1994 by The Folger Shakespeare Library

All rights reserved, including the right to reproduce this book or portions thereof in any form whatsoever. For information, address Simon & Schuster Subsidiary Rights Department, 1230 Avenue of the Americas, New York, NY 10020.

This Simon & Schuster trade paperback edition May 2020

SIMON & SCHUSTER and colophon are registered trademarks of Simon & Schuster, Inc.

For information about special discounts for bulk purchases, please contact Simon & Schuster Special Sales at 1-866-506-1949 or business@simonandschuster.com.

The Simon & Schuster Speakers Bureau can bring authors to your live event. For more information or to book an event, contact the Simon & Schuster Speakers Bureau at 1-866-248-3049 or visit our website at www.simonspeakers.com.

Manufactured in the United States of America

10   9   8   7   6

ISBN 978-1-9821-2251-5
ISBN 978-1-5011-4993-1 (ebook)

# From the Director of the Folger Shakespeare Library

It is hard to imagine a world without Shakespeare. Since their composition more than four hundred years ago, Shakespeare's plays and poems have traveled the globe, inviting those who see and read his works to make them their own.

Readers of the New Folger Editions are part of this ongoing process of "taking up Shakespeare," finding our own thoughts and feelings in language that strikes us as old or unusual and, for that very reason, new. We still struggle to keep up with a writer who could think a mile a minute, whose words paint pictures that shift like clouds. These expertly edited texts, presented here with accompanying explanatory notes and up-to-date critical essays, are distinctive because of what they do: they allow readers not simply to keep up, but to engage deeply with a writer whose works invite us to think, and think again.

These New Folger Editions of Shakespeare's plays are also special because of where they come from. The Folger Shakespeare Library in Washington, D.C., where the Editions are produced, is the single greatest documentary source of Shakespeare's works. An unparalleled collection of early modern books, manuscripts, and artwork connected to Shakespeare, the Folger's holdings have been consulted extensively in the preparation of these texts. The Editions also reflect the expertise gained through the regular performance of Shakespeare's works in the Folger's Elizabethan Theatre.

I want to express my deep thanks to editors Barbara Mowat and Paul Werstine for creating these indispensable editions of Shakespeare's works, which incorporate the best of textual scholarship with a richness of commentary that is both inspired and engaging. Readers who want to know more about Shakespeare and his plays can follow the paths these distinguished scholars have trod by visiting the Folger itself, where a range of physical and digital resources (available online) exists to supplement the material in these texts. I commend to you these words, and hope that they inspire.

*Michael Witmore*
Director, Folger Shakespeare Library

# Contents

# Editors' Preface

In recent years, ways of dealing with Shakespeare's texts and with the interpretation of his plays have been undergoing significant change. This edition, while retaining many of the features that have always made the Folger Shakespeare so attractive to the general reader, at the same time reflects these current ways of thinking about Shakespeare. For example, modern readers, actors, and teachers have become interested in the differences between, on the one hand, the early forms in which Shakespeare's plays were first published and, on the other hand, the forms in which editors through the centuries have presented them. In response to this interest, we have based our edition on what we consider the best early printed version of a particular play (explaining our rationale in a section called "An Introduction to This Text") and have marked our changes in the text—unobtrusively, we hope, but in such a way that the curious reader can be aware that a change has been made and can consult the "Textual Notes" to discover what appeared in the early printed version.

Current ways of looking at the plays are reflected in our brief introductions, in many of the commentary notes, in the annotated lists of "Further Reading," and especially in each play's "Modern Perspective," an essay written by an outstanding scholar who brings to the reader his or her fresh assessment of the play in the light of today's interests and concerns.

As in the Folger Library General Reader's Shakespeare, which this edition replaces, we include explanatory notes designed to help make Shakespeare's language clearer to a modern reader, and we place the notes on the page facing the text that they explain. We also follow the earlier edition in including illustrations —of objects, of clothing, of mythological figures—from books and manuscripts in the Folger Library collection. We provide fresh accounts of the life of Shakespeare, of the publishing of his plays, and of the theaters in which his plays were performed, as well as an introduction to the text itself. We also include a section called "Reading Shakespeare's Language," in which we try to help readers learn to "break the code" of Elizabethan poetic language.

For each section of each volume, we are indebted to a host of generous experts and fellow scholars. The "Reading Shakespeare's Language" sections, for example, could not have been written had not Arthur King, of Brigham Young University, and Randal Robinson, author of *Unlocking Shakespeare's Language,* led the way in untangling Shakespearean language puzzles and shared their insights and methodologies generously with us. "Shakespeare's Life" profited by the careful reading given it by S. Schoenbaum, "Shakespeare's Theater" was read and strengthened by Andrew Gurr and John Astington, and "The Publication of Shakespeare's Plays" is indebted to the comments of Peter W. M. Blayney. Among the texts we consulted in editing *Henry IV, Part 1,* we found David Bevington's edition of the play in the Oxford Shakespeare series particularly helpful. We, as editors, take sole responsibility for any errors in our editions.

We are grateful to the authors of the "Modern Perspectives"; to Leeds Barroll and David Bevington for their generous encouragement; to the Huntington and Newberry Libraries for fellowship support; to King's College for the grants it has provided to Paul Werstine; to the Social Sciences and Humanities Research Council of Canada, which provided him with a Research Time

Stipend for 1990–91; to Paul Menzer and Brandon Miller, who drafted "Further Reading" material; to Margaret Horsley for help with Oldcastle and Falstaff; to the University of British Columbia (and especially to Anthony Dawson and Herbert Rosengarten for their hospitality during a crucial stage in the preparation of this text); and to the Folger Institute's Center for Shakespeare Studies for its fortuitous sponsorship of a workshop on "Shakespeare's Texts for Students and Teachers" (funded by the National Endowment for the Humanities and led by Richard Knowles of the University of Wisconsin), a workshop from which we learned an enormous amount about what is wanted by college and high school teachers of Shakespeare today.

Our biggest debt is to the Folger Shakespeare Library: to Werner Gundersheimer, Director of the Library, who made possible our edition; to Jean Miller, the Library's Art Curator, who combs the Library holdings for illustrations, and to Julie Ainsworth, Head of the Photography Department, who carefully photographs them; to Peggy O'Brien, Director of Education, who gave us expert advice about the needs being expressed by Shakespeare teachers and students (and to Martha Christian and other "master teachers" who used our texts in manuscript in their classrooms); to the staff of the Academic Programs Division, especially Mary Tonkinson, Lena Cowen Orlin, Amy Adler, Molly Haws, and Jessica Hymowitz; and, finally, to the staff of the Library Reading Room, whose patience and support are invaluable.

Barbara A. Mowat and Paul Werstine

King Henry IV.
From John Speed, *A prospect of the most famous part of the world* (1631).

# Shakespeare's *Henry IV, Part 1*

At the center of *Henry IV, Part 1* (which is called "Part 1" because it has a sequel, "Part 2") are several family relationships—primarily pairs of fathers and sons, but also brothers, husbands and wives, and uncles and nephews. King Henry and his son, Prince Hal, form one major father-son pair. When the play opens, Henry is in despair because Hal lives a dissolute life. Henry himself has won (rather than inherited) the throne of England; Hal's way of living can be seen as calling into public question Henry's and his family's right to the throne. In seeming contrast to the king and prince are the father-son pair of Hotspur (Lord Henry Percy) and his father, the earl of Northumberland. Hotspur accomplishes deeds that "a prince can boast of"—as Henry is reminded—and Henry openly envies Northumberland "his Harry," wishing that it could be proved that the two sons had been exchanged in their cradles so that Henry could be rid of Hal and could claim the gallant Hotspur as his own.

In the meantime, Hal himself has entered into a quasi-father-son relationship with a disreputable knight, Sir John Falstaff. Much of the action of the play can be seen as the interactions of these pairs of fathers and sons. The fathers, Henry and Northumberland (along with Northumberland's brother, Worcester), fight for control of England while Henry and Falstaff seem to fight for Hal's love and loyalty. At the same time, the sons Hal and Hotspur fight for the place of honor in the eyes of the English nobility.

Another strand of action centers on a different set of family relationships. Hotspur's stand against King Henry, engineered by his uncle Worcester and colluded in by Hotspur's father, focuses on Hotspur's brother-in-law, Mortimer. As this play presents English history, this is the Mortimer whom Richard II had proclaimed heir to the throne. Mortimer has led "the men of Hereford-shire" to fight against the great Welsh magician Owen Glendower, has been defeated and captured, and has married Glendower's daughter. King Henry has declared Mortimer's defeat a defection and, because Mortimer is now his captor's son-in-law, has pronounced Mortimer a traitor whom Henry will not ransom. Hotspur, in declaring war on England's king, sees himself as fighting for the honor and rescue of his wife's brother.

This play's highlighting of family patterns and family struggles is most clear in such scenes as 2.4 and 3.2, the two father-son scenes in mid-play. The first, parodic scene is staged in the tavern when Falstaff and Hal pretend to be father and son, followed by the second scene played out in earnest between King Henry and Prince Hal. Between these two scenes comes 3.1, the remarkable domestic scene in Wales, where Mortimer, the supposed heir to the throne, and Hotspur, valiant leader of rebel forces, are presented primarily as husbands and brothers-in-law and where Owen Glendower, legendary wizard and military commander, is presented as doting father and concerned father-in-law.

Perhaps it is no coincidence that several of the important details that, in the play, bring father-son and other family relationships into prominence are Shakespeare's own creations—are not found, that is, in the chronicles of English history that provide the play's historical narrative. To mention only a few examples: Hal's offer to fight Hotspur in single combat, Hal's rescue of his father in battle, and Hal's final battle with Hotspur—none of these appear in the chronicles. (The fact that Hal and

Hotspur are presented in the play as being the same age, when, in fact, Hotspur was older than King Henry himself, may not be a change that Shakespeare himself made, but may instead indicate that Shakespeare was here following Samuel Daniel's *Civil Wars* [1595] rather than Holinshed's *Chronicles*.) Second, the domestic scene in Wales depends upon major changes of chronicle material. In the chronicles, the meeting to divide the kingdom and to draw up the indentures was not attended by the rebel lords but was conducted by their representatives, and it did not take place at Glendower's home but at the residence of the archbishop of Bangor. Thus the presentation of the rebel lords in a family setting required a significant rewriting of history.

Such rewriting and the play's resulting focus on family relationships have two important effects. First, they pull us into the play: Henry, Hal, and Hotspur are not so much distant historical figures as they are persons caught up in relationships and struggles that resemble family situations even today. Second, the play's focus on the family reminds us that the wars for control of England, Scotland, and Wales in the fourteenth and fifteenth centuries were basically family struggles. When the oldest son of King Edward III died prematurely, leaving behind an infant son to inherit the kingdom (as Richard II) at Edward III's death, the stage was set for the bloody centuries that followed, as brothers, cousins, and nephews fought each other to win and retain the tantalizing prize of the crown.

After you have read the play, we invite you to turn to the back of this book and read *"Henry IV, Part 1: A Modern Perspective,"* by Professor Alexander Leggatt of the University of Toronto. You will also find at the back of the book a brief discussion of Sir John Falstaff and his historical model, Sir John Oldcastle.

# Reading Shakespeare's Language

For many people today, reading Shakespeare's language can be a problem—but it is a problem that can be solved. Those who have studied Latin (or even French or German or Spanish) and those who are used to reading poetry will have little difficulty understanding the language of Shakespeare's poetic drama. Others, though, need to develop the skills of untangling unusual sentence structures and of recognizing and understanding poetic compressions, omissions, and wordplay. And even those skilled in reading unusual sentence structures may have occasional trouble with Shakespeare's words. Four hundred years of "static" intervene between his speaking and our hearing. Most of his immense vocabulary is still in use, but a few of his words are not, and, worse, some of his words now have meanings quite different from those they had in the sixteenth century. In the theater, most of these difficulties are solved for us by actors who study the language and articulate it for us so that the essential meaning is heard—or, when combined with stage action, is at least *felt*. When reading on one's own, one must do what each actor does: go over the lines (often with a dictionary close at hand) until the puzzles are solved and the lines yield up their poetry and the characters speak in words and phrases that are, suddenly, rewarding and wonderfully memorable.

## Shakespeare's Words

As you begin to read the opening scenes of a play by Shakespeare, you may notice occasional unfamiliar words. Some are unfamiliar simply because we no longer use them. In the opening scenes of *1 Henry IV,* for example, you will find the words *therefor* (i.e., for that purpose), *marry* (a mild oath, originally an oath "by the Virgin Mary"), *an* (i.e., if), *jerkin* (i.e., a close-fitting jacket), and *zounds* (an oath "by Christ's wounds"). Words of this kind are explained in notes to the text and will become familiar the more of Shakespeare's plays you read.

In *1 Henry IV,* as in all of Shakespeare's writing, more problematic are the words that we still use but that we use with a different meaning. In the opening scenes of *1 Henry IV,* for example, the word *sullen* has the meaning of "dull," *close* is used where we would say "struggle," *surprised* where we would say "captured," and *riot* where we would say "dissipation, loose living." Such words will be explained in the notes to the text, but they, too, will become familiar as you continue to read Shakespeare's language.

Some words are strange not because of the "static" introduced by changes in language over the past centuries but because these are words that Shakespeare is using to build a dramatic world that has its own space, time, history, and background mythology. In *1 Henry IV,* within the larger world of early-fifteenth-century England and Wales that the play creates, Shakespeare uses one set of words to construct Henry IV's court and the stately houses and courtly battleground confrontations of Henry's time, and he uses a second set of words to construct the lower-class world of thieves, vintners, hostesses, hostlers, and setters who frequent the taverns of Eastcheap and the inns along "the London road." The courtly world of Henry IV and his allies and enemies is built through references to "Plantagenet," to "revolted Percy," and to "Richard that dead is"; to "swift Severn," to "Holmedon," and to "the sepulcher of Christ"; to

Eastcheap.

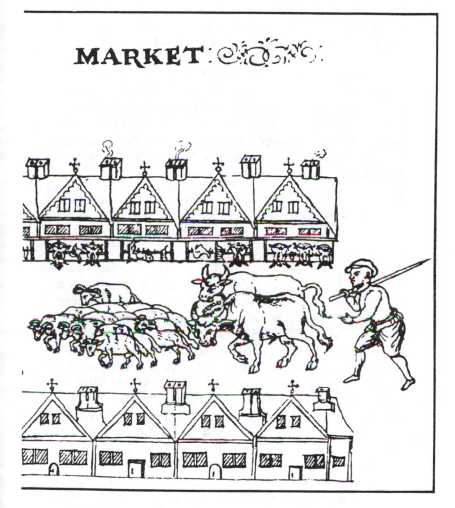

From Hugh Alley, *A caveat for the city of London* (1598).

"new broils . . . commenced in stronds afar remote," to the "furious close of civil butchery," and to "the detested blot of murderous subornation." This is the world inhabited by Henry IV, Hotspur, Northumberland, and Worcester—and, when he chooses, by Prince Hal. The tavern world of Falstaff and his fellows is created through references to Moorditch, Gad's Hill, and Eastcheap, to sack, to bawds, to leaping-houses, to buff jerkins and robes of durance, and to Phoebus and Diana. This also is Prince Hal's world, so long as he chooses to be a part of it. The words that create these two language worlds will become increasingly familiar to you as you read further into the play.

## Shakespeare's Sentences

In an English sentence, meaning is quite dependent on the place given each word. "The dog bit the boy" and "The boy bit the dog" mean very different things, even though the individual words are the same. Because English places such importance on the positions of words in sentences, on the way words are arranged, unusual arrangements can puzzle a reader. Shakespeare frequently shifts his sentences away from "normal" English arrangements—often to create the rhythm he seeks, sometimes to use a line's poetic rhythm to emphasize a particular word, sometimes to give a character his or her own speech patterns or to allow the character to speak in a special way. When we attend a good performance of a play, the actors will have worked out the sentence structures and will articulate the sentences so that the meaning is clear. In reading for yourself, do as the actor does. That is, when you become puzzled by a character's speech, check to see if words are being presented in an unusual sequence.

Look first for the placement of subject and verb. Shakespeare often places the verb before the subject (e.g., instead of "He goes" we find "Goes he") or places the subject between the two parts of a verb (e.g., instead of "We will go" we find "Will we go"). In *1 Henry IV*, we find an inverted subject-verb construction in King Henry's *"Find we* a time" (1.1.2) as well as in his "a power of English *shall we levy*" (1.1.22). Prince Hal's "Yet herein *will I imitate* the sun" (1.2.204) is another example of inverted subject and verb.

Such inversions rarely cause much confusion. More problematic is Shakespeare's frequent placing of the object before the subject and verb (e.g., instead of "I hit him" we might find "Him I hit"). King Henry's "two-and-twenty knights / Balked in their own blood, did Sir Walter see" (1.1.68–69) is an example of such an inversion (the normal order would be "Sir Walter did see two-and-twenty knights balked in their own blood"). Another example is King Henry's "The prisoners / Which he in this adventure hath surprised / To his own use he keeps" (1.1.91–93), where the normal order would be "He keeps to his own use the prisoners which he hath surprised in this adventure."

Inversions are not the only unusual sentence structures in Shakespeare's language. Often in his sentences words that would normally appear together are separated from each other. (Again, this is often done to create a particular rhythm or to stress a particular word.) Take, for example, King Henry's "The edge of war, like an ill-sheathèd knife, / No more shall cut his master" (1.1.17–18); here the phrase "like an ill-sheathèd knife" separates the subject ("The edge of war") from its verb ("shall cut"). Or take Prince Hal's lines: "My reformation, glitt'ring o'er my fault, / Shall show more goodly and attract more eyes" (1.2.220–21), where the normal construction "My reformation shall show more goodly" is interrupted by the phrase "glitt'ring o'er my fault." Hotspur uses a similar construction when he says "I then, all smarting with my wounds being cold, / To be so pestered with a popinjay, / Out of my grief and my impatience / Answered neglectingly I know not what" (1.3.50–53), where the basic sentence elements ("I answered neglectingly") are separated by several interrupting phrases. In order to create for yourself sentences that seem more like the English of everyday speech, you may wish to rearrange the words, putting together the word clusters ("the edge of war shall cut," "my reformation shall show," "I answered neglectingly"). You will usually find that the sentence will gain in clarity but will lose its rhythm or shift its emphasis.

Locating and rearranging words that "belong together" is especially necessary in passages that separate basic sentence elements by long delaying or expanding interruptions—a structure that is used frequently in *1 Henry IV*. When King Henry describes the civil strife that has just ended and the hoped-for crusade to the Holy Land, he uses such an interrupted construction:

> *Those opposèd eyes,*
> *Which,* like the meteors of a troubled heaven,
> All of one nature, of one substance bred,
> *Did lately meet in* the intestine shock
> And furious close of *civil butchery,*
> *Shall now,* in mutual well-beseeming ranks,
> *March all one way....*          (1.1.9–15)

Here the basic sentence elements ("Those opposed eyes which did lately meet in civil butchery shall now march all one way") are interrupted by phrases and figures of speech that characterize the formal rhetoric of King Henry. Hotspur uses an interrupted construction (as well as a verb-object inversion) when attacking his father and his uncle for their past and present behaviors:

> But shall it be that you that set the crown
> Upon the head of this forgetful man
> And for his sake wear the detested blot
> Of murderous subornation—shall it be
> That you *a world of curses undergo,*
> Being the agents or base second means,
> The cords, the ladder, or the hangman rather?
>
> (1.3.164–70)

Here the basic sentence elements ("But shall it be that you undergo a world of curses") are interrupted by details that catch the audience up in Hotspur's narrative of the past, reminding the audience of a story that they would have known from Shakespeare's *Richard II* and giving the audience Hotspur's perspective on that story. The sentence structure forces the audience to attend to the narrative details while listening for the sentence's completion. In *1 Henry IV* as in many other of Shakespeare's plays (*Hamlet,* for instance), long interrupted sentences are used frequently, sometimes to catch the audience up in the narrative and sometimes as a characterizing device.

In some of his plays (again, *Hamlet* is a good example), rather than separating basic sentence elements, Shakespeare simply holds them back, delaying them until much subordinate material has already been given. This kind of delaying structure is rarely used in *1 Henry IV*—though we do find it in such speeches as Prince Hal's "Unless hours were cups of sack, and minutes capons, and clocks the tongues of bawds, and dials the signs of leaping-houses, and the blessed sun himself a fair hot wench in flame-colored taffeta, *I see no reason why thou shouldst be so superfluous to demand the time of the day"* (1.2.7–13), where a "normally constructed" English sentence would have begun with the basic sentence elements ("I see no reason . . .").

More often in *1 Henry IV*, we find very long sentences where the basic sentence elements are distributed over several lines as detail piles on detail. King Henry, Prince Hal, and Hotspur all use such sentences, though each speaks sentences constructed in ways that characterize the particular speaker. An example of such a sentence appears in King Henry's opening speech:

>                      *Therefore, friends,*
> *As far as to the sepulcher of Christ—*
> Whose soldier now, under whose blessèd cross
> We are impressèd and engaged to fight—
> *Forthwith a power of English shall we levy,*
> Whose arms were molded in their mothers' womb
> To chase these pagans in those holy fields
> Over whose acres walked those blessèd feet
> Which fourteen hundred years ago were nailed
> For our advantage on the bitter cross.
>                         (1.1.18–27)

Finally, in many of Shakespeare's plays, sentences are sometimes complicated not because of unusual structures or interruptions but because Shakespeare omits words and parts of words that English sentences normally require. (In conversation, we, too, often omit words. We say "Heard from him yet?" and our hearer supplies the missing "Have you.") Frequent reading of Shakespeare—and of other poets—trains us to supply such missing words. In his later plays, Shakespeare uses omissions both of verbs and of nouns to great dramatic effect. In *1 Henry IV* omissions are extremely rare and seem to be used to affect the tone of the speech or for the sake of speech rhythm. For example, in King Henry's "But let him from my thoughts" (1.1.90) the omission of the word "go" creates a regular iambic pentameter line and perhaps conveys some of the intensity of the king's feelings. A similar rhythmic and tonal effect is created in Hotspur's "I will not send them. I will after straight / And tell him so" (1.3.128–29), where "after straight" is used in place of "go after him straightway" (i.e., immediately).

## Shakespearean Wordplay

Shakespeare plays with language so often and so variously that entire books are written on the topic. Here we will mention only two kinds of wordplay, puns and metaphors. A pun is a play on words that sound the same but that have different meanings, or—as is usually the case in *1 Henry IV*—on a single word that has more than one meaning. In *1 Henry IV* 1.2.18–22, for example, Falstaff plays on four different meanings of the word "grace" in a dialogue exchange with Prince Hal, first addressing him by the title "thy Grace," then arguing that this is an inaccurate title, since "grace thou wilt have none" (where "grace" means both "virtue" and "God's grace"); this series of puns concludes with Falstaff's claim that Hal will have "not so much" grace "as will serve to be a prologue to an egg and butter"— where a "grace" is a short prayer before a meal. A few lines later, Falstaff puns again, saying to Hal, "let men say we be men of good government, being governed, as the sea is, by our noble and chaste mistress the moon, under whose countenance we steal" (1.2.28–31)—

where "under whose countenance we steal" means both "beneath whose face we move stealthily" and "under whose protection we commit theft."

Hotspur is another character in *1 Henry IV* whose language sometimes employs puns. When, for example, Hotspur defends the behavior of Mortimer, claiming that Mortimer's many wounds received in the battle prove that he is no traitor, Hotspur says, "Never did bare and rotten policy / Color her working with such deadly wounds" (1.3.111–12), where the verb "color" means (1) misrepresent and (2) paint, as with a cosmetic (with the verb "color" referring literally to Mortimer's staining himself with blood). Because of the presence in *1 Henry IV* of Falstaff and Hotspur, this play, although a history, uses puns frequently. Thus the language needs to be listened to carefully if one is to catch all its meanings.

A metaphor is a play on words in which one object or idea is expressed as if it were something else, something with which it shares common features. In the opening lines of *1 Henry IV*,

> So shaken as we are, so wan with care,
> Find we a time for frighted peace to pant
> And breathe short-winded accents of new broils
> To be commenced in strands afar remote.
> No more the thirsty entrance of this soil
> Shall daub her lips with her own children's blood,
>
> 						(1.1.1–6)

metaphoric language is used to describe the horrors of the civil war just ended. The first metaphor (in lines 2–3) presents peace as a hunted animal trying to catch its breath; the second (in lines 5–6) pictures England, with its blood-stained soil, as a mother whose lips are red with the blood of her own children.

Later in the play, Worcester uses metaphoric language when he tells Hotspur about the highly secret information Worcester is about to reveal:

> And now I will unclasp a secret book,
> And to your quick-conceiving discontents
> I'll read you matter deep and dangerous. . . .
>                                  (1.3.193–95)

Here the telling of information is imaged as the opening of, and reading from, a clandestine book that contains dangerous material.

Hotspur responds to Worcester's language with metaphoric language of his own. He declares himself ready to seek for honor no matter what the danger; his declaration takes the form of a metaphor in which honor is a heroine in need of a hero's rescue:

> By heaven, methinks it were an easy leap
> To pluck bright honor from the pale-faced moon,
> Or dive into the bottom of the deep,
> Where fathom line could never touch the ground,
> And pluck up drownèd honor by the locks. . . .
>                                  (1.3.206–10)

In *1 Henry IV*, metaphor is most often used—as it is here in Hotspur's speech—to lift a character's rhetoric to a "high style," demonstrating his linguistic powers, his control over language. Thus this play differs from many of Shakespeare's plays in which metaphor is used when the idea being conveyed is hard to express, or when a character seems to find an emotion beyond normal expression. In such plays, the speaker is given metaphorical language that helps to carry the idea or the feeling to his or her listener—and to the audience.

## Implied Stage Action

Finally, in reading Shakespeare's plays we should always remember that what we are reading is a performance script. The dialogue is written to be spoken by actors who, at the same time, are moving, gesturing, picking up objects, weeping, shaking their fists. Some stage action is described in what are called "stage directions"; some is suggested within the dialogue itself. We need to learn to be alert to such signals as we stage the play in our imaginations. When, in *1 Henry IV* 2.4.389–400, Falstaff says to Prince Hal, as they stage their rehearsal of Hal's visit to King Henry, "This chair shall be my state," it is clear that Falstaff here takes his seat; when Hal responds, "Here is my leg," one knows from the language of the time that this means that Hal here makes an elaborate bow. At several places in *1 Henry IV*, signals to the reader are not quite so clear. When, in 3.1.220–76, Glendower says to Mortimer, "She bids you on the wanton rushes lay you down / And rest your gentle head upon her lap," Mortimer's response, "With all my heart I'll sit and hear her sing," suggests that at some point Mortimer sits down and perhaps rests his head in his wife's lap. Hotspur's order to his own wife, which follows immediately ("Come, Kate, thou art perfect in lying down. / Come, quick, quick, that I may lay my head in thy lap"), probably indicates that Hotspur and his wife also sit; Lady Percy's response, "Go, you giddy goose," casts some doubt on whether she does in fact obey him, but her remark a few lines later, "Lie still, you thief, and hear the lady sing in Welsh," makes the stage action fairly clear. But there is no hint in the dialogue about when any of the husbands and wives stand. Thus the director and the actors—and we as readers—must choose the moment for Hotspur, for example, to stand,

and must decide whether or not his wife stands at the same time or whether he walks off and leaves her sitting—decisions that may have a large impact on our response to these characters. (Because the dialogue in this scene gives so little direction, we have chosen not to insert stage directions for the characters' movements.)

Learning to read the language of stage action repays one many times over when one reaches a crucial scene like 5.4, with its series of sword fights, deaths, and mock deaths—a scene in which imagined stage action vitally affects our response to the play.

It is immensely rewarding to work carefully with Shakespeare's language so that the words, the sentences, the wordplay, and the implied stage action all become clear—as readers for the past four centuries have discovered. It may be more pleasurable to attend a good performance of a play—though not everyone has thought so. But the joy of being able to stage one of Shakespeare's plays in one's imagination, to return to passages that continue to yield further meanings (or further questions) the more one reads them—these are pleasures that, for many, rival (or at least augment) those of the performed text, and certainly make it worth considerable effort to "break the code" of Elizabethan poetic drama and let free the remarkable language that makes up a Shakespeare text.

# Shakespeare's Life

Surviving documents that give us glimpses into the life of William Shakespeare show us a playwright, poet, and actor who grew up in the market town of Stratford-upon-Avon, spent his professional life in London, and returned to Stratford a wealthy landowner. He was born in April 1564, died in April 1616, and is buried inside the chancel of Holy Trinity Church in Stratford.

We wish we could know more about the life of the world's greatest dramatist. His plays and poems are testaments to his wide reading—especially to his knowledge of Virgil, Ovid, Plutarch, Holinshed's *Chronicles*, and the Bible—and to his mastery of the English language, but we can only speculate about his education. We know that the King's New School in Stratford-upon-Avon was considered excellent. The school was one of the English "grammar schools" established to educate young men, primarily in Latin grammar and literature. As in other schools of the time, students began their studies at the age of four or five in the attached "petty school," and there learned to read and write in English, studying primarily the catechism from the Book of Common Prayer. After two years in the petty school, students entered the lower form (grade) of the grammar school, where they began the serious study of Latin grammar and Latin texts that would occupy most of the remainder of their school days. (Several Latin texts that Shakespeare used repeatedly in writing his plays and poems were texts that schoolboys memorized and recited.) Latin comedies were introduced early in the lower form; in the upper form, which the boys entered at age ten or eleven, students wrote their own Latin orations and declamations, studied Latin historians and rhetoricians, and began the study of Greek using the Greek New Testament.

Since the records of the Stratford "grammar school" do not survive, we cannot prove that William Shake-

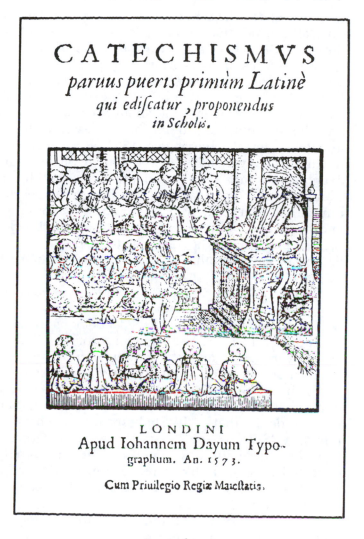

# CATECHISMVS
*paruus pueris primùm Latinè*
*qui ediscatur , proponendus*
*in Scholis.*

LONDINI
Apud Iohannem Dayum Typo-
graphum. An. 1573.

Cum Priuilegio Regiæ Maieftatis,

A catechism.
Title page of *Catechismvs paruus pueris primum Latine* . . . (1573).

speare attended the school; however, every indication (his father's position as an alderman and bailiff of Stratford, the playwright's own knowledge of the Latin classics, scenes in the plays that recall grammar-school experiences—for example, *The Merry Wives of Windsor,* 4.1) suggests that he did. We also lack generally accepted documentation about Shakespeare's life after his schooling ended and his professional life in London began. His marriage in 1582 (at age eighteen) to Anne Hathaway and the subsequent births of his daughter Susanna (1583) and the twins Judith and Hamnet (1585) are recorded, but how he supported himself and where he lived are not known. Nor do we know when and why he left Stratford for the London theatrical world, nor how he rose to be the important figure in that world that he had become by the early 1590s.

We do know that by 1592 he had achieved some prominence in London as both an actor and a playwright. In that year was published a book by the playwright Robert Greene attacking an actor who had the audacity to write blank-verse drama and who was "in his own conceit [i.e., opinion] the only Shake-scene in a country." Since Greene's attack includes a parody of a line from one of Shakespeare's early plays, there is little doubt that it is Shakespeare to whom he refers, a "Shake-scene" who had aroused Greene's fury by successfully competing with university-educated dramatists like Greene himself. It was in 1593 that Shakespeare became a published poet. In that year he published his long narrative poem *Venus and Adonis;* in 1594, he followed it with *The Rape of Lucrece.* Both poems were dedicated to the young earl of Southampton (Henry Wriothesley), who may have become Shakespeare's patron.

The Globe Theater.
From Claes Jansz Visscher, *Londinum Florentissima
Britanniae Urbs* . . . (c. 1625).

It seems no coincidence that Shakespeare wrote these narrative poems at a time when the theaters were closed because of the plague, a contagious epidemic disease that devastated the population of London. When the theaters reopened in 1594, Shakespeare apparently resumed his double career of actor and playwright and began his long (and seemingly profitable) service as an acting-company shareholder. Records for December of 1594 show him to be a leading member of the Lord Chamberlain's Men. It was this company of actors, later named the King's Men, for whom he would be a principal actor, dramatist, and shareholder for the rest of his career.

So far as we can tell, that career spanned about twenty years. In the 1590s, he wrote his plays on English history as well as several comedies and at least two tragedies (*Titus Andronicus* and *Romeo and Juliet*). These histories, comedies, and tragedies are the plays credited to him in 1598 in a work, *Palladis Tamia*, that in one chapter compares English writers with "Greek, Latin, and Italian Poets." There the author, Francis Meres, claims that Shakespeare is comparable to the Latin dramatists Seneca for tragedy and Plautus for comedy, and calls him "the most excellent in both kinds for the stage." He also names him "Mellifluous and honey-tongued Shakespeare": "I say," writes Meres, "that the Muses would speak with Shakespeare's fine filed phrase, if they would speak English." Since Meres also mentions Shakespeare's "sugared sonnets among his private friends," it is assumed that many of Shakespeare's sonnets (not published until 1609) were also written in the 1590s.

In 1599, Shakespeare's company built a theater for themselves across the river from London, naming it the Globe. The plays that are considered by many to be

Shakespeare's major tragedies (*Hamlet, Othello, King Lear*, and *Macbeth*) were written while the company was resident in this theater, as were such comedies as *Twelfth Night* and *Measure for Measure*. Many of Shakespeare's plays were performed at court (both for Queen Elizabeth I and, after her death in 1603, for King James I), some were presented at the Inns of Court (the residences of London's legal societies), and some were doubtless performed in other towns, at the universities, and at great houses when the King's Men went on tour; otherwise, his plays from 1599 to 1608 were, so far as we know, performed only at the Globe. Between 1608 and 1612, Shakespeare wrote several plays—among them *The Winter's Tale* and *The Tempest* —presumably for the company's new indoor Blackfriars theater, though the plays seem to have been performed also at the Globe and at court. Surviving documents describe a performance of *The Winter's Tale* in 1611 at the Globe, for example, and performances of *The Tempest* in 1611 and 1613 at the royal palace of Whitehall.

Shakespeare wrote very little after 1612, the year in which he probably wrote *King Henry VIII*. (It was at a performance of *Henry VIII* in 1613 that the Globe caught fire and burned to the ground.) Sometime between 1610 and 1613 he seems to have returned to live in Stratford-upon-Avon, where he owned a large house and considerable property, and where his wife and his two daughters and their husbands lived. (His son Hamnet had died in 1596.) During his professional years in London, Shakespeare had presumably derived income from the acting company's profits as well as from his own career as an actor, from the sale of his play manuscripts to the acting company, and, after 1599, from his shares as an owner of the Globe. It was presumably that income, carefully invested in land and other property, which made him the wealthy man that surviving documents show him to have become. It is also assumed that William Shakespeare's growing wealth and reputation played some part in inclining the crown, in 1596, to grant John Shakespeare, William's father, the coat of arms that he had so long sought. William Shakespeare died in Stratford on April 23, 1616 (according to the epitaph carved under his bust in Holy Trinity Church) and was buried on April 25. Seven years after his death, his collected plays were published as *Mr. William Shakespeares Comedies, Histories, & Tragedies* (the work now known as the First Folio).

The years in which Shakespeare wrote were among the most exciting in English history. Intellectually, the discovery, translation, and printing of Greek and Roman classics were making available a set of works and worldviews that interacted complexly with Christian texts and beliefs. The result was a questioning, a vital intellectual ferment, that provided energy for the period's amazing dramatic and literary output and that fed directly into Shakespeare's plays. The Ghost in *Hamlet,* for example, is wonderfully complicated in part because he is a figure from Roman tragedy—the spirit of the dead returning to seek revenge—who at the same time inhabits a Christian hell (or purgatory); Hamlet's description of humankind reflects at one moment the Neoplatonic wonderment at mankind ("What a piece of work is a man!") and, at the next, the Christian disparagement of human sinners ("And yet, to me, what is this quintessence of dust?").

As intellectual horizons expanded, so also did geographical and cosmological horizons. New worlds—both North and South America—were explored, and in them were found human beings who lived and worshiped in ways radically different from those of Renaissance Europeans and Englishmen. The universe during these years also seemed to shift and expand. Copernicus had earlier theorized that the earth was not the center of the cosmos but revolved as a planet around the sun. Galileo's telescope, created in 1609, allowed scientists to see that Copernicus had been correct: the universe was not organized with the earth at the center, nor was it so nicely circumscribed as people had, until that time, thought. In terms of expanding horizons, the impact of these discoveries on people's beliefs—religious, scientific, and philosophical—cannot be overstated.

London, too, rapidly expanded and changed during the years (from the early 1590s to around 1610) that Shakespeare lived there. London—the center of England's government, its economy, its royal court, its overseas trade—was, during these years, becoming an exciting metropolis, drawing to it thousands of new citizens every year. Troubled by overcrowding, by poverty, by recurring epidemics of the plague, London was also a mecca for the wealthy and the aristocratic, and for those who sought advancement at court, or power in government or finance or trade. One hears in Shakespeare's plays the voices of London—the struggles for power, the fear of venereal disease, the language of buying and selling. One hears as well the voices of Stratford-upon-Avon—references to the nearby Forest of Arden; to sheep herding, to small-town gossip, to village fairs and markets. Part of the richness of Shakespeare's work is the influence felt there of the various worlds in which he lived: the world of metropolitan London, the world of small-town and rural England, the world of the theater, and the worlds of craftsmen and shepherds.

That Shakespeare inhabited such worlds we know from surviving London and Stratford documents, as well as from the evidence of the plays and poems themselves. From such records we can sketch the dramatist's life. We know from his works that he was a voracious reader. We know from legal and business documents that he was a multifaceted theater man who became a wealthy landowner. We know a bit about his family life and a fair amount about his legal and financial dealings. Most scholars today depend upon such evidence as they draw their picture of the world's greatest playwright. Such, however, has not always been the case. Until the late eighteenth century, the William Shakespeare who lived in most biographies was the creation of legend and tradition. This was the Shakespeare who was supposedly caught poaching deer at Charlecote, the estate of Sir Thomas Lucy close by Stratford; this was the Shakespeare who fled from Sir Thomas's vengeance and made his way in London by taking care of horses outside a playhouse; this was the Shakespeare who reportedly could barely read but whose natural gifts were extraordinary, whose father was a butcher who allowed his gifted son sometimes to help in the butcher shop, where William supposedly killed calves "in a high style," making a speech for the occasion. It was this legendary William Shakespeare whose Falstaff (in *1* and *2 Henry IV*) so pleased Queen Elizabeth that she demanded a play about Falstaff in love, and demanded that it be written in fourteen days (hence the existence of *The Merry Wives of Windsor*). It was this legendary Shakespeare who reached the top of his acting career in the roles of the Ghost in *Hamlet* and old Adam in *As You Like It*—and who died of a fever contracted by drinking too hard at "a merry meeting" with the poets Michael Drayton and Ben Jonson. This legendary Shakespeare is a rambunctious, undisciplined man, as attractively "wild" as his plays were seen by earlier generations to be. Unfortunately, there is no trace of evidence to support these wonderful stories.

Perhaps in response to the disreputable Shakespeare of legend—or perhaps in response to the fragmentary and, for some, all-too-ordinary Shakespeare documented by surviving records—some people since the mid-nineteenth century have argued that William Shakespeare could not have written the plays that bear his name. These persons have put forward some dozen names as more likely authors, among them Queen Elizabeth, Sir Francis Bacon, Edward de Vere (earl of Oxford), and Christopher Marlowe. Such attempts to find what for these people is a more believable author of the plays is a tribute to the regard in which the plays are held. Unfortunately for their claims, the documents that exist that provide evidence for the facts of Shakespeare's life tie him inextricably to the body of plays and poems that bear his name. Unlikely as it seems to those who want the works to have been written by an aristocrat, a university graduate, or an "important" person, the plays and poems seem clearly to have been produced by a man from Stratford-upon-Avon with a very good "grammar-school" education and a life of experience in London and in the world of the London theater. How this particular man produced the works that dominate the cultures of much of the world almost four hundred years after his death is one of life's mysteries—and one that will continue to tease our imaginations as we continue to delight in his plays and poems.

# Shakespeare's Theater

The actors of Shakespeare's time are known to have performed plays in a great variety of locations. They played at court (that is, in the great halls of such royal residences as Whitehall, Hampton Court, and Greenwich); they played in halls at the universities of Oxford and Cambridge, and at the Inns of Court (the residences in London of the legal societies); and they also played in the private houses of great lords and civic officials. Sometimes acting companies went on tour from London into the provinces, often (but not only) when outbreaks of bubonic plague in the capital forced the closing of theaters to reduce the possibility of contagion in crowded audiences. In the provinces the actors usually staged their plays in churches (until around 1600) or in guildhalls. While surviving records show only a handful of occasions when actors played at inns while on tour, London inns were important playing places up until the 1590s.

The building of theaters in London had begun only shortly before Shakespeare wrote his first plays in the 1590s. These theaters were of two kinds: outdoor or public playhouses that could accommodate large numbers of playgoers, and indoor or private theaters for much smaller audiences. What is usually regarded as the first London outdoor public playhouse was called simply the Theatre. James Burbage—the father of Richard Burbage, who was perhaps the most famous actor in Shakespeare's company—built it in 1576 in an area north of the city of London called Shoreditch. Among the more famous of the other public playhouses that capitalized on the new fashion were the Curtain and the

From the frontispiece of William Alabaster, *Roxana* (1632).

Fortune (both also built north of the city), the Rose, the Swan, the Globe, and the Hope (all located on the Bankside, a region just across the Thames south of the city of London). All these playhouses had to be built outside the jurisdiction of the city of London because many civic officials were hostile to the performance of drama and repeatedly petitioned the royal council to abolish it.

The theaters erected on the Bankside (a region under the authority of the Church of England, whose head was the monarch) shared the neighborhood with houses of prostitution and with the Paris Garden, where the blood sports of bearbaiting and bullbaiting were carried on. There may have been no clear distinction between playhouses and buildings for such sports, for we know that the Hope was used for both plays and baiting and that Philip Henslowe, owner of the Rose and, later, partner in the ownership of the Fortune, was also a partner in a monopoly on baiting. All these forms of entertainment were easily accessible to Londoners by boat across the Thames or over London Bridge.

Evidently Shakespeare's company prospered on the Bankside. They moved there in 1599. Threatened by difficulties in renewing the lease on the land where their first theater (the Theatre) had been built, Shakespeare's company took advantage of the Christmas holiday in 1598 to dismantle the Theatre and transport its timbers across the Thames to the Bankside, where, in 1599, these timbers were used in the building of the Globe. The weather in late December 1598 is recorded as having been especially harsh. It was so cold that the Thames was "nigh [nearly] frozen," and there was heavy snow. Perhaps the weather aided Shakespeare's company in eluding their landlord, the snow hiding their activity and the freezing of the Thames allowing them to slide the timbers across to the Bankside without paying tolls for repeated trips over London Bridge. Attractive as this narrative is, it remains just as likely that the heavy snow hampered transport of the timbers in wagons through the London streets to the river. It also must be remembered that the Thames was, according to report, only "nigh frozen" and therefore as impassable as it ever was. Whatever the precise circumstances of this fascinating event in English theater history, Shakespeare's company was able to begin playing at their new Globe theater on the Bankside in 1599. After the first Globe burned down in 1613 during the staging of Shakespeare's *Henry VIII* (its thatch roof was set alight by cannon fire called for by the performance), Shakespeare's company immediately rebuilt on the same location. The second Globe seems to have been a grander structure than its predecessor. It remained in use until the beginning of the English Civil War in 1642, when Parliament officially closed the theaters. Soon thereafter it was pulled down.

The public theaters of Shakespeare's time were very different buildings from our theaters today. First of all, they were open-air playhouses. As recent excavations of the Rose and the Globe confirm, some were polygonal or roughly circular in shape; the Fortune, however, was square. The most recent estimates of their size put the diameter of these buildings at 72 feet (the Rose) to 100 feet (the Globe), but we know that they held vast audiences of two or three thousand, who must have been squeezed together quite tightly. Some of these spectators paid extra to sit or stand in the two or three levels of roofed galleries that extended, on the upper levels, all the way around the theater and surrounded an open space. In this space were the stage and, perhaps, the tiring house (what we would call dressing rooms), as well as the so-called yard. In the yard stood the spectators who chose to pay less, the ones whom Hamlet contemptuously called "groundlings." For a roof they had only the sky, and so they were exposed to all kinds of weather. They stood on a floor that was sometimes made of mortar and sometimes of ash mixed with the shells of hazelnuts. The latter provided a porous and therefore dry footing for the crowd, and the shells may have been more comfortable to stand on because they were not as hard as mortar. Availability of shells may not have been a problem if hazelnuts were a favorite food for Shakespeare's audiences to munch on as they watched his plays. Archaeologists who are today unearthing the remains of theaters from this period have discovered quantities of these nutshells on theater sites.

Unlike the yard, the stage itself was covered by a roof. Its ceiling, called "the heavens," is thought to have been elaborately painted to depict the sun, moon, stars, and planets. Just how big the stage was remains hard to determine. We have a single sketch of part of the interior of the Swan. A Dutchman named Johannes de Witt visited this theater around 1596 and sent a sketch of it back to his friend, Arend van Buchel. Because van Buchel found de Witt's letter and sketch of interest, he copied both into a book. It is van Buchel's copy, adapted, it seems, to the shape and size of the page in his book, that survives. In this sketch, the stage appears to be a large rectangular platform that thrusts far out into the yard, perhaps even as far as the center of the circle formed by the surrounding galleries. This drawing, combined with the specifications for the size of the stage in the building contract for the Fortune, has led scholars to conjecture that the stage on which Shakespeare's plays were performed must have measured approximately 43 feet in width and 27 feet in depth, a vast acting area. But the digging up of a large part of the Rose by archaeologists has provided evidence of a quite different stage design. The Rose stage was a platform tapered at the corners and much shallower than what seems to be depicted in the van Buchel sketch. Indeed, its measurements seem to be about 37.5 feet across at its widest point and only 15.5 feet deep. Because the surviving indications of stage size and design differ from each other so much, it is possible that the stages in other theaters, like the Theatre, the Curtain, and the Globe (the outdoor playhouses where we know that Shakespeare's plays were performed), were different from those at both the Swan and the Rose.

After about 1608 Shakespeare's plays were staged not only at the Globe but also at an indoor or private playhouse in Blackfriars. This theater had been constructed in 1596 by James Burbage in an upper hall of a former Dominican priory or monastic house. Although Henry VIII had dissolved all English monasteries in the 1530s (shortly after he had founded the Church of England), the area remained under church, rather than hostile civic, control. The hall that Burbage had purchased and renovated was a large one in which Parliament had once met. In the private theater that he constructed, the stage, lit by candles, was built across the narrow end of the hall, with boxes flanking it. The rest of the hall offered seating room only. Because there was no provision for standing room, the largest audience it could hold was less than a thousand, or about a quarter of what the Globe could accommodate. Admission to Blackfriars was correspondingly more expensive. Instead of a penny to stand in the yard at the Globe, it cost a minimum of sixpence to get into Blackfriars. The best seats at the Globe (in the Lords' Room in the gallery above and behind the stage) cost sixpence; but the boxes flanking the stage at Blackfriars were half a crown, or five times sixpence. Some spectators who were particularly interested in displaying themselves paid even more to sit on stools on the Blackfriars stage.

Whether in the outdoor or indoor playhouses, the stages of Shakespeare's time were different from ours. They were not separated from the audience by the dropping of a curtain between acts and scenes. Therefore the playwrights of the time had to find other ways of signaling to the audience that one scene (to be imagined as occurring in one location at a given time) had ended and the next (to be imagined at perhaps a different location at a later time) had begun. The customary way used by Shakespeare and many of his contemporaries was to have everyone onstage exit at the end of one scene and have one or more different characters enter to begin the next. In a few cases, where characters remain onstage from one scene to another, the dialogue or stage action makes the change of location clear, and the characters are generally to be imagined as having moved from one place to another. For example, in *Romeo and Juliet*, Romeo and his friends remain onstage in Act 1 from scene 4 to scene 5, but they are represented as having moved between scenes from the street that leads to Capulet's house into Capulet's house itself. The new location is signaled in part by the appearance onstage of Capulet's servingmen carrying napkins, something they would not take into the streets. Playwrights had to be quite resourceful in the use of hand properties, like the napkin, or in the use of dialogue to specify where the action was taking place in their plays because, in contrast to most of today's theaters, the playhouses of Shakespeare's time did not use movable scenery to dress the stage and make the setting precise. As another consequence of this difference, however, the playwrights of Shakespeare's time did not have to specify exactly where the action of their plays was set when they did not choose to do so, and much of the action of their plays is tied to no specific place.

Usually Shakespeare's stage is referred to as a "bare stage," to distinguish it from the stages of the last two or three centuries with their elaborate sets. But the stage in Shakespeare's time was not completely bare. Philip Henslowe, owner of the Rose, lists in his inventory of stage properties a rock, three tombs, and two mossy banks. Stage directions in plays of the time also call for such things as thrones (or "states"), banquets (presumably tables with plaster replicas of food on them), and beds and tombs to be pushed onto the stage. Thus the stage often held more than the actors.

The actors did not limit their performing to the stage alone. Occasionally they went beneath the stage, as the Ghost appears to do in the first act of *Hamlet*. From there they could emerge onto the stage through a trapdoor. They could retire behind the hangings across the back of the stage (or the front of the tiring house), as, for example, the actor playing Polonius does when he hides behind the arras. Sometimes the hangings could be drawn back during a performance to "discover" one or more actors behind them. When performance required that an actor appear "above," as when Juliet is imagined to stand at the window of her chamber in the famous and misnamed "balcony scene," then the actor probably climbed the stairs to the gallery over the back of the stage and temporarily shared it with some of the spectators. The stage was also provided with ropes and winches so that actors could descend from, and re-ascend to, the "heavens."

Perhaps the greatest difference between dramatic performances in Shakespeare's time and ours was that in Shakespeare's England the roles of women were played by boys. (Some of these boys grew up to take male roles in their maturity.) There were no women in the acting companies, only in the audience. It had not always been so in the history of the English stage. There are records of women on English stages in the thirteenth and fourteenth centuries, two hundred years before Shakespeare's plays were performed. After the accession of James I in 1603, the queen of England and her ladies took part in entertainments at court called masques, and with the re-opening of the theaters in 1660 at the restoration of Charles II, women again took their place on the public stage.

The chief competitors for the companies of adult actors such as the one to which Shakespeare belonged and for which he wrote were companies of exclusively boy actors. The competition was most intense in the early 1600s. There were then two principal children's companies: the Children of Paul's (the choirboys from St. Paul's Cathedral, whose private playhouse was near the cathedral); and the Children of the Chapel Royal (the choirboys from the monarch's private chapel, who performed at the Blackfriars theater built by Burbage in 1596, which Shakespeare's company had been stopped from using by local residents who objected to crowds). In *Hamlet* Shakespeare writes of "an aerie [nest] of children, little eyases [hawks], that cry out on the top of question and are most tyrannically clapped for 't. These are now the fashion and . . . be-rattle the common stages [attack the public theaters]." In the long run, the adult actors prevailed. The Children of Paul's dissolved around 1606. By about 1608 the Children of the Chapel Royal had been forced to stop playing at the Blackfriars theater, which was then taken over by the King's Men, Shakespeare's own troupe.

Acting companies and theaters of Shakespeare's time were organized in different ways. For example, Philip Henslowe owned the Rose and leased it to companies of actors, who paid him from their takings. Henslowe would act as manager of these companies, initially paying playwrights for their plays and buying properties, recovering his outlay from the actors. Shakespeare's company, however, managed itself, with the principal actors, Shakespeare among them, having the status of "sharers" and the right to a share in the takings, as well as the responsibility for a part of the expenses. Five of the sharers themselves, Shakespeare among them, owned the Globe. As actor, as sharer in an acting company and in ownership of theaters, and as playwright, Shakespeare was about as involved in the theatrical industry as one could imagine. Although Shakespeare and his fellows prospered, their status under the law was conditional upon the protection of powerful patrons. "Common players"—those who did not have patrons or masters—were classed in the language of the law with "vagabonds and sturdy beggars." So the actors had to secure for themselves the official rank of servants of patrons. Among the patrons under whose protection Shakespeare's company worked were the lord chamberlain and, after the accession of King James in 1603, the king himself.

We are now perhaps on the verge of learning a great

deal more about the theaters in which Shakespeare and his contemporaries performed—or at least of opening up new questions about them. Already about 70 percent of the Rose has been excavated, as has about 10 percent of the second Globe, the one built in 1614. It is to be hoped that soon more will be available for study. These are exciting times for students of Shakespeare's stage.

# The Publication of Shakespeare's Plays

Eighteen of Shakespeare's plays found their way into print during the playwright's lifetime, but there is nothing to suggest that he took any interest in their publication. These eighteen appeared separately in editions called quartos. Their pages were not much larger than the one you are now reading, and these little books were sold unbound for a few pence. The earliest of the quartos that still survive were printed in 1594, the year that both *Titus Andronicus* and a version of the play now called *2 King Henry VI* became available. While almost every one of these early quartos displays on its title page the name of the acting company that performed the play, only about half provide the name of the playwright, Shakespeare. The first quarto edition to bear the name Shakespeare on its title page is *Love's Labor's Lost* of 1598. A few of these quartos were popular with the book-buying public of Shakespeare's lifetime; for example, quarto *Richard II* went through five editions between 1597 and 1615. But most of the quartos were far from best-sellers; *Love's Labor's Lost* (1598), for instance, was not reprinted in quarto until 1631. After Shakespeare's death, two more of his plays appeared in quarto format: *Othello* in 1622 and *The Two Noble Kinsmen,* coauthored with John Fletcher, in 1634.

In 1623, seven years after Shakespeare's death, *Mr. William Shakespeares Comedies, Histories, & Tragedies* was published. This printing offered readers in a single book thirty-six of the thirty-eight plays now thought to have been written by Shakespeare, including eighteen that had never been printed before. And it offered them in a style that was then reserved for serious literature and scholarship. The plays were arranged in double columns on pages nearly a foot high. This large page size is called "folio," as opposed to the smaller "quarto," and the 1623 volume is usually called the Shakespeare First Folio. It is reputed to have sold for the lordly price of a pound. (One copy at the Folger Library is marked fifteen shillings—that is, three-quarters of a pound.)

In a preface to the First Folio entitled "To the great Variety of Readers," two of Shakespeare's former fellow actors in the King's Men, John Heminge and Henry Condell, wrote that they themselves had collected their dead companion's plays. They suggested that they had seen his own papers: "we have scarce received from him a blot in his papers." The title page of the Folio declared that the plays within it had been printed "according to the True Original Copies." Comparing the Folio to the quartos, Heminge and Condell disparaged the quartos, advising their readers that "before you were abused with divers stolen and surreptitious copies, maimed, and deformed by the frauds and stealths of injurious impostors." Many Shakespeareans of the eighteenth and nineteenth centuries believed Heminge and Condell and regarded the Folio plays as superior to anything in the quartos.

Once we begin to examine the Folio plays in detail, it becomes less easy to take at face value the word of Heminge and Condell about the superiority of the Folio texts. For example, of the first nine plays in the Folio (one quarter of the entire collection), four were essentially reprinted from earlier quarto printings that Heminge and Condell had disparaged; and four have now been identified as printed from copies written in the hand of a professional scribe of the 1620s named Ralph Crane; the ninth, *The Comedy of Errors,* was apparently also printed from a manuscript, but one whose origin cannot be readily identified. Evidently then, eight of the first nine plays in the First Folio were not printed, in spite of what the Folio title page announces, "according to the True Original Copies," or Shakespeare's own papers, and the source of the ninth is unknown. Since today's editors have been forced to treat Heminge and Condell's pronouncements with skepticism, they must choose whether to base their own editions upon quartos or the Folio on grounds other than Heminge and Condell's story of where the quarto and Folio versions originated.

Editors have often fashioned their own narratives to explain what lies behind the quartos and Folio. They have said that Heminge and Condell meant to criticize only a few of the early quartos, the ones that offer much shorter and sometimes quite different, often garbled, versions of plays. Among the examples of these are the 1600 quarto of *Henry V* (the Folio offers a much fuller version) or the 1603 *Hamlet* quarto (in 1604 a different, much longer form of the play got into print as a quarto). Early in this century editors speculated that these questionable texts were produced when someone in the audience took notes from the plays' dialogue during performances and then employed "hack poets" to fill out the notes. The poor results were then sold to a publisher and presented in print as Shakespeare's plays. More recently this story has given way to another in which the shorter versions are said to be recreations from memory of Shakespeare's plays by actors who wanted to stage them in the provinces but lacked manuscript copies. Most of the quartos offer much better texts than these so-called bad quartos. Indeed, in most of the quartos we find texts that are at least equal to or better than what is printed in the Folio. Many of this century's Shakespeare enthusiasts have persuaded themselves that most of the quartos were set into type directly from Shakespeare's own papers, although there is nothing on which to base this conclusion except the desire for it to be true. Thus speculation continues about how the Shakespeare plays got to be printed. All that we have are the printed texts.

The book collector who was most successful in bringing together copies of the quartos and the First Folio was Henry Clay Folger, founder of the Folger Shakespeare Library in Washington, D.C. While it is estimated that there survive around the world only about 230 copies of the First Folio, Mr. Folger was able to acquire more than seventy-five copies, as well as a large number of fragments, for the library that bears his name. He also amassed a substantial number of quartos. For example, only fourteen copies of the First Quarto of *Love's Labor's Lost* are known to exist, and three are at the Folger Shakespeare Library. As a consequence of Mr. Folger's labors, twentieth-century scholars visiting the Folger Library have been able to learn a great deal about sixteenth- and seventeenth-century printing and, particularly, about the printing of Shakespeare's plays. And Mr. Folger did not stop at the First Folio, but collected many copies of later editions of Shakespeare, beginning with the Second Folio (1632), the Third (1663–64), and the Fourth (1685). Each of these later folios was based on its immediate predecessor and was edited anonymously. The first editor of Shakespeare whose name we know was Nicholas Rowe, whose first edition came out in 1709. Mr. Folger collected this edition and many, many more by Rowe's successors.

# An Introduction to This Text

*Henry IV, Part 1* was first printed in 1598 as a quarto. All that survives of that printing (known to scholars as Q0) is a single copy in the Folger Library of eight of its pages. These Q0 pages contain the lines numbered in the present edition as 1.3.206–2.2.117—lines which, in the present edition, are based directly on Q0. The rest of the present edition is based directly on the first printing of the play that survives in full.* This is also a quarto (Q1), and it was also printed in 1598 by the same printer responsible for Q0, which appears to have served as printer's copy for Q1. *Henry IV, Part 1* was a popular book; it went through five more editions in quarto before its appearance in the First Folio of 1623. The Folio text was printed from a slightly edited copy of the Fifth Quarto of 1613 (Q5). Whoever prepared Q5 to be printer's copy for the Folio restored some Q1 readings, but also introduced other changes, the authority

---

*We have also consulted the computerized text of the First Quarto provided by the Text Archive of the Oxford University Computing Centre, to which we are grateful.

for which is indeterminable. We have therefore not accepted these changes into the present edition.

For the convenience of the reader, we have modernized the punctuation and the spelling of the quartos. Sometimes we go so far as to modernize certain old forms of words; for example, when *a* means "he," we change it to *he;* we change *mo* to *more* and *ye* to *you.* But it has not been our editorial practice in any of the plays to modernize some words that sound distinctly different from modern forms. For example, when the early printed texts read *sith* or *apricocks* or *porpentine,* we have not modernized to *since, apricots, porcupine.* When the forms *an, and,* or *and if* appear instead of the modern form *if,* we have reduced *and* to *an* but have not changed any of these forms to their modern equivalent, *if.* We also modernize and, where necessary, correct passages in foreign languages, unless an error in the early printed text can be reasonably explained as a joke.

Whenever we change the wording of the quartos or add anything to their stage directions, we mark the change by enclosing it in superior half-brackets (⌐ ¬). We want our readers to be immediately aware when we have intervened. (Only when we correct an obvious typographical error in the quartos does the change not get marked.) Whenever we change the quartos' wording or change their punctuation so that meaning changes, we list the change in the textual notes at the back of the book, even if all we have done is fix an obvious error.

We, like a great many editors before us, regularize a number of the proper names. This issue is particularly vexed in *Henry IV, Part 1* because the character Falstaff, as well as his companions Bardolph and Peto, appear occasionally in the earliest printed texts of both *Henry IV, Part 1* and its sequel, *Henry IV, Part 2,* under quite different names. There is considerable evidence that Sir John Falstaff was originally called Sir John Oldcastle, the name of a fifteenth-century proto-Protestant martyr who was celebrated by sixteenth-century Protestant historians. In the First Quarto of *Henry IV, Part 2*, the speech prefix for one of Falstaff's speeches is *"Old.,"* and there survives in *Henry IV, Part 1* what appears to be a joke on Falstaff's former name when Prince Hal addresses him as "my old lad of the castle" (1.2.44). According to a nearly contemporary report, Shakespeare and his acting company were obliged to abandon the name Oldcastle by the martyr's descendant William Brooke, Lord Cobham, a powerful aristocrat who served as lord chamberlain to Elizabeth I in 1596–97. It is just possible that similar circumstances forced changes in the names of Peto and Bardolph, who are once referred to in the text of *Henry IV, Part 1* as "Haruey and Rossill" (i.e., Harvey and Russell). Perhaps, the influential figures who bore those names in Shakespeare's time objected, as Lord Cobham did, to having their ancestors put onstage.

Some editors have recently argued that the names Oldcastle, Harvey, and Russell should be substituted for Falstaff, Peto, and Bardolph so as to return the play to the form in which Shakespeare first wrote it. These editors assert that the only changes that were made to the play between the form in which it was originally staged and the form in which it has come down to us in print were the name changes. Against this view stands the fact that the only version of the play that has come down to us is the one in which the characters are named Falstaff, Peto, and Bardolph. Because we have only this version, it is impossible to know how it may differ from any other version, including the one in which the characters were named Oldcastle, Haruey, and Rossill.

That is, to claim that Q1 is the original in all respects but in the name changes is to claim more than can be known. Our choice therefore is to print the names as they appear in the quartos, with the exception that, in 1.2, we regularize "Haruey" to "Peto," and, in 1.2 and 2.4, we regularize "Rossill" and *"Ross."* to "Bardolph." We expand the often severely abbreviated forms of names used as speech headings in early printed texts into the full names of the characters. Variations in the speech headings of the early printed texts are recorded in the textual notes.

This edition differs from many earlier ones in its efforts to aid the reader in imagining the play as a performance rather than as a series of fictional events. For example, near the end of 3.3, Prince Hal tells Bardolph to "bear this letter to Lord John of Lancaster, . . . this to my Lord of Westmoreland" and, in the fiction of the play, gives Bardolph two letters. But in the staging of the play, one actor, in the role of Prince Hal, gives another, in the role of Bardolph, not some letters, but some papers representing letters. And so our stage direction reads *"handing Bardolph papers"* rather than "letters." Whenever it is reasonably certain, in our view, that a speech is accompanied by a particular action, we provide a stage direction describing the action. (Occasional exceptions to this rule occur when the action is so obvious that to add a stage direction would insult the reader.) Stage directions for the entrance of characters in mid-scene are, with rare exceptions, placed so that they immediately precede the characters' participation in the scene, even though these entrances may appear somewhat earlier in the early printed texts. Whenever we move a stage direction, we record this change in the textual notes. Latin stage directions (e.g., *Exeunt*) are translated into English (e.g., *They exit*).

In the present edition, as well, we mark with a dash any change of address within a speech, unless a stage direction intervenes. When the *-ed* ending of a word is to be pronounced, we mark it with an accent. Like editors for the past two centuries we print metrically linked lines in the following way:

HOTSPUR
  We'll fight with him tonight.
  WORCESTER                             It may not be.

However, when there are a number of short verse lines that can be linked in more than one way, we do not, with rare exceptions, indent any of them.

## The Explanatory Notes

The notes that appear on the pages facing the text are designed to provide readers with the help that they may need to enjoy the play. Whenever the meaning of a word in the text is not readily available in a good contemporary dictionary, we offer the meaning in a note. Sometimes we provide a note even when the relevant meaning is to be found in the dictionary but when the word has acquired since Shakespeare's time other potentially confusing meanings. In our notes, we try to offer modern synonyms for Shakespeare's words. We also try to indicate to the reader the connection between the word in the play and the modern synonym. For example, Shakespeare sometimes uses the word *head* to mean "source," but, for modern readers, there may be no connection evident between these two words. We provide the connection by explaining Shakespeare's usage as follows: **"head:** fountainhead, source." On some occasions, a whole phrase or clause needs explanation. Then we rephrase in our own words the difficult passage, and add at the end synonyms for individual words in the passage. When scholars have been unable to determine the meaning of a word or a phrase, we acknowledge the uncertainty.

At Shrowesbury in the place then called Olfeilde a great and
bloody battaill was fought by the percies Henry surnamed
Hotspure, and Thomas Earle of Worcester, against King
Henry the 4. Wherein the sayd Lord Henry slayne and L.
Thomas taken and beheaded with ý losse of 6600. Souldiers
on both parts Anno 1403.

The battle of Shrewsbury.
From John Speed, *A prospect of the most famous part of
the world* (1631).

The History of

# HENRY IV
## Part 1

# The Line of Edward III

[Dates of reign are given in brackets.]

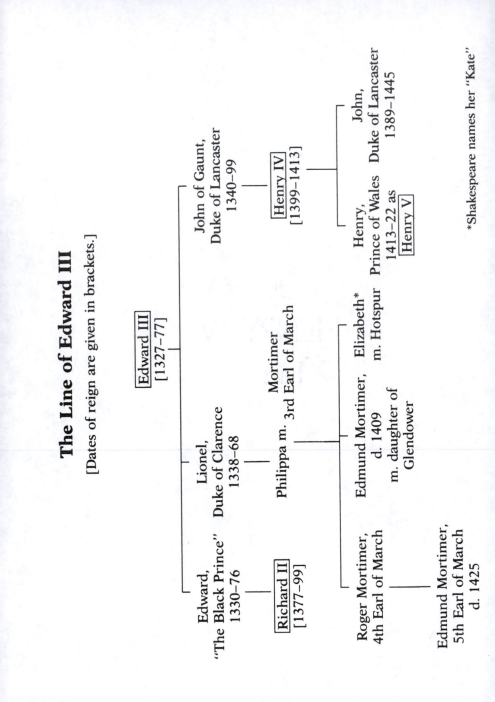

Edward III
[1327–77]

Edward, "The Black Prince" 1330–76

Lionel, Duke of Clarence 1338–68

John of Gaunt, Duke of Lancaster 1340–99

Richard II [1377–99]

Philippa m. Mortimer 3rd Earl of March

Henry IV [1399–1413]

Edmund Mortimer, d. 1409 m. daughter of Glendower

Elizabeth* m. Hotspur

Henry, Prince of Wales 1413–22 as Henry V

John, Duke of Lancaster 1389–1445

Roger Mortimer, 4th Earl of March

Edmund Mortimer, 5th Earl of March d. 1425

*Shakespeare names her "Kate"

# Characters in the Play

KING HENRY IV, formerly Henry Bolingbroke

PRINCE HAL, Prince of Wales and heir to the throne (also called Harry and Harry Monmouth)

LORD JOHN OF LANCASTER, younger son of King Henry
EARL OF WESTMORELAND
SIR WALTER BLUNT

HOTSPUR (Sir Henry, or Harry, Percy)
LADY PERCY (also called Kate)
EARL OF NORTHUMBERLAND, Henry Percy, Hotspur's father
EARL OF WORCESTER, Thomas Percy, Hotspur's uncle

EDMUND MORTIMER, earl of March
LADY MORTIMER (also called "the Welsh lady")
OWEN GLENDOWER, a Welsh lord, father of Lady Mortimer

DOUGLAS (Archibald, earl of Douglas)
ARCHBISHOP (Richard Scroop, archbishop of York)
SIR MICHAEL, a priest or knight associated with the archbishop
SIR RICHARD VERNON, an English knight

SIR JOHN FALSTAFF
POINS (also called Edward, Yedward, and Ned)
BARDOLPH
PETO
GADSHILL, setter for the robbers

3

HOSTESS of the tavern (also called Mistress Quickly)
VINTNER, or keeper of the tavern
FRANCIS, an apprentice tapster

Carriers, Ostlers, Chamberlain, Travelers, Sheriff, Servants, Lords, Attendants, Messengers, Soldiers

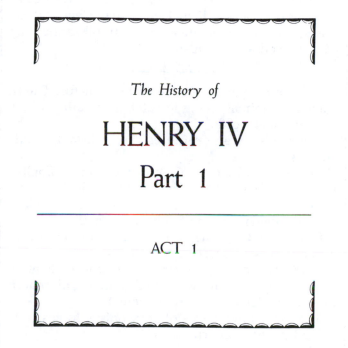

*The History of*

# HENRY IV
## Part 1

ACT 1

**1.1**  King Henry meets with his advisers to discuss his proposed crusade to the Holy Land, but the discussion turns instead to new battles on England's borders. In Wales, an English nobleman named Mortimer has been captured by Owen Glendower; in the north, England's forces have prevailed over the Scots, but Hotspur, a young English nobleman, refuses to yield his prisoners to King Henry. In the face of these crises, the crusade is once again put off as the king calls a meeting at Windsor.

---

2. **frighted peace: Peace** is here pictured as a frightened animal trying to catch its breath.
3. **accents:** words
4. **strands afar remote:** i.e., distant lands **strands:** shores
5-6. **No . . . blood:** i.e., no longer must English soil drink the blood of its own people  **daub:** smear, paint
7. **her fields:** i.e., the fields of England
8-9. **armèd . . . paces:** i.e., the iron-shod hooves of the cavalry's horses
9-18. **Those . . . master:** i.e., instead of fighting each other in civil war, Englishmen will march together (against a common enemy)
9. **opposèd eyes:** eyes of antagonistic forces
12. **intestine:** internal
13. **close:** struggle
14. **mutual:** i.e., joined in common purpose; **well-beseeming:** suitable; or, attractive
18. **his:** its

*(continued)*

*Enter the King, Lord John of Lancaster, ⌜and the⌝ Earl
of Westmoreland, with others.*

KING
  So shaken as we are, so wan with care,
  Find we a time for frighted peace to pant
  And breathe short-winded accents of new broils
  To be commenced in strands afar remote.
  No more the thirsty entrance of this soil          5
  Shall daub her lips with her own children's blood.
  No more shall trenching war channel her fields,
  Nor bruise her flow'rets with the armèd hoofs
  Of hostile paces. Those opposèd eyes,
  Which, like the meteors of a troubled heaven,    10
  All of one nature, of one substance bred,
  Did lately meet in the intestine shock
  And furious close of civil butchery,
  Shall now, in mutual well-beseeming ranks,
  March all one way and be no more opposed     15
  Against acquaintance, kindred, and allies.
  The edge of war, like an ill-sheathèd knife,
  No more shall cut his master. Therefore, friends,
  As far as to the sepulcher of Christ—
  Whose soldier now, under whose blessèd cross    20
  We are impressèd and engaged to fight—

7

19. **sepulcher of Christ:** i.e., the Holy Sepulcher in Jerusalem (From 1095 to c. 1450, a series of wars— the Crusades—were fought by Christians to recover the sepulcher from the Muslims. At the end of Shakespeare's *Richard II*, King Henry promises to fight such a war in order to gain God's forgiveness for Henry's part in Richard's death.)

21. **We:** i.e., I (the royal "we"); **impressèd:** drafted, conscripted

22. **a power:** an army

24. **these pagans:** i.e., the Muslims

30. **Therefor:** for that purpose

31. **Of:** from; **gentle:** noble; **cousin:** i.e., kinsman (Henry and Westmoreland were related by marriage.)

33. **dear expedience:** important expedition

34. **this haste:** i.e., this urgent matter; **hot in question:** actively discussed

35. **limits of the charge:** (1) estimates of the cost; or (2) duties and commands

36. **all athwart:** i.e., across our path and thwarting our purposes

37. **post:** i.e., a messenger riding a post horse; **loaden:** laden, loaded

40. **irregular:** perhaps a reference to Glendower's guerrilla style of fighting; or perhaps synonymous with **wild,** a reference to Glendower's powers as a Welsh sorcerer

43. **corpse:** corpses

48. **Brake:** broke

50. **uneven:** rough

52. **Holy-rood Day:** i.e., September 14, Holy Cross Day (The year of this battle between Harry Percy and Archibald, earl of Douglas, was 1402.)

Forthwith a power of English shall we levy,
Whose arms were molded in their mothers' womb
To chase these pagans in those holy fields
Over whose acres walked those blessèd feet                    25
Which fourteen hundred years ago were nailed
For our advantage on the bitter cross.
But this our purpose now is twelve month old,
And bootless 'tis to tell you we will go.
Therefor we meet not now. Then let me hear                    30
Of you, my gentle cousin Westmoreland,
What yesternight our council did decree
In forwarding this dear expedience.

WESTMORELAND
My liege, this haste was hot in question,
And many limits of the charge set down                        35
But yesternight, when all athwart there came
A post from Wales loaden with heavy news,
Whose worst was that the noble Mortimer,
Leading the men of Herefordshire to fight
Against the irregular and wild Glendower,                     40
Was by the rude hands of that Welshman taken,
A thousand of his people butcherèd,
Upon whose dead corpse there was such misuse,
Such beastly shameless transformation
By those Welshwomen done, as may not be                       45
Without much shame retold or spoken of.

KING
It seems then that the tidings of this broil
Brake off our business for the Holy Land.

WESTMORELAND
This matched with other did, my gracious lord.
For more uneven and unwelcome news                            50
Came from the north, and thus it did import:
On Holy-rood Day the gallant Hotspur there,
Young Harry Percy, and brave Archibald,
That ever valiant and approvèd Scot,

57–58. **As . . . told:** i.e., as we can assume by what was heard

59. **them:** i.e., the news

60. **pride:** intensity

62. **Here . . . friend:** It is possible that Sir Walter Blunt is onstage and that Henry gestures to him at this point, though the fact that Blunt is given no lines and that Henry describes Blunt's appearance suggests that Blunt is not present, and that Henry's line means that Blunt is "here in the court." Either of these readings would mean that Henry has entered the scene knowing Blunt's news, which he waits until this moment to reveal. It is also possible that a messenger brings Henry a letter, which Henry here reads and reports.

66. **smooth and welcome:** Henry's response to Westmoreland's **uneven and unwelcome** at line 50

67. **discomfited:** defeated

69. **Balked:** i.e., piled up in ridges, as if by a plow

74. **spoil:** plunder, loot

82. **minion:** darling

84. **riot:** dissipation, loose living

85–89. **O, that . . . mine:** Henry's statement draws on the old belief that fairies exchanged one newborn for another or for a fairy child.

At Holmedon met, where they did spend                           55
A sad and bloody hour—
As by discharge of their artillery
And shape of likelihood the news was told,
For he that brought them, in the very heat
And pride of their contention did take horse,                   60
Uncertain of the issue any way.

KING
Here is ⌐a⌐ dear, a true-industrious friend,
Sir Walter Blunt, new lighted from his horse,
Stained with the variation of each soil
Betwixt that Holmedon and this seat of ours,                    65
And he hath brought us smooth and welcome news.
The Earl of Douglas is discomfited;
Ten thousand bold Scots, two-and-twenty knights,
Balked in their own blood, did Sir Walter see
On Holmedon's plains. Of prisoners Hotspur took                 70
Mordake, Earl of Fife and eldest son
To beaten Douglas, and the Earl of Atholl,
Of Murray, Angus, and Menteith.
And is not this an honorable spoil?
A gallant prize? Ha, cousin, is it not?                         75

WESTMORELAND
In faith, it is a conquest for a prince to boast of.

KING
Yea, there thou mak'st me sad, and mak'st me sin
In envy that my Lord Northumberland
Should be the father to so blest a son,
A son who is the theme of Honor's tongue,                       80
Amongst a grove the very straightest plant,
Who is sweet Fortune's minion and her pride;
Whilst I, by looking on the praise of him,
See riot and dishonor stain the brow
Of my young Harry. O, that it could be proved                   85
That some night-tripping fairy had exchanged
In cradle-clothes our children where they lay,

88. **Percy:** the surname of the earl of Northumberland and his family; **Plantagenet:** a surname applied to the royal house of England between 1154 and 1485

90. **from:** i.e., go out of

92. **surprised:** captured

93. **To . . . use:** i.e., to enjoy their ransoms himself

96. **Malevolent . . . aspects:** an astrological image, in which Worcester is like a planet that, no matter what its position or **aspect,** portends evil for Henry

97. **Which:** i.e., Worcester's teaching; **makes him prune himself:** i.e., makes Hotspur prepare himself for action (like a hawk pruning away broken feathers in preparation for a fight)

**1.2** Prince Hal and Sir John Falstaff taunt each other, Hal warning Falstaff that he will one day be hanged as a thief and Falstaff insisting that, when Hal becomes king, thieves will have a friend in court. Poins enters to enlist them in an upcoming robbery. Hal refuses, but, after Falstaff leaves, Poins persuades Hal to join in a plot to rob and embarrass Falstaff and the other thieves. Alone, Hal reveals that he will soon end his association with his companions and that, after his "reformation," he will shine all the brighter against his background of irresponsible living.

2. **fat-witted:** thick-brained, stupid

3. **sack:** sherry

5. **truly:** correctly

5–6. **wouldst truly know:** i.e., really want to know

And called mine "Percy," his "Plantagenet"!
Then would I have his Harry, and he mine.
But let him from my thoughts. What think you, coz,      90
Of this young Percy's pride? The prisoners
Which he in this adventure hath surprised
To his own use he keeps, and sends me word
I shall have none but Mordake, Earl of Fife.
WESTMORELAND
This is his uncle's teaching. This is Worcester,      95
Malevolent to you in all aspects,
Which makes him prune himself, and bristle up
The crest of youth against your dignity.
KING
But I have sent for him to answer this.
And for this cause awhile we must neglect      100
Our holy purpose to Jerusalem.
Cousin, on Wednesday next our council we
Will hold at Windsor. So inform the lords.
But come yourself with speed to us again,
For more is to be said and to be done      105
Than out of anger can be utterèd.
WESTMORELAND      I will, my liege.

*They exit.*

⌜Scene 2⌝
*Enter Prince of Wales, and Sir John Falstaff.*

FALSTAFF      Now, Hal, what time of day is it, lad?
PRINCE      Thou art so fat-witted with drinking of old
      sack, and unbuttoning thee after supper, and
      sleeping upon benches after noon, that thou hast
      forgotten to demand that truly which thou wouldst      5
      truly know. What a devil hast thou to do with
      the time of the day? Unless hours were cups of
      sack, and minutes capons, and clocks the tongues

9. **dials:** sun dials; **leaping-houses:** brothels

11–12. **why . . . demand:** i.e., why you should be so inane as to ask

14. **you come near me:** i.e., you're near the mark

15. **go by:** (1) walk under the light of; (2) tell time by

15–16. **seven stars:** the constellation also known as the Pleiades

16. **Phoebus:** god of the sun, or, here, the sun itself

16–17. **wand'ring knight:** i.e., a knight errant

17. **sweet wag:** dear fellow

18. **thy Grace:** your Majesty (with a pun on **grace** as "virtue," or as "God's grace")

22. **prologue . . . butter:** another pun on **grace,** a short prayer before a meal

23. **roundly:** i.e., speak bluntly

24. **Marry:** i.e., indeed (a mild oath)

25. **squires . . . body:** A "squire of the body" was an officer who attended on the person of a dignitary. Falstaff is perhaps punning on night/knight.

26. **beauty:** probably a pun on "booty" or loot; **be:** i.e., be called; **Diana:** goddess of the moon (See page 66.)

27. **foresters:** officials in charge of forest lands

30–31. **under . . . steal:** (1) beneath whose face we move stealthily; (2) under whose protection we commit theft

38. **swearing "Lay by":** i.e., ordering people to give up their money

38–39. **crying "Bring in":** i.e., calling to the waiter for more wine

39. **the ladder:** the steps leading up to the **gallows** (See page 82.)

of bawds, and dials the signs of leaping-houses,
and the blessed sun himself a fair hot wench in          10
flame-colored taffeta, I see no reason why thou
shouldst be so superfluous to demand the time
of the day.

FALSTAFF   Indeed, you come near me now, Hal, for we
that take purses go by the moon and the seven          15
stars, and not by Phoebus, he, that wand'ring
knight so fair. And I prithee, sweet wag, when thou
art king, as God save thy Grace—Majesty, I should
say, for grace thou wilt have none—

PRINCE   What, none?          20

FALSTAFF   No, by my troth, not so much as will serve to
be prologue to an egg and butter.

PRINCE   Well, how then? Come, roundly, roundly.

FALSTAFF   Marry then, sweet wag, when thou art king,
let not us that are squires of the night's body be          25
called thieves of the day's beauty. Let us be Diana's
foresters, gentlemen of the shade, minions of the
moon, and let men say we be men of good government, being governed, as the sea is, by our noble
and chaste mistress the moon, under whose counte-          30
nance we steal.

PRINCE   Thou sayest well, and it holds well too, for the
fortune of us that are the moon's men doth ebb and
flow like the sea, being governed, as the sea is, by
the moon. As for proof now: a purse of gold most          35
resolutely snatched on Monday night and most
dissolutely spent on Tuesday morning, got with
swearing "Lay by" and spent with crying "Bring
in"; now in as low an ebb as the foot of the ladder,
and by and by in as high a flow as the ridge of the          40
gallows.

FALSTAFF   By the Lord, thou sayst true, lad. And is not
my hostess of the tavern a most sweet wench?

44. **Hybla:** a place in ancient Sicily, famous for its honey bees; **old . . . castle:** This reference, along with other evidence, persuades editors that the character called Falstaff was originally named Oldcastle. See "Historical Background: Sir John Falstaff and Sir John Oldcastle," pages 235–41.

45. **buff jerkin:** leather military jacket (worn by sheriff's officers, for example)

45–46. **robe of durance:** Hal puns on **durance** as "confinement, imprisonment" and as a kind of coarse, imitation-leather cloth

48. **quiddities:** quibbles

48, 50. **What a plague, what a pox:** mild oaths, though Hal's use of **pox** (which can refer to venereal disease) makes his oath more pointed

52. **called . . . reckoning:** i.e., asked for the bill (The phrase normally means "made her give an account of herself.")

61. **heir apparent:** i.e., the next king

63. **resolution:** (thieves') firmness of purpose

64. **fubbed . . . with:** i.e., cheated (fobbed) . . . by; **curb:** metal part of a horse's bridle; **old father Antic:** The word **antic** referred to theatrical characters or dancers who were clothed grotesquely and who acted fantastically. It also meant "antique," i.e., ancient. Both meanings are appropriate here.

68. **rare:** excellent; **brave:** splendid, admirable

73. **jumps:** agrees, fits

74. **humor:** temperament, disposition; **waiting . . . court:** i.e., awaiting cases to try as a judge (Hal responds as if Falstaff had meant "being in attendance at the royal court.")

76. **suits:** petitions

*(continued)*

PRINCE    As the honey of Hybla, my old lad of the castle. And is not a buff jerkin a most sweet robe of durance?          45

FALSTAFF    How now, how now, mad wag? What, in thy quips and thy quiddities? What a plague have I to do with a buff jerkin?

PRINCE    Why, what a pox have I to do with my hostess          50 of the tavern?

FALSTAFF    Well, thou hast called her to a reckoning many a time and oft.

PRINCE    Did I ever call for thee to pay thy part?

FALSTAFF    No, I'll give thee thy due. Thou hast paid all          55 there.

PRINCE    Yea, and elsewhere, so far as my coin would stretch, and where it would not, I have used my credit.

FALSTAFF    Yea, and so used it that were it not here          60 apparent that thou art heir apparent—But I prithee, sweet wag, shall there be gallows standing in England when thou art king? And resolution thus fubbed as it is with the rusty curb of old father Antic the law? Do not thou, when thou art king, hang a          65 thief.

PRINCE    No, thou shalt.

FALSTAFF    Shall I? O rare! By the Lord, I'll be a brave judge.

PRINCE    Thou judgest false already. I mean thou shalt          70 have the hanging of the thieves, and so become a rare hangman.

FALSTAFF    Well, Hal, well, and in some sort it jumps with my humor as well as waiting in the court, I can tell you.          75

PRINCE    For obtaining of suits?

FALSTAFF    Yea, for obtaining of suits, whereof the hangman hath no lean wardrobe. 'Sblood, I am as melancholy as a gib cat or a lugged bear.

77–78. **suits . . . wardrobe:** The hangman was given the clothing of those he executed.

78. **'Sblood:** an oath "by Christ's blood"

79. **gib cat . . . bear:** The tomcat and the bear pulled by the head were proverbially melancholy, as were the **old lion, lover's lute, bagpipe,** and **hare.**

83. **Moorditch:** a foul ditch in the north of London (See page 20.)

85. **comparative:** i.e., quick to make similes

87. **vanity:** that which is vain or worthless

88. **commodity:** supply

89. **rated:** reproved, scolded

90–91. **marked him not:** paid no attention to him

91–93. **he talked . . . too:** Falstaff here echoes Proverbs 1.20 and 1.24 ("Wisdom crieth . . . in the streets . . . and no man regardeth"). Hal responds by repeating the verses of Scripture.

96. **damnable iteration:** perhaps, a devilish way of quoting Scripture; or, perhaps, a way of using Scripture that will damn you

102. **an:** if

105. **take a purse:** i.e., commit a robbery

106. **Zounds:** an oath "by God's wounds"; **make one:** i.e., be one of the party

107. **baffle me:** subject me to public disgrace

110–11. **'Tis . . . vocation:** The Bible urges Christians to labor in the vocations to which they are called (see 1 Corinthians 7.20 and Ephesians 4.1).

112–13. **set a match:** i.e., arranged a robbery

113. **if . . . merit:** i.e., if the salvation of one's soul rested on one's actions, rather than on God's grace (The issue of salvation by grace or by good works was hotly debated in Shakespeare's day.)

**PRINCE**    Or an old lion, or a lover's lute.    80

**FALSTAFF**    Yea, or the drone of a Lincolnshire bagpipe.

**PRINCE**    What sayest thou to a hare, or the melancholy of Moorditch?

**FALSTAFF**    Thou hast the most unsavory ⌜similes,⌝ and art indeed the most comparative, rascaliest, sweet    85
young prince. But, Hal, I prithee trouble me no more with vanity. I would to God thou and I knew where a commodity of good names were to be bought. An old lord of the council rated me the other day in the street about you, sir, but I marked    90
him not, and yet he talked very wisely, but I regarded him not, and yet he talked wisely, and in the street, too.

**PRINCE**    Thou didst well, for wisdom cries out in the streets and no man regards it.    95

**FALSTAFF**    O, thou hast damnable iteration, and art indeed able to corrupt a saint. Thou hast done much harm upon me, Hal, God forgive thee for it. Before I knew thee, Hal, I knew nothing, and now am I, if a man should speak truly, little better than    100
one of the wicked. I must give over this life, and I will give it over. By the Lord, an I do not, I am a villain. I'll be damned for never a king's son in Christendom.

**PRINCE**    Where shall we take a purse tomorrow, Jack?    105

**FALSTAFF**    Zounds, where thou wilt, lad. I'll make one. An I do not, call me villain and baffle me.

**PRINCE**    I see a good amendment of life in thee, from praying to purse-taking.

**FALSTAFF**    Why, Hal, 'tis my vocation, Hal. 'Tis no sin    110
for a man to labor in his vocation.

*Enter Poins.*

Poins!—Now shall we know if Gadshill have set a match. O, if men were to be saved by merit, what

115. **Stand:** a highwayman's command to his victim

116. **true:** honest

121–22. **thy soul . . . leg:** Falstaff is accused of selling his soul to the devil for food and drink on a day of strict fasting.

128. **Else:** otherwise; **cozening:** cheating

132. **Canterbury:** site of the shrine of Thomas à Becket; **offerings:** donations

133. **vizards:** masks

135. **bespoke:** arranged for

136. **Eastcheap:** an area of London filled with markets and taverns (See pages xviii–xix.)

141. **hang you:** i.e., have you hanged

142. **chops:** fat cheeks

145. **honesty:** honor

147–48. **stand . . . shillings:** i.e., rob a victim of ten shillings (See the note on **stand** at line 115.) The phrase can also mean "represent the royal blood." (A **royal** was a coin worth ten shillings.)

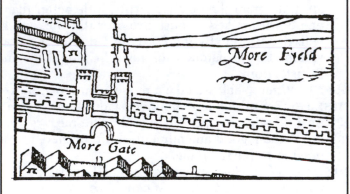

Moorditch. (1.2.83)
From R. Agas, *Map of London attributed to Ralph Agas, ca. 1560* (1905).

20

hole in hell were hot enough for him? This is the
most omnipotent villain that ever cried "Stand!" to      115
a true man.

PRINCE   Good morrow, Ned.

POINS   Good morrow, sweet Hal.—What says Mon-
sieur Remorse? What says Sir John Sack-and-
Sugar? Jack, how agrees the devil and thee about      120
thy soul that thou soldest him on Good Friday last
for a cup of Madeira and a cold capon's leg?

PRINCE   Sir John stands to his word. The devil shall
have his bargain, for he was never yet a breaker of
proverbs. He will give the devil his due.      125

POINS, ⌜*to Falstaff*⌝   Then art thou damned for keeping
thy word with the devil.

PRINCE   Else he had been damned for cozening the
devil.

POINS   But, my lads, my lads, tomorrow morning, by      130
four o'clock early at Gad's Hill, there are pilgrims
going to Canterbury with rich offerings, and traders
riding to London with fat purses. I have vizards for
you all. You have horses for yourselves. Gadshill lies
tonight in Rochester. I have bespoke supper tomor-      135
row night in Eastcheap. We may do it as secure as
sleep. If you will go, I will stuff your purses full of
crowns. If you will not, tarry at home and be
hanged.

FALSTAFF   Hear you, Yedward, if I tarry at home and      140
go not, I'll hang you for going.

POINS   You will, chops?

FALSTAFF   Hal, wilt thou make one?

PRINCE   Who, I rob? I a thief? Not I, by my faith.

FALSTAFF   There's neither honesty, manhood, nor      145
good fellowship in thee, nor thou cam'st not of
the blood royal, if thou darest not stand for ten
shillings.

PRINCE   Well then, once in my days I'll be a madcap.

FALSTAFF   Why, that's well said.      150

158–61. **God . . . believed:** language used at the close of religious services

163. **want countenance:** lack support and encouragement (from high-ranking persons)

165–66. **latter spring, Allhallown summer:** Both phrases allude to Falstaff's age. **latter:** late, second; **Allhallown:** i.e., Allhallows, or All Saints' Day (November 1)

171. **waylaid:** set the trap for

172. **they, them:** Falstaff and his fellow thieves

176–77. **wherein . . . fail:** i.e., where we may, if we please, fail (to meet them)

180. **like:** likely

181. **habits:** clothes

181–82. **every other appointment:** everything about our outfits

185. **sirrah:** a familiar form of "sir" (Poins's use of it here shows his sense that he may treat Hal familiarly.); **cases of buckram:** suits of buckram cloth

186. **for the nonce:** for the occasion; **immask:** i.e., hide; **noted:** well-known

PRINCE   Well, come what will, I'll tarry at home.

FALSTAFF   By the Lord, I'll be a traitor then when thou
  art king.

PRINCE   I care not.

POINS   Sir John, I prithee leave the Prince and me   155
  alone. I will lay him down such reasons for this
  adventure that he shall go.

FALSTAFF   Well, God give thee the spirit of persuasion,
  and him the ears of profiting, that what thou
  speakest may move, and what he hears may be   160
  believed, that the true prince may, for recreation
  sake, prove a false thief, for the poor abuses of the
  time want countenance. Farewell. You shall find me
  in Eastcheap.

PRINCE   Farewell, ⌜thou⌝ latter spring. Farewell, All-   165
  hallown summer.                           ⌜*Falstaff exits.*⌝

POINS   Now, my good sweet honey lord, ride with us
  tomorrow. I have a jest to execute that I cannot
  manage alone. Falstaff, ⌜Peto, Bardolph,⌝ and Gadshill shall rob those men that we have already   170
  waylaid. Yourself and I will not be there. And when
  they have the booty, if you and I do not rob them,
  cut this head off from my shoulders.

PRINCE   How shall we part with them in setting forth?

POINS   Why, we will set forth before or after them, and   175
  appoint them a place of meeting, wherein it is at our
  pleasure to fail; and then will they adventure upon
  the exploit themselves, which they shall have no
  sooner achieved but we'll set upon them.

PRINCE   Yea, but 'tis like that they will know us by our   180
  horses, by our habits, and by every other appointment to be ourselves.

POINS   Tut, our horses they shall not see; I'll tie them
  in the wood. Our vizards we will change after we
  leave them. And, sirrah, I have cases of buckram   185
  for the nonce, to immask our noted outward garments.

188. **doubt:** fear; **too hard for us:** i.e., stronger than we are

189. **for:** i.e., as for

190. **turned back:** i.e., ran away

192. **forswear arms:** give up wearing a sword; **virtue:** power, worth

193. **incomprehensible:** immense, boundless

195. **wards:** defensive motions

202. **know you:** am aware of what you are

203. **unyoked:** uncontrolled; **humor . . . idleness:** inclination to behave irresponsibly

205. **Who:** i.e., which; **base:** menial; **contagious:** corrupting

206–10. **his, he, himself, he, him:** All of these words refer to the **sun.**

212. **sport:** play

213. **they:** i.e., holidays

214. **accidents:** events (Proverbial: "That which is rare is precious.")

218. **hopes:** expectations

219. **on . . . ground:** against a dark background

**PRINCE**   Yea, but I doubt they will be too hard for us.

**POINS**   Well, for two of them, I know them to be as
true-bred cowards as ever turned back; and for the      190
third, if he fight longer than he sees reason, I'll
forswear arms. The virtue of this jest will be the
incomprehensible lies that this same fat rogue will
tell us when we meet at supper: how thirty at least
he fought with, what wards, what blows, what      195
extremities he endured; and in the reproof of this
lives the jest.

**PRINCE**   Well, I'll go with thee. Provide us all things
necessary and meet me tomorrow night in Eastcheap. There I'll sup. Farewell.      200

**POINS**   Farewell, my lord.          *Poins exits.*

**PRINCE**
I know you all, and will awhile uphold
The unyoked humor of your idleness.
Yet herein will I imitate the sun,
Who doth permit the base contagious clouds      205
To smother up his beauty from the world,
That, when he please again to be himself,
Being wanted, he may be more wondered at
By breaking through the foul and ugly mists
Of vapors that did seem to strangle him.      210
If all the year were playing holidays,
To sport would be as tedious as to work,
But when they seldom come, they wished-for come,
And nothing pleaseth but rare accidents.
So when this loose behavior I throw off      215
And pay the debt I never promisèd,
By how much better than my word I am,
By so much shall I falsify men's hopes;
And, like bright metal on a sullen ground,
My reformation, glitt'ring o'er my fault,      220
Shall show more goodly and attract more eyes
Than that which hath no foil to set it off.

224. **Redeeming:** i.e., recovering by paying that which is owed (The idea of **redeeming time** is both proverbial and biblical. See, e.g., Ephesians 5.16.)

**1.3**  King Henry meets with Hotspur, Hotspur's father (Northumberland), and his uncle (Worcester) to demand that Hotspur yield his prisoners to the crown. Hotspur agrees to do so only if Henry will ransom Mortimer, Hotspur's brother-in-law, from captivity in Wales. Henry refuses and exits. Hotspur is enraged by Henry's accusation that Mortimer is a traitor and is happy to go along with a plot devised by Worcester and Northumberland to oust Henry from the throne.

——————

2. **Unapt:** not inclined
3. **found me:** discovered me (to be so), found me out; or, found me so
5. **myself:** i.e., a king
6. **condition:** disposition, temperament
10. **Our house:** i.e., the Percy family
13. **holp:** helped; **portly:** imposing, majestic
17. **peremptory:** obstinate (pronounced **pèremptory**)
19. **moody  frontier . . . brow:** i.e., a subject's frowning forehead   **frontier:** forehead
20. **us, we:** i.e., me, I (the royal "we")

I'll so offend to make offense a skill,
Redeeming time when men think least I will.

*He exits.*


⌜Scene 3⌝
*Enter the King, Northumberland, Worcester, Hotspur,*
⌜*and*⌝ *Sir Walter Blunt, with others.*

KING, ⌜*to Northumberland, Worcester, and Hotspur*⌝
My blood hath been too cold and temperate,
Unapt to stir at these indignities,
And you have found me, for accordingly
You tread upon my patience. But be sure
I will from henceforth rather be myself,          5
Mighty and to be feared, than my condition,
Which hath been smooth as oil, soft as young down,
And therefore lost that title of respect
Which the proud soul ne'er pays but to the proud.
WORCESTER
Our house, my sovereign liege, little deserves     10
The scourge of greatness to be used on it,
And that same greatness too which our own hands
Have holp to make so portly.
NORTHUMBERLAND    My lord—
KING
Worcester, get thee gone, for I do see           15
Danger and disobedience in thine eye.
O sir, your presence is too bold and peremptory,
And majesty might never yet endure
The moody frontier of a servant brow.
You have good leave to leave us. When we need     20
Your use and counsel, we shall send for you.

*Worcester exits.*

You were about to speak.
NORTHUMBERLAND              Yea, my good lord.

27. **delivered:** reported

28. **envy . . . or misprision:** malice or misunder-standing

32. **dry:** thirsty; **extreme:** pronounced èxtreme

35. **new reaped:** i.e., freshly shaved; or, with beard freshly trimmed

36. **Showed:** looked; **harvest home:** the end of harvesting

39. **pouncet box:** small container filled with a fragrant substance (See page 34.); **ever and anon:** now and then

40. **gave his nose:** brought up to his nose

41. **Who therewith angry:** i.e., which, being angry that the pouncet box had been taken away

42. **Took . . . snuff:** (1) took offense; (2) sniffed angrily, or, perhaps, sneezed; **still:** continually

44. **them:** i.e., the soldiers

45. **slovenly:** disgusting; **corse:** corpse

46. **his nobility:** i.e., himself

47. **holiday . . . terms:** To "speak holiday" meant to use choice language. **lady terms:** words used by ladies

51. **popinjay:** (1) parrot; (2) vain, conceited person

52. **grief:** anger; or, pain

53. **neglectingly:** negligently, carelessly

57–58. **God . . . mark:** here, an expression of impatience

Those prisoners in your Highness' name demanded,
Which Harry Percy here at Holmedon took,                    25
Were, as he says, not with such strength denied
As is delivered to your Majesty.
Either envy, therefore, or misprision
Is guilty of this fault, and not my son.
HOTSPUR
My liege, I did deny no prisoners.                          30
But I remember, when the fight was done,
When I was dry with rage and extreme toil,
Breathless and faint, leaning upon my sword,
Came there a certain lord, neat and trimly dressed,
Fresh as a bridegroom, and his chin new reaped             35
Showed like a stubble land at harvest home.
He was perfumèd like a milliner,
And 'twixt his finger and his thumb he held
A pouncet box, which ever and anon
He gave his nose and took 't away again,                   40
Who therewith angry, when it next came there,
Took it in snuff; and still he smiled and talked.
And as the soldiers bore dead bodies by,
He called them untaught knaves, unmannerly,
To bring a slovenly unhandsome corse                       45
Betwixt the wind and his nobility.
With many holiday and lady terms
He questioned me, amongst the rest demanded
My prisoners in your Majesty's behalf.
I then, all smarting with my wounds being cold,            50
To be so pestered with a popinjay,
Out of my grief and my impatience
Answered neglectingly I know not what—
He should, or he should not; for he made me mad
To see him shine so brisk and smell so sweet               55
And talk so like a waiting-gentlewoman
Of guns, and drums, and wounds—God save the
  mark!—

59. **sovereignest:** most excellent

60. **parmacety:** i.e., spermaceti, a waxy substance used as a medicinal ointment, taken from the head of the sperm whale

62. **saltpeter:** the chief ingredient of gunpowder

64. **Which . . . destroyed:** i.e., the saltpeter had destroyed many brave men

65. **but for:** except for

67. **bald unjointed:** trivial, incoherent

70. **Come current for:** i.e., be accepted as

75. **with . . . retold:** i.e., taking into account the rest of the story

77. **impeach:** (1) attack, discredit; (2) make treasonous

78. **so:** i.e., provided that

79. **yet . . . deny:** he still denies

80–81. **But . . . That:** i.e., unless

81. **straight:** immediately

82–87. **His brother-in-law . . . married:** Shakespeare follows the chronicles of the time in treating two Edmund Mortimers as if they were a single person. (Sir Edmund Mortimer, brother to Hotspur's wife, was captured by Glendower and married Glendower's daughter; his nephew, Edmund Mortimer, was fifth earl of March and had a strong claim to the throne. See family chart, page 2, and lines 147–63 below.)

89. **indent with fears:** i.e., make a covenant with those we should fear

And telling me the sovereignest thing on earth
Was parmacety for an inward bruise,                              60
And that it was great pity, so it was,
This villainous saltpeter should be digged
Out of the bowels of the harmless earth,
Which many a good tall fellow had destroyed
So cowardly, and but for these vile guns                         65
He would himself have been a soldier.
This bald unjointed chat of his, my lord,
I answered indirectly, as I said,
And I beseech you, let not his report
Come current for an accusation                                   70
Betwixt my love and your high Majesty.

BLUNT
The circumstance considered, good my lord,
Whate'er Lord Harry Percy then had said
To such a person and in such a place,
At such a time, with all the rest retold,                        75
May reasonably die and never rise
To do him wrong or any way impeach
What then he said, so he unsay it now.

KING
Why, yet he doth deny his prisoners,
But with proviso and exception                                   80
That we at our own charge shall ransom straight
His brother-in-law, the foolish Mortimer,
Who, on my soul, hath willfully betrayed
The lives of those that he did lead to fight
Against that great magician, damned Glendower,                   85
Whose daughter, as we hear, that Earl of March
Hath lately married. Shall our coffers then
Be emptied to redeem a traitor home?
Shall we buy treason and indent with fears
When they have lost and forfeited themselves?                    90
No, on the barren mountains let him starve,
For I shall never hold that man my friend

94. **revolted Mortimer:** i.e., Mortimer, who has thrown off his allegiance

96. **fall off:** i.e., go over to the enemy

97. **But by:** except through

99. **mouthèd:** i.e., open like mouths

100. **Severn's . . . bank:** i.e., the sedge-covered bank of the river Severn

102. **confound:** spend

103. **changing hardiment:** exchanging brave deeds

104. **breathed:** i.e., stopped to catch their breath

107. **Who:** i.e., the Severn River; **affrighted with:** frightened by

109. **his crisp head:** i.e., its rough water (literally, his curly hair) The words play on the image of the river as a frightened man running from the bloody looks of the fighters.

110. **combatants:** pronounced **còmbatants**

111. **policy:** cunning

112. **Color:** misrepresent; paint, as with cosmetics (literally, stain with blood); **her:** its

115. **with revolt:** i.e., with the charge of having changed his allegiance

116. **belie:** misrepresent

118. **alone:** i.e., in single combat

120. **sirrah:** familiar form of "sir," used here to emphasize the king's position of authority over Hotspur

123. **kind:** manner

125. **license your departure:** give you leave to depart

Whose tongue shall ask me for one penny cost
To ransom home revolted Mortimer.
HOTSPUR  Revolted Mortimer!                                   95
He never did fall off, my sovereign liege,
But by the chance of war. To prove that true
Needs no more but one tongue for all those wounds,
Those mouthèd wounds, which valiantly he took
When on the gentle Severn's sedgy bank              100
In single opposition hand to hand
He did confound the best part of an hour
In changing hardiment with great Glendower.
Three times they breathed, and three times did they
    drink,                                                     105
Upon agreement, of swift Severn's flood,
Who then, affrighted with their bloody looks,
Ran fearfully among the trembling reeds
And hid his crisp head in the hollow bank,
Blood-stainèd with these valiant combatants.       110
Never did bare and rotten policy
Color her working with such deadly wounds,
Nor never could the noble Mortimer
Receive so many, and all willingly.
Then let not him be slandered with revolt.          115
KING
Thou dost belie him, Percy; thou dost belie him.
He never did encounter with Glendower.
I tell thee, he durst as well have met the devil alone
As Owen Glendower for an enemy.
Art thou not ashamed? But, sirrah, henceforth      120
Let me not hear you speak of Mortimer.
Send me your prisoners with the speediest means,
Or you shall hear in such a kind from me
As will displease you.—My lord Northumberland,
We license your departure with your son.—           125
Send us your prisoners, or you will hear of it.
                    *King exits ⌜with Blunt and others.⌝*

128. **I . . . straight:** i.e., I'll go after him right now

130. **Albeit . . . head:** i.e., even if I risk my head

131. **choler:** anger

134. **Zounds:** an oath "by Christ's wounds"

135. **Want mercy:** lack mercy (from God)

140. **ingrate:** ungrateful; **cankered:** malignant; spiteful; **Bolingbroke:** King Henry's family name

141. **made . . . mad:** i.e., put . . . in a rage

143. **forsooth:** here, an expression of impatience

146. **an eye of death:** perhaps, a deathlike look of fear; or, perhaps, a look threatening death

148. **he:** i.e., Mortimer (See note on lines 82–87, above.)

149. **next of blood:** i.e., heir to the throne

151–55. **And . . . murderèd:** This story is dramatized by Shakespeare in *Richard II*.

151. **unhappy:** unfortunate

152. **in us:** i.e., committed by us

A pouncet box. (1.3.39)
From Walther Hermann Ryff, *Confect Bock* (1563).

HOTSPUR

    An if the devil come and roar for them,
    I will not send them. I will after straight
    And tell him so, for I will ease my heart,
    Albeit I make a hazard of my head.           130

NORTHUMBERLAND

    What, drunk with choler? Stay and pause awhile.
    Here comes your uncle.

*Enter Worcester.*

HOTSPUR                  Speak of Mortimer?

    Zounds, I will speak of him, and let my soul
    Want mercy if I do not join with him.        135
    Yea, on his part I'll empty all these veins
    And shed my dear blood drop by drop in the dust,
    But I will lift the downtrod Mortimer
    As high in the air as this unthankful king,
    As this ingrate and cankered Bolingbroke.     140

NORTHUMBERLAND

    Brother, the King hath made your nephew mad.

WORCESTER

    Who struck this heat up after I was gone?

HOTSPUR

    He will forsooth have all my prisoners,
    And when I urged the ransom once again
    Of my wife's brother, then his cheek looked pale,    145
    And on my face he turned an eye of death,
    Trembling even at the name of Mortimer.

WORCESTER

    I cannot blame him. Was not he proclaimed
    By Richard, that dead is, the next of blood?

NORTHUMBERLAND

    He was; I heard the proclamation.          150
    And then it was when the unhappy king—
    Whose wrongs in us God pardon!—did set forth
    Upon his Irish expedition;

158. **soft:** i.e., wait a minute

159. **brother:** i.e., brother-in-law

163. **wished him . . . starve:** i.e., wanted Mortimer . . . to starve

167. **Of . . . subornation:** i.e., of having instigated a murder (The following lines make it clear that he is referring to the death of Richard II.)

169. **base:** contemptible; **second means:** agents

172. **line:** rank, station; **predicament:** dangerous situation

173. **range:** occupy a place (with wordplay on its more usual meaning of "wander around, stray")

177. **gage them:** bind themselves (either by offering themselves as guarantee or risking themselves as a wager)

180. **thorn, canker:** i.e., the prickly wild rose (*Rosa canina*)

From whence he, intercepted, did return
To be deposed and shortly murderèd.                          155
WORCESTER
  And for whose death we in the world's wide mouth
  Live scandalized and foully spoken of.
HOTSPUR
  But soft, I pray you. Did King Richard then
  Proclaim my brother Edmund Mortimer
  Heir to the crown?                                    160
NORTHUMBERLAND   He did; myself did hear it.
HOTSPUR
  Nay then, I cannot blame his cousin king
  That wished him on the barren mountains starve.
  But shall it be that you that set the crown
  Upon the head of this forgetful man                    165
  And for his sake wear the detested blot
  Of murderous subornation—shall it be
  That you a world of curses undergo,
  Being the agents or base second means,
  The cords, the ladder, or the hangman rather?          170
  O, pardon me that I descend so low
  To show the line and the predicament
  Wherein you range under this subtle king.
  Shall it for shame be spoken in these days,
  Or fill up chronicles in time to come,                 175
  That men of your nobility and power
  Did gage them both in an unjust behalf
  (As both of you, God pardon it, have done)
  To put down Richard, that sweet lovely rose,
  And plant this thorn, this canker, Bolingbroke?         180
  And shall it in more shame be further spoken
  That you are fooled, discarded, and shook off
  By him for whom these shames you underwent?
  No, yet time serves wherein you may redeem
  Your banished honors and restore yourselves             185
  Into the good thoughts of the world again,

187. **disdained:** i.e., disdainful

193. **unclasp:** Books were often fastened by means of metal clasps. (See page 40.)

195. **matter:** i.e., subject matter

198. **footing:** surface

199. **he:** such a man; **or:** i.e., whether he

201. **So:** i.e., provided that

202. **them:** i.e., danger and honor

203. **lion:** a symbol of the monarch (Both **rouse** and **start** mean to cause game to run or fly from hiding.)

208. **deep:** i.e., sea

211. **So:** i.e., provided; **her:** i.e., honor, pictured here as a woman in need of rescue

213. **out . . . fellowship:** i.e., curses on sharing honor's favors with others

214. **figures:** (1) figures of speech; (2) images

215. **attend:** pay attention to

217. **I . . . mercy:** i.e., I beg your pardon

"The King himself is to be feared as the lion." (3.3.158)
From John Speed, *A prospect of the most famous part of the world* (1631).

Revenge the jeering and disdained contempt
Of this proud king, who studies day and night
To answer all the debt he owes to you
Even with the bloody payment of your deaths.                    190
Therefore I say—
WORCESTER                Peace, cousin, say no more.
And now I will unclasp a secret book,
And to your quick-conceiving discontents
I'll read you matter deep and dangerous,                        195
As full of peril and adventurous spirit
As to o'erwalk a current roaring loud
On the unsteadfast footing of a spear.
HOTSPUR
If he fall in, good night, or sink or swim!
Send danger from the east unto the west,                        200
So honor cross it from the north to south,
And let them grapple. O, the blood more stirs
To rouse a lion than to start a hare!
NORTHUMBERLAND, ⌜*to Worcester*⌝
Imagination of some great exploit
Drives him beyond the bounds of patience.                       205
⌜HOTSPUR⌝
By heaven, methinks it were an easy leap
To pluck bright honor from the pale-faced moon,
Or dive into the bottom of the deep,
Where fathom line could never touch the ground,
And pluck up drownèd honor by the locks,                        210
So he that doth redeem her thence might wear
Without corrival all her dignities.
But out upon this half-faced fellowship!
WORCESTER
He apprehends a world of figures here,
But not the form of what he should attend.—                     215
Good cousin, give me audience for a while.
HOTSPUR
I cry you mercy.

221. **a Scot of them:** i.e., a single Scot

224. **start away:** i.e., will not stay still

234. **still:** constantly, always

237. **Save:** i.e., except

238. **sword . . . buckler:** These were weapons worn mostly by servants and lower-class men.

249. **stung with pismires:** i.e., as if stung by ants

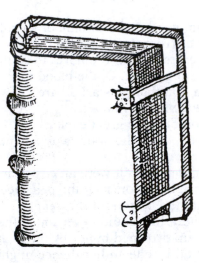

A book fastened with clasps. (1.3.193)
From *Notita vtraque cum Orientis tum Occidentis* (1552).

WORCESTER          Those same noble Scots
  That are your prisoners—
HOTSPUR                              I'll keep them all.          220
  By God, he shall not have a Scot of them.
  No, if a Scot would save his soul, he shall not.
  I'll keep them, by this hand!
WORCESTER                              You start away
  And lend no ear unto my purposes:          225
  Those prisoners you shall keep—
HOTSPUR   Nay, I will. That's flat!
  He said he would not ransom Mortimer,
  Forbade my tongue to speak of Mortimer.
  But I will find him when he lies asleep,          230
  And in his ear I'll hollo "Mortimer."
  Nay, I'll have a starling shall be taught to speak
  Nothing but "Mortimer," and give it him
  To keep his anger still in motion.
WORCESTER   Hear you, cousin, a word.          235
HOTSPUR
  All studies here I solemnly defy,
  Save how to gall and pinch this Bolingbroke.
  And that same sword-and-buckler Prince of Wales—
  But that I think his father loves him not
  And would be glad he met with some mischance—          240
  I would have him poisoned with a pot of ale.
WORCESTER
  Farewell, kinsman. I'll talk to you
  When you are better tempered to attend.
NORTHUMBERLAND, ⌜*to Hotspur*⌝
  Why, what a wasp-stung and impatient fool
  Art thou to break into this woman's mood,          245
  Tying thine ear to no tongue but thine own!
HOTSPUR
  Why, look you, I am ⌜whipped⌝ and scourged with
    rods,
  Nettled and stung with pismires, when I hear

250. **politician:** shrewd schemer

253. **madcap duke his uncle:** i.e., the duke of York, Richard's uncle; **kept:** lived, stayed

257. **Ravenspurgh:** a seaport on the Humber River, where Bolingbroke landed when he returned to England from exile

258. **Berkeley Castle:** a castle near Bristol

260. **candy:** i.e., sweet, melting; **deal:** quantity

261. **fawning greyhound:** The dog was often used as the symbol of flattery.

262. **Look when:** i.e., whenever, as soon as

263. **gentle:** i.e., noble

264. **cozeners:** cheats (with a pun on "cousin-ers," i.e., those who call me "cousin")

266. **to it:** i.e., go to it

267. **stay your leisure:** i.e., wait until you have time for us

270. **Deliver them up:** free them; **straight:** straightway, immediately

271. **mean:** means

272. **For powers:** i.e., for raising an army; **divers:** diverse, various

276. **bosom:** i.e., confidence

280. **bears hard:** resents

281. **His . . . Scroop:** The earl of Scroop was executed for treason in 1399; Shakespeare follows the chronicles in making him the brother of the archbishop of York.

282. **estimation:** conjecture

Of this vile politician, Bolingbroke.                                                250
In Richard's time—what do you call the place?
A plague upon it! It is in Gloucestershire.
'Twas where the madcap duke his uncle kept,
His uncle York, where I first bowed my knee
Unto this king of smiles, this Bolingbroke.                                   255
'Sblood, when you and he came back from
    Ravenspurgh.
NORTHUMBERLAND   At Berkeley Castle.
HOTSPUR   You say true.
Why, what a candy deal of courtesy                                           260
This fawning greyhound then did proffer me:
"Look when his infant fortune came to age,"
And "gentle Harry Percy," and "kind cousin."
O, the devil take such cozeners!—God forgive me!
Good uncle, tell your tale. I have done.                                      265
WORCESTER
Nay, if you have not, to it again.
We will stay your leisure.
HOTSPUR                          I have done, i' faith.
WORCESTER
Then once more to your Scottish prisoners:
Deliver them up without their ransom straight,                     270
And make the Douglas' son your only mean
For powers in Scotland, which, for divers reasons
Which I shall send you written, be assured
Will easily be granted.—You, my lord,
Your son in Scotland being thus employed,                          275
Shall secretly into the bosom creep
Of that same noble prelate well beloved,
The Archbishop.
HOTSPUR   Of York, is it not?
WORCESTER   True, who bears hard                                     280
His brother's death at Bristol, the Lord Scroop.
I speak not this in estimation,

285. **stays:** waits

288. **Before . . . slip:** i.e., you always unleash the dogs before the quarry is stirring

290. **power:** forces

293. **aimed:** devised

294. **'tis . . . speed:** i.e., we have great reason to make haste

295. **a head:** i.e., an army

296. **bear . . . can:** i.e., no matter how carefully we conduct ourselves

299. **pay us home:** i.e., repay us completely (The term is from fencing, where a *home thrust* is a sword thrust that hits a vital spot. Here, the deadly sense of the term is suggested.)

305. **suddenly:** soon, shortly

307. **powers:** forces

308. **happily:** successfully (with a play on its usual meaning)

310. **Which:** i.e., our fortunes

As what I think might be, but what I know
Is ruminated, plotted, and set down,
And only stays but to behold the face          285
Of that occasion that shall bring it on.
HOTSPUR
I smell it. Upon my life it will do well.
NORTHUMBERLAND
Before the game is afoot thou still let'st slip.
HOTSPUR
Why, it cannot choose but be a noble plot.
And then the power of Scotland and of York          290
To join with Mortimer, ha?
WORCESTER                              And so they shall.
HOTSPUR
In faith, it is exceedingly well aimed.
WORCESTER
And 'tis no little reason bids us speed
To save our heads by raising of a head,          295
For bear ourselves as even as we can,
The King will always think him in our debt,
And think we think ourselves unsatisfied,
Till he hath found a time to pay us home.
And see already how he doth begin          300
To make us strangers to his looks of love.
HOTSPUR
He does, he does. We'll be revenged on him.
WORCESTER
Cousin, farewell. No further go in this
Than I by letters shall direct your course.
When time is ripe, which will be suddenly,          305
I'll steal to Glendower and Lord Mortimer,
Where you and Douglas and our powers at once,
As I will fashion it, shall happily meet
To bear ⌜our⌝ fortunes in our own strong arms,
Which now we hold at much uncertainty.          310

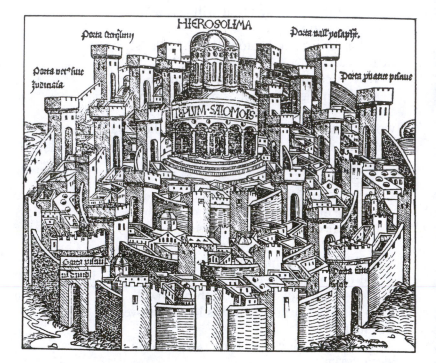

Jerusalem. (1.1.19)
From Hartmann Schedel, *Liber chronicorum* (1493).

NORTHUMBERLAND
　Farewell, good brother. We shall thrive, I trust.
HOTSPUR
　Uncle, adieu. O, let the hours be short
　Till fields and blows and groans applaud our sport.
　　　　　　　　　　　　　　　　　　　*They exit.*

The History of

# HENRY IV
## Part 1

---

ACT 2

**2.1** Gadshill, the "setter" for Falstaff and his fellow thieves, seeks information at an inn about the travelers whom they plan to rob.

---

O SD. **Carrier:** one who hauls merchandise, produce, etc.; **lantern:** This signals to the audience that the scene takes place at night.

1. **An:** if; **four . . . day:** i.e., four o'clock in the morning

2. **Charles's Wain:** i.e., "Charlemagne's wagon," a constellation of stars also known as the Big Dipper

3. **horse:** i.e., horses

4. **ostler:** one who takes care of horses at an inn

5. **Anon:** i.e., just a minute

6. **Tom:** probably addressed to the Second Carrier, who is just entering; **Cut:** A cut is a horse with a docked tail, or a gelding; here, it seems to be the horse's name.

7. **flocks:** locks of wool; **point:** i.e., the pommel of the saddle; **wrung:** chafed

8. **withers:** ridge between the horse's shoulders; **out of all cess:** beyond estimation, excessively

9. **Peas and beans:** i.e., cheap food for horses

9–10. **dank . . . dog:** i.e., damp as can be

10. **next:** i.e., quickest; **jades:** horses

11. **bots:** intestinal worms

11–12. **Robin ostler:** i.e., Robin, the ostler

16. **house:** inn; **London road:** i.e., the road leading to London

17. **tench:** a freshwater fish related to the carp (According to Pliny's *Natural History*, "the very fleas that skip so merrily in summertime . . . is thought to

*(continued)*

# ⌐ACT 2⌐

⌐Scene 1⌐

*Enter a Carrier with a lantern in his hand.*

FIRST CARRIER  Heigh-ho! An it be not four by the day,
I'll be hanged. Charles's Wain is over the new
chimney, and yet our horse not packed.—What,
ostler!

OSTLER, ⌐*within*⌐  Anon, anon.                                        5

FIRST CARRIER  I prithee, Tom, beat Cut's saddle. Put a
few flocks in the point. Poor jade is wrung in the
withers out of all cess.

*Enter another Carrier, ⌐with a lantern.⌐*

SECOND CARRIER  Peas and beans are as dank here as a
dog, and that is the next way to give poor jades the       10
bots. This house is turned upside down since Robin
ostler died.

FIRST CARRIER  Poor fellow never joyed since the price
of oats rose. It was the death of him.

SECOND CARRIER  I think this be the most villainous       15
house in all London road for fleas. I am stung like a
tench.

FIRST CARRIER  Like a tench? By the Mass, there is
ne'er a king christen could be better bit than I have
been since the first cock.                                            20

SECOND CARRIER  Why, they will allow us ne'er a jor-

51

trouble the poor fishes in their sleep" [trans. Philemon Holland, 1601].)

19. **king christen:** i.e., Christian king

20. **first cock:** i.e., midnight

21–22. **jordan:** chamber pot

22. **leak . . . chimney:** urinate in the fireplace (**Your** is used as an impersonal pronoun with no definite meaning.)

22–23. **your chamber-lye:** urine; **loach:** another freshwater fish

24. **What:** an interjection, here suggesting impatience; **come away:** i.e., come along

26. **a gammon of bacon:** i.e., a ham

27. **races:** roots

27–28. **Charing Cross:** a market town west of London (now part of the city)

29. **God's body:** an oath by the body of Christ; **pannier:** a large basket hung over a horse's back

31. **never:** i.e., not

32. **as good . . . drink:** a colloquial expression ("as good a deed as to take a drink")

32–33. **the pate on thee:** i.e., your head

33. **a very villain:** i.e., a complete scoundrel

34. **Hast . . . thee?:** i.e., can't you be trusted?

39. **soft:** i.e., wait a minute

43. **when, canst tell:** a colloquial way of saying no

48. **Time enough:** i.e., in time

50–51. **will . . . company:** i.e., want to travel with company

51. **great charge:** i.e., a lot of money or other possessions

52. **chamberlain:** one responsible for the bedrooms in the inn

dan, and then we leak in your chimney, and your
chamber-lye breeds fleas like a loach.

FIRST CARRIER  What, ostler, come away and be
hanged. Come away.                                            25

SECOND CARRIER  I have a gammon of bacon and two
races of ginger to be delivered as far as Charing
Cross.

FIRST CARRIER  God's body, the turkeys in my pannier
are quite starved.—What, ostler! A plague on thee!          30
Hast thou never an eye in thy head? Canst not hear?
An 'twere not as good deed as drink to break the
pate on thee, I am a very villain. Come, and be
hanged. Hast no faith in thee?

*Enter Gadshill.*

GADSHILL  Good morrow, carriers. What's o'clock?            35
⌈FIRST⌉ CARRIER  I think it be two o'clock.

GADSHILL  I prithee, lend me thy lantern to see my
gelding in the stable.

FIRST CARRIER  Nay, by God, soft. I know a trick worth
two of that, i' faith.                                       40

GADSHILL, ⌈*to Second Carrier*⌉  I pray thee, lend me
thine.

SECOND CARRIER  Ay, when, canst tell? "Lend me thy
lantern," quoth he. Marry, I'll see thee hanged
first.                                                       45

GADSHILL  Sirrah carrier, what time do you mean to
come to London?

SECOND CARRIER  Time enough to go to bed with a
candle, I warrant thee. Come, neighbor Mugs,
we'll call up the gentlemen. They will along with      50
company, for they have great charge.

⌈*Carriers*⌉ *exit.*

GADSHILL  What ho, chamberlain!

*Enter Chamberlain.*

53. **At . . . pickpurse:** i.e., "Here I am, said the pickpocket to his victim" (a colloquial expression)

54. **even as fair as:** i.e., just as good as saying

55–56. **thou variest . . . purses:** i.e., your work is no more different from picking purses

56. **giving direction:** i.e., supervising

57. **laboring:** i.e., doing the actual work

58. **Good morrow:** good morning

58–59. **It . . . yesternight:** i.e., what I told you last night is still true

59–60. **franklin . . . Kent:** i.e., a wealthy landowner from the Weald (forest) of Kent (a large district southeast of London)

62. **auditor:** an official who examines monetary accounts (perhaps an officer of the king's Exchequer)

64–65. **eggs and butter:** i.e., breakfast

65. **presently:** at once

66–67. **Saint Nicholas' clerks:** i.e., robbers, highwaymen (The patron saint of travelers, St. Nicholas, became the saint of robbers as well. The name also suggests "Old Nick," the devil.)

74. **Troyans:** Trojans (a slang term for "good fellows," "companions"), here referring to Prince Hal

75. **the which:** i.e., who; **sport sake:** i.e., fun

76. **the profession:** i.e., of robbery

78. **make all whole:** i.e., have any scandal covered up; or, have any resulting problems smoothed over

78–81. **I am joined . . . malt-worms:** i.e., my companions are not base scoundrels **foot-land-rakers:** i.e., footpads, highwaymen on foot **long-staff . . . strikers:** i.e., thieves with poles who steal paltry sums **mad . . . malt-worms:** i.e., beer drinkers with mustaches and florid faces

*(continued)*

CHAMBERLAIN   At hand, quoth pickpurse.

GADSHILL   That's even as fair as "at hand, quoth the
 Chamberlain," for thou variest no more from          55
 picking of purses than giving direction doth from
 laboring: thou layest the plot how.

CHAMBERLAIN   Good morrow, Master Gadshill. It holds
 current that I told you yesternight: there's a franklin in the Wild of Kent hath brought three hundred    60
 marks with him in gold. I heard him tell it to one of
 his company last night at supper—a kind of auditor,
 one that hath abundance of charge too, God knows
 what. They are up already and call for eggs and
 butter. They will away presently.                     65

GADSHILL   Sirrah, if they meet not with Saint Nicholas'
 clerks, I'll give thee this neck.

CHAMBERLAIN   No, I'll none of it. I pray thee, keep that
 for the hangman, for I know thou worshipest Saint
 Nicholas as truly as a man of falsehood may.          70

GADSHILL   What talkest thou to me of the hangman? If
 I hang, I'll make a fat pair of gallows, for if I hang,
 old Sir John hangs with me, and thou knowest he is
 no starveling. Tut, there are other Troyans that
 thou dream'st not of, the which for sport sake are     75
 content to do the profession some grace, that
 would, if matters should be looked into, for their
 own credit sake make all whole. I am joined with no
 foot-land-rakers, no long-staff sixpenny strikers,
 none of these mad mustachio purple-hued malt-          80
 worms, but with nobility and tranquillity, burgo-
 masters and great oneyers, such as can hold in, such
 as will strike sooner than speak, and speak sooner
 than drink, and drink sooner than pray, and yet,
 zounds, I lie, for they pray continually to their saint  85
 the commonwealth, or rather not pray to her but
 prey on her, for they ride up and down on her and
 make her their boots.

81. **nobility:** i.e., noblemen; **tranquillity:** perhaps, those who have easy lives

82. **great oneyers:** i.e., great ones; **hold in:** i.e., keep their own counsel

88. **boots:** booty, profit (The Chamberlain responds with the obvious pun.)

90. **in foul way:** i.e., on a muddy road

91. **liquored:** covered with grease

92. **as in a castle:** i.e., with complete safety (with a probable reference to Sir John Oldcastle)

93. **receipt of:** recipe for; **fern seed:** popularly thought to make one invisible

98. **purchase:** plunder, booty

101. **Go to:** an expression of impatience; **Homo . . . men:** Gadshill quotes from *Lily's Latin Grammar* to defend his oath "as I am a true man." **Homo:** Latin for "man"

103. **muddy:** immoral, "dirty"; stupid


**2.2** Falstaff, Peto, Bardolph, and Gadshill rob the travelers and are, in turn, robbed by Prince Hal and Poins in disguise.

––––––––––

2. **frets:** fusses, fumes (with a pun on **frets** meaning to become frayed, like **gummed velvet**, velvet that has been treated with resin and frays easily)

3. **Stand close:** i.e., hide

12–13. **by the square:** exactly, precisely

13. **break my wind:** i.e., wheeze like a broken-winded horse; expel intestinal gas

CHAMBERLAIN   What, the commonwealth their boots?
Will she hold out water in foul way?                          90
GADSHILL   She will, she will. Justice hath liquored her.
We steal as in a castle, cocksure. We have the
receipt of fern seed; we walk invisible.
CHAMBERLAIN   Nay, by my faith, I think you are more
beholding to the night than to fern seed for your          95
walking invisible.
GADSHILL   Give me thy hand. Thou shalt have a share in
our purchase, as I am a true man.
CHAMBERLAIN   Nay, rather let me have it as you are a
false thief.                                                  100
GADSHILL   Go to. *Homo* is a common name to all men.
Bid the ostler bring my gelding out of the stable.
Farewell, you muddy knave.
                                            ⌜*They exit.*⌝


⌜Scene 2⌝
*Enter Prince, Poins,* ⌜*Bardolph,*⌝ *and Peto.*

POINS   Come, shelter, shelter! I have removed Falstaff's
horse, and he frets like a gummed velvet.
PRINCE   Stand close.   ⌜*Poins, Bardolph, and Peto exit.*⌝

*Enter Falstaff.*

FALSTAFF   Poins! Poins, and be hanged! Poins!
PRINCE   Peace, you fat-kidneyed rascal. What a brawl-       5
ing dost thou keep!
FALSTAFF   Where's Poins, Hal?
PRINCE   He is walked up to the top of the hill. I'll go
seek him.                           ⌜*Prince exits.*⌝
FALSTAFF   I am accursed to rob in that thief's company.     10
The rascal hath removed my horse and tied him I
know not where. If I travel but four foot by the
square further afoot, I shall break my wind. Well, I

14. **doubt not but:** i.e., expect; **for all this:** i.e., in spite of all this

19. **medicines:** potions

20. **else:** otherwise

22. **ere:** before

22–23. **as . . . drink:** See note on 2.1.32.

23. **to turn true man:** i.e., to become honest

24. **veriest varlet:** i.e., worst scoundrel

26. **with:** i.e., for

29. **Whew:** perhaps Falstaff's attempt to whistle; or, perhaps, his exclamation of disgust

34. **list:** i.e., listen

39. **colt:** trick (Hal responds with a pun on **colt** as "horse.")

45. **Out:** an interjection of reproach

46–47. **Hang . . . garters:** Falstaff's version of the proverb "He may hang himself in his own garters"

47. **peach:** appeach, turn informer

doubt not but to die a fair death for all this, if I
'scape hanging for killing that rogue. I have for-        15
sworn his company hourly any time this two-and-
twenty years, and yet I am bewitched with the
rogue's company. If the rascal have not given me
medicines to make me love him, I'll be hanged. It
could not be else: I have drunk medicines.—Poins!        20
Hal! A plague upon you both.—Bardolph! Peto!—
I'll starve ere I'll rob a foot further. An 'twere not as
good a deed as drink to turn true man and to leave
these rogues, I am the veriest varlet that ever
chewed with a tooth. Eight yards of uneven ground        25
is threescore and ten miles afoot with me, and the
stony-hearted villains know it well enough. A plague
upon it when thieves cannot be true one to another!
(*They whistle,* ⌐*within.*⌐) Whew! A plague upon you
all!        30

⌐*Enter the Prince, Poins, Peto, and Bardolph.*⌐

Give me my horse, you rogues. Give me my horse
and be hanged!
PRINCE    Peace, you fat guts! Lie down, lay thine ear
close to the ground, and list if thou canst hear the
tread of travelers.        35
FALSTAFF    Have you any levers to lift me up again being down? 'Sblood, I'll not bear my own flesh so
far afoot again for all the coin in thy father's Exchequer. What a plague mean you to colt me
thus?        40
PRINCE    Thou liest. Thou art not colted; thou art un-
colted.
FALSTAFF    I prithee, good Prince Hal, help me to my
horse, good king's son.
PRINCE    Out, you rogue! Shall I be your ostler?        45
FALSTAFF    Hang thyself in thine own heir-apparent
garters! If I be ta'en, I'll peach for this. An I have

48. **made on:** i.e., written about

49–50. **when . . . afoot:** (1) when our plot is so advanced, moving forward so well; (2) when your joke on me is so blatant, making me go on foot

53. **setter:** the thief who "sets" (arranges) the robbery (Gadshill may enter masked.)

55. **Case you:** i.e., put on your masks

57. **'Tis . . . Exchequer:** i.e., it is royal, or government, revenue

60. **make us all:** i.e., make our fortunes, make us wealthy

62. **front:** i.e., confront

69. **John of Gaunt:** Falstaff puns on **gaunt** as "thin."

71. **proof:** test

75–76. **if . . . hanged:** i.e., no matter what

78. **hard by:** i.e., nearby

79. **happy . . . dole:** a proverbial expression for wishing good luck   **dole:** lot in life, destiny

not ballads made on you all and sung to filthy
tunes, let a cup of sack be my poison—when a jest
is so forward, and afoot too! I hate it.      50

*Enter Gadshill.*

GADSHILL   Stand.

FALSTAFF   So I do, against my will.

POINS   O, 'tis our setter. I know his voice.

⌜BARDOLPH⌝   What news?

⌜GADSHILL⌝   Case you, case you. On with your vizards.      55
There's money of the King's coming down the hill.
'Tis going to the King's Exchequer.

FALSTAFF   You lie, you rogue. 'Tis going to the King's
Tavern.

GADSHILL   There's enough to make us all.      60

FALSTAFF   To be hanged.

PRINCE   Sirs, you four shall front them in the narrow
lane. Ned Poins and I will walk lower. If they 'scape
from your encounter, then they light on us.

PETO   How many be there of them?      65

GADSHILL   Some eight or ten.

FALSTAFF   Zounds, will they not rob us?

PRINCE   What, a coward, Sir John Paunch?

FALSTAFF   Indeed, I am not John of Gaunt, your grandfather, but yet no coward, Hal.      70

PRINCE   Well, we leave that to the proof.

POINS   Sirrah Jack, thy horse stands behind the hedge.
When thou need'st him, there thou shalt find him.
Farewell and stand fast.

FALSTAFF   Now cannot I strike him, if I should be      75
hanged.

PRINCE, ⌜*aside to Poins*⌝   Ned, where are our disguises?

POINS, ⌜*aside to Prince*⌝   Here, hard by. Stand close.
⌜*The Prince and Poins exit.*⌝

FALSTAFF   Now, my masters, happy man be his dole,
say I. Every man to his business.      80
⌜*They step aside.*⌝

87. **caterpillars:** a conventional term of abuse for those seen as feeding off the commonwealth; **bacon-fed:** i.e., fat

92. **gorbellied:** potbellied, corpulent

92–93. **undone:** ruined

93. **chuffs:** a term of abuse for country people or misers; **your store:** all you own

94. **bacons:** i.e., fatties

95. **grandjurors:** i.e., wealthy enough to serve on a grand jury

95–96. **jure you:** a general threat of violence, playing on the sound of "juror"

97. **true:** honest

98. **could . . . I:** i.e., if you and I could

99. **argument:** something to talk about

104. **equity:** i.e., ability to judge character

"The most villainous house . . . for fleas." (2.1.15-16)
From *Hortus sanitatis* (1536).

*Enter the Travelers.*

⌜FIRST⌝ TRAVELER   Come, neighbor, the boy shall lead
   our horses down the hill. We'll walk afoot awhile
   and ease our legs.
THIEVES, ⌜*advancing*⌝   Stand!
TRAVELERS   Jesus bless us!                                    85
FALSTAFF   Strike! Down with them! Cut the villains'
   throats! Ah, whoreson caterpillars, bacon-fed
   knaves, they hate us youth. Down with them!
   Fleece them!
TRAVELERS   O, we are undone, both we and ours for-    90
   ever!
FALSTAFF   Hang, you gorbellied knaves! Are you undone? No, you fat chuffs. I would your store were
   here. On, bacons, on! What, you knaves, young men
   must live. You are grandjurors, are you? We'll jure    95
   you, faith.
      *Here they rob them and bind them. They ⌜all⌝ exit.*

   *Enter the Prince and Poins, ⌜disguised.⌝*

PRINCE   The thieves have bound the true men. Now
   could thou and I rob the thieves and go merrily to
   London, it would be argument for a week, laughter
   for a month, and a good jest forever.                    100
POINS   Stand close, I hear them coming.
                          ⌜*They step aside.*⌝

   *Enter the Thieves again.*

FALSTAFF   Come, my masters, let us share, and then to
   horse before day. An the Prince and Poins be not
   two arrant cowards, there's no equity stirring.
   There's no more valor in that Poins than in a wild    105
   duck.
                          *As they are sharing, the Prince*
                          *and Poins set upon them.*

113. **officer:** constable
115. **lards:** i.e., covers with fat

**2.3**  Hotspur reads a letter from a nobleman who refuses to join the rebellion against King Henry. Lady Percy enters to ask Hotspur what has been troubling him so much lately, but he will not confide in her.

---

2. **in respect of:** because of
3. **house:** family (Hotspur, lines 5–6, gives the word its usual meaning.)
9. **Lord Fool:** We are not told whose letter Hotspur is reading.
12. **uncertain:** not reliable; **unsorted:** unsuitable
13. **light . . . counterpoise:** The image here is of weights put into opposing balance scales.

Scales. (2.3.13)
From Silvestro Pietrasanta, *Symbola heroica* (1682).

64

PRINCE   Your money!

POINS   Villains!

*They all run away, and Falstaff, after a blow or two,*
*runs away too, leaving the booty behind them.*

PRINCE

Got with much ease. Now merrily to horse.

The thieves are all scattered, and possessed with          110
  fear

So strongly that they dare not meet each other.

Each takes his fellow for an officer.

Away, good Ned. Falstaff sweats to death,

And lards the lean earth as he walks along.                115

Were 't not for laughing, I should pity him.

POINS   How the fat rogue roared!

*They exit.*


⌜Scene 3⌝

*Enter Hotspur alone, reading a letter.*

⌜HOTSPUR⌝   *But, for mine own part, my lord, I could be*
*well contented to be there, in respect of the love I*
*bear your house.* He could be contented; why is he
not, then? In respect of the love he bears our
house—he shows in this he loves his own barn          5
better than he loves our house. Let me see some
more. *The purpose you undertake is dangerous.*
Why, that's certain. 'Tis dangerous to take a cold,
to sleep, to drink; but I tell you, my Lord Fool, out
of this nettle, danger, we pluck this flower, safety.     10
*The purpose you undertake is dangerous, the friends*
*you have named uncertain, the time itself unsorted,*
*and your whole plot too light for the counterpoise*
*of so great an opposition.* Say you so, say you so?
I say unto you again, you are a shallow, cowardly       15
hind, and you lie. What a lack-brain is this! By

23. **by:** close to

31–32. **in . . . heart:** i.e., in his very sincere cowardice

32. **will he:** i.e., he will go; **lay open:** reveal

34. **buffets:** fisticuffs (one part of me against another); **moving . . . with:** i.e., approaching such a coward about

43. **stomach:** appetite

45. **start:** i.e., jump, move suddenly

47. **my treasures . . . thee:** i.e., the pleasures I should be enjoying as your wife

48. **curst:** bad-tempered

49. **watched:** stayed awake

Diana. (1.2.26)
From Johann Engel, *Astrolabium* (1488).

66

the Lord, our plot is a good plot as ever was laid, our friends true and constant—a good plot, good friends, and full of expectation; an excellent plot, very good friends. What a frosty-spirited rogue is this! Why, my Lord of York commends the plot and the general course of the action. Zounds, an I were now by this rascal, I could brain him with his lady's fan. Is there not my father, my uncle, and myself, Lord Edmund Mortimer, my Lord of York, and Owen Glendower? Is there not besides the Douglas? Have I not all their letters to meet me in arms by the ninth of the next month, and are they not some of them set forward already? What a pagan rascal is this—an infidel! Ha, you shall see now, in very sincerity of fear and cold heart, will he to the King and lay open all our proceedings. O, I could divide myself and go to buffets for moving such a dish of skim milk with so honorable an action! Hang him, let him tell the King. We are prepared. I will set forward tonight.

*Enter his Lady.*

How now, Kate? I must leave you within these two
hours.

LADY PERCY
O my good lord, why are you thus alone?
For what offense have I this fortnight been
A banished woman from my Harry's bed?
Tell me, sweet lord, what is 't that takes from thee
Thy stomach, pleasure, and thy golden sleep?
Why dost thou bend thine eyes upon the earth
And start so often when thou sit'st alone?
Why hast thou lost the fresh blood in thy cheeks
And given my treasures and my rights of thee
To thick-eyed musing and curst melancholy?
In thy faint slumbers I by thee have watched,

51. **manage:** i.e., *manege,* horsemanship

53. **retires:** military retreats

54. **palisadoes:** palisades, fences made of pales or stakes; **frontiers:** ramparts

55. **basilisks:** very large cannon; **culverin:** smaller cannon

62. **motions:** emotions; movements

64. **hest:** command; purpose

66. **heavy:** weighty; sad, woeful

69. **packet:** i.e., packet of letters, dispatches

72. **even:** i.e., just

76. **back:** mount; **straight:** right away; **Esperance:** the Percy motto, which means "hope"

And heard thee murmur tales of iron wars,                    50
Speak terms of manage to thy bounding steed,
Cry "Courage! To the field!" And thou hast talked
Of sallies and retires, of trenches, tents,
Of palisadoes, frontiers, parapets,
Of basilisks, of cannon, culverin,                           55
Of prisoners' ransom, and of soldiers slain,
And all the currents of a heady fight.
Thy spirit within thee hath been so at war,
And thus hath so bestirred thee in thy sleep,
That beads of sweat have stood upon thy brow                 60
Like bubbles in a late-disturbèd stream,
And in thy face strange motions have appeared,
Such as we see when men restrain their breath
On some great sudden hest. O, what portents are
    these?                                                   65
Some heavy business hath my lord in hand,
And I must know it, else he loves me not.
HOTSPUR
What, ho!

⌜*Enter a Servant.*⌝

         Is Gilliams with the packet gone?
SERVANT   He is, my lord, an hour ago.                       70
HOTSPUR
Hath Butler brought those horses from the sheriff?
SERVANT
One horse, my lord, he brought even now.
HOTSPUR
What horse? ⌜A⌝ roan, a crop-ear, is it not?
SERVANT
It is, my lord.
HOTSPUR          That roan shall be my throne.               75
Well, I will back him straight. O, Esperance!
Bid Butler lead him forth into the park.
                           ⌜*Servant exits.*⌝

80. **carries you away:** i.e., makes you so wild (Hotspur responds as if she means the words literally.)

83. **such . . . spleen:** i.e., such a changeable temperament (The **spleen** was considered the seat of many strong emotions, and the **weasel** was proverbially quarrelsome.)

88. **line:** reinforce, strengthen; **go:** travel (Hotspur gives the word its meaning of "walk.")

90. **paraquito:** little parrot

97. **mammets:** dolls; **tilt:** battle as in a tournament

98. **cracked crowns:** broken heads

99. **pass them current:** make them acceptable (with a pun on the sense of **crown** as the French coin, which, even when **cracked,** should be made to pass as genuine currency); **Gods:** i.e., God save

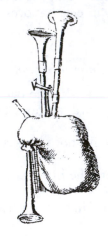

A bagpipe. (1.2.81)
From Giovanni Francesco Bonomi, *Chiron Achillis, siue Nauarchus humanae vitae* (1691).

70

LADY PERCY   But hear you, my lord.
HOTSPUR   What say'st thou, my lady?
LADY PERCY   What is it carries you away?                    80
HOTSPUR   Why, my horse, my love, my horse.
LADY PERCY   Out, you mad-headed ape!
   A weasel hath not such a deal of spleen
   As you are tossed with. In faith,
   I'll know your business, Harry, that I will.            85
   I fear my brother Mortimer doth stir
   About his title, and hath sent for you
   To line his enterprise; but if you go—
HOTSPUR
   So far afoot, I shall be weary, love.
LADY PERCY
   Come, come, you paraquito, answer me                    90
   Directly unto this question that I ask.
   In faith, I'll break thy little finger, Harry,
   An if thou wilt not tell me all things true.
HOTSPUR   Away!
   Away, you trifler. Love, I love thee not.               95
   I care not for thee, Kate. This is no world
   To play with mammets and to tilt with lips.
   We must have bloody noses and cracked crowns,
   And pass them current too.—Gods me, my horse!—
   What say'st thou, Kate? What wouldst thou have          100
      with me?
LADY PERCY
   Do you not love me? Do you not indeed?
   Well, do not then, for since you love me not,
   I will not love myself. Do you not love me?
   Nay, tell me if you speak in jest or no.                105
HOTSPUR   Come, wilt thou see me ride?
   And when I am a-horseback I will swear
   I love thee infinitely. But hark you, Kate,
   I must not have you henceforth question me
   Whither I go, nor reason whereabout.                    110

116. **closer:** more able to keep a secret
124. **of force:** perforce, of necessity


**2.4** At a tavern in Eastcheap, Prince Hal and Poins amuse themselves by tormenting a young waiter while waiting for Falstaff to return. Falstaff comes in telling a story about having been robbed by a large body of men with whom he fought bravely. Hal then reveals that it was he and Poins who robbed Falstaff. A messenger arrives from King Henry to summon Hal to court. Falstaff and Hal stage mock versions of the scene to take place between Hal and his father. These impromptu performances are halted by the arrival of a sheriff in search of Falstaff and his gang, whom Hal conceals.

---

1. **fat room:** perhaps, room full of thick air; or, perhaps, vat room
2. **lend . . . hand:** i.e., help me
4. **loggerheads:** blockheads
5. **hogsheads:** wine barrels; **sounded:** (1) played like a musical instrument; (2) measured the depths, as with a sounding line
6. **sworn brother:** i.e., best buddy (as if we had sworn an oath to defend each other)
7. **leash:** set of three (a hunting term applied to animals); **drawers:** tapsters
9. **take it:** maintain; or, take their oath; **upon . . . salvation:** i.e., as they hope to be saved
11. **jack:** (1) fellow; (2) Jack Falstaff
12. **Corinthian:** good sport; **lad of mettle:** spirited fellow

Whither I must, I must; and to conclude
This evening must I leave you, gentle Kate.
I know you wise, but yet no farther wise
Than Harry Percy's wife; constant you are,
But yet a woman; and for secrecy                    115
No lady closer, for I well believe
Thou wilt not utter what thou dost not know,
And so far will I trust thee, gentle Kate.

LADY PERCY   How? So far?

HOTSPUR
Not an inch further. But hark you, Kate,            120
Whither I go, thither shall you go too.
Today will I set forth, tomorrow you.
Will this content you, Kate?

LADY PERCY                         It must, of force.

*They exit.*


⌜Scene 4⌝
*Enter Prince and Poins.*

PRINCE   Ned, prithee, come out of that fat room and
  lend me thy hand to laugh a little.

POINS   Where hast been, Hal?

PRINCE   With three or four loggerheads amongst three
  or fourscore hogsheads. I have sounded the very        5
  bass string of humility. Sirrah, I am sworn brother
  to a leash of drawers, and can call them all by their
  Christian names, as Tom, Dick, and Francis. They
  take it already upon their salvation that though I be
  but Prince of Wales, yet I am the king of courtesy,    10
  and tell me flatly I am no proud jack, like Falstaff,
  but a Corinthian, a lad of mettle, a good boy—by
  the Lord, so they call me—and when I am king of
  England, I shall command all the good lads in
  Eastcheap. They call drinking deep "dyeing scar-       15

16. **breathe . . . watering:** i.e., stop to take a breath while drinking

17. **Play it off:** i.e., drink it down

19. **tinker:** mender of pots and pans

21. **action:** i.e., noble military engagement

24. **underskinker:** assistant tapster

27. **Anon:** i.e., coming, right away; **Score:** i.e., mark down the charges for a drink

28. **bastard:** sweet wine; **Half-moon:** the name of a room in the tavern

30. **by-room:** side room

32. **leave:** i.e., stop

38–39. **Pomgarnet:** a room in the tavern

42. **serve:** i.e., as an apprentice (usually a seven-year term)

46. **By 'r Lady:** by our Lady (the Virgin Mary)

46–47. **a long . . . pewter:** i.e., a long apprenticeship to learn how to be a tapster   **lease:** contract

48–49. **indenture:** i.e., contract of apprenticeship

let," and when you breathe in your watering, they
cry "Hem!" and bid you "Play it off!" To conclude, I
am so good a proficient in one quarter of an hour
that I can drink with any tinker in his own language
during my life. I tell thee, Ned, thou hast lost much          20
honor that thou wert not with me in this action; but,
sweet Ned—to sweeten which name of Ned, I give
thee this pennyworth of sugar, clapped even now
into my hand by an underskinker, one that never
spake other English in his life than "Eight shillings          25
and sixpence," and "You are welcome," with this
shrill addition, "Anon, anon, sir.—Score a pint of
bastard in the Half-moon," or so. But, Ned, to
drive away the time till Falstaff come, I prithee, do
thou stand in some by-room while I question my          30
puny drawer to what end he gave me the sugar, and
do thou never leave calling "Francis," that his tale
to me may be nothing but "Anon." Step aside, and
I'll show thee a ⌜precedent.⌝          ⌜*Poins exits.*⌝

POINS, ⌜*within*⌝  Francis!          35
PRINCE  Thou art perfect.
⌜POINS, *within*⌝  Francis!

*Enter ⌜Francis, the⌝ Drawer.*

FRANCIS  Anon, anon, sir.—Look down into the Pom-
garnet, Ralph.
PRINCE  Come hither, Francis.          40
FRANCIS  My lord?
PRINCE  How long hast thou to serve, Francis?
FRANCIS  Forsooth, five years, and as much as to—
POINS, ⌜*within*⌝  Francis!
FRANCIS  Anon, anon, sir.          45
PRINCE  Five year! By 'r Lady, a long lease for the
clinking of pewter! But, Francis, darest thou be
so valiant as to play the coward with thy inden-
ture, and show it a fair pair of heels, and run
from it?          50

56. **Michaelmas next:** i.e., next Feast of Michael the Archangel (September 29)

71–73. **this . . . Spanish-pouch:** Hal presumably describes the tavern owner to whom Francis is apprenticed, noting his close-fitting short leather coat with crystal buttons, his closely cropped head (**not-pated**), his quartz-crystal ring, his dark-wool stockings fastened with worsted garters, his unctuous way of talking, and his Spanish-leather vintner's pouch.

75–78. **Why . . . much:** This speech has been variously explained as (1) nonsense meant to mystify Francis, (2) a warning to Francis not to rob his master, (3) a mocking reference to Francis's having missed his chance to be given a thousand pounds.

75–76. **your only drink:** i.e., the best of all drinks

77. **doublet:** close-fitting jacket

82 SD. **amazed:** utterly confused, dumbfounded (as if lost in a maze)

FRANCIS    O Lord, sir, I'll be sworn upon all the books
 in England, I could find in my heart—
POINS, ⌜*within*⌝    Francis!
FRANCIS    Anon, sir.
PRINCE    How old art thou, Francis?     55
FRANCIS    Let me see. About Michaelmas next, I shall
 be—
POINS, ⌜*within*⌝    Francis!
FRANCIS    Anon, sir.—Pray, stay a little, my lord.
PRINCE    Nay, but hark you, Francis, for the sugar thou 60
 gavest me—'twas a pennyworth, was 't not?
FRANCIS    O Lord, I would it had been two!
PRINCE    I will give thee for it a thousand pound. Ask
 me when thou wilt, and thou shalt have it.
POINS, ⌜*within*⌝    Francis!     65
FRANCIS    Anon, anon.
PRINCE    Anon, Francis? No, Francis. But tomorrow,
 Francis; or, Francis, o' Thursday; or indeed, Fran-
 cis, when thou wilt. But, Francis—
FRANCIS    My lord?     70
PRINCE    Wilt thou rob this leathern-jerkin, crystal-
 button, not-pated, agate-ring, puke-stocking, cad-
 dis-garter, smooth-tongue, Spanish-pouch—
FRANCIS    O Lord, sir, who do you mean?
PRINCE    Why then, your brown bastard is your only 75
 drink, for look you, Francis, your white canvas
 doublet will sully. In Barbary, sir, it cannot come to
 so much.
FRANCIS    What, sir?
POINS, ⌜*within*⌝    Francis!     80
PRINCE    Away, you rogue! Dost thou not hear them
 call?
 *Here they both call him. The Drawer stands amazed,*
    *not knowing which way to go.*

   *Enter Vintner.*

93. **match:** agreement, bargain

93–94. **with this jest of:** i.e., in this game with

94. **issue:** outcome

95. **humors:** moods, whims

96–97. **Goodman:** a form of address for a lower-class man

97. **pupil:** i.e., young

102. **yet:** i.e., yet be

104. **parcel:** i.e., words or items; **reckoning:** tavern bill

105. **kills me:** i.e., kills

113, 115. **brawn, Ribs, Tallow:** i.e., Falstaff (All three words allude to fat meat.)

114. **Rivo:** a shout used in drinking bouts

Eastcheap. (1.2.136)
From Hugh Alley, *A caveat for the city of London* (1598).

VINTNER  What, stand'st thou still and hear'st such a
calling? Look to the guests within. ⌐*Francis exits.*¬
My lord, old Sir John with half a dozen more are at      85
the door. Shall I let them in?

PRINCE  Let them alone awhile, and then open the
door. ⌐*Vintner exits.*¬ Poins!

*Enter Poins.*

POINS  Anon, anon, sir.

PRINCE  Sirrah, Falstaff and the rest of the thieves are      90
at the door. Shall we be merry?

POINS  As merry as crickets, my lad. But hark you,
what cunning match have you made with this jest
of the drawer. Come, what's the issue?

PRINCE  I am now of all humors that have showed      95
themselves humors since the old days of Goodman Adam to the pupil age of this present twelve
o'clock at midnight.

⌐*Enter Francis, in haste.*¬

What's o'clock, Francis?

FRANCIS  Anon, anon, sir.          ⌐*Francis exits.*¬    100

PRINCE  That ever this fellow should have fewer words
than a parrot, and yet the son of a woman! His
industry is upstairs and downstairs, his eloquence
the parcel of a reckoning. I am not yet of Percy's
mind, the Hotspur of the north, he that kills me      105
some six or seven dozen of Scots at a breakfast,
washes his hands, and says to his wife "Fie upon
this quiet life! I want work." "O my sweet Harry,"
says she, "how many hast thou killed today?"
"Give my roan horse a drench," says he, and an-      110
swers "Some fourteen," an hour after. "A trifle, a
trifle." I prithee, call in Falstaff. I'll play Percy,
and that damned brawn shall play Dame Mortimer his wife. *"Rivo!"* says the drunkard. Call in
Ribs, call in Tallow.      115

117. **A plague of:** i.e., curses on

119–20. **Ere . . . them:** i.e., I'll give up this life and take up sewing and mending  **netherstocks:** stockings  **foot:** perhaps, make new feet for

123. **Titan:** i.e., the sun

124. **that:** i.e., the butter

126. **that compound:** perhaps, melting butter; or, perhaps, Falstaff's round hot face "kissing" the cup of sack

127. **lime:** calcium oxide, added to wine by unscrupulous vintners to make it sparkle

130–31. **Go thy ways:** i.e., off you go

133. **a . . . herring:** i.e., thin and weak, like a fish that has just spawned

134. **good men:** i.e., men of courage

135. **the while:** i.e., the present age

136–37. **weaver . . . psalms:** Weavers were known for singing and for belonging to Protestant sects that favored psalm-singing.

139. **woolsack:** large bale of wool (with perhaps plays on "wool" with reference to weavers, and on "sack")

141. **dagger of lath:** a wooden dagger carried by a comic character called the Vice

*Enter Falstaff, ⌐Gadshill, Peto, Bardolph;*
*and Francis, with wine.⌐*

POINS  Welcome, Jack. Where hast thou been?

FALSTAFF  A plague of all cowards, I say, and a vengeance too! Marry and amen!—Give me a cup of
sack, boy.—Ere I lead this life long, I'll sew netherstocks and mend them, and foot them too. A plague      120
of all cowards!—Give me a cup of sack, rogue!—Is
there no virtue extant?              *He drinketh.*

PRINCE  Didst thou never see Titan kiss a dish of
butter—pitiful-hearted Titan!—that melted at the
sweet tale of the sun's? If thou didst, then behold      125
that compound.

FALSTAFF, ⌐*to Francis*⌐  You rogue, here's lime in this
sack too.—There is nothing but roguery to be
found in villainous man, yet a coward is worse than
a cup of sack with lime in it. A villainous coward! Go      130
thy ways, old Jack. Die when thou wilt. If manhood,
good manhood, be not forgot upon the face of the
earth, then am I a shotten herring. There lives not
three good men unhanged in England, and one of
them is fat and grows old, God help the while. A bad      135
world, I say. I would I were a weaver. I could sing
psalms, or anything. A plague of all cowards, I say
still.

PRINCE  How now, woolsack, what mutter you?

FALSTAFF  A king's son! If I do not beat thee out of thy      140
kingdom with a dagger of lath, and drive all thy
subjects afore thee like a flock of wild geese, I'll
never wear hair on my face more. You, Prince of
Wales!

PRINCE  Why, you whoreson round man, what's the      145
matter?

FALSTAFF  Are not you a coward? Answer me to that—
and Poins there?

161. **All . . . that:** i.e., it doesn't matter

165. **this day morning:** i.e., this morning

170. **at half-sword:** i.e., in close combat

171. **together:** altogether

173. **doublet:** close-fitting short jacket; **buckler:** small shield (See note on 1.3.238.)

175. **Ecce signum:** behold the sign (an echo of religious language); **dealt:** i.e., fought

176. **All . . . do:** i.e., no matter what I did, it wasn't enough

179–80. **sons of darkness:** Biblical: "You are all the children of light . . . : we are not of the night, neither of darkness" (1 Thessalonians 5.5).

"The ridge of the gallows." (1.2.40-41)
From Raphael Holinshed, *The chronicles of England* (1577).

POINS   Zounds, you fat paunch, an you call me coward,
by the Lord, I'll stab thee.     150

FALSTAFF   I call thee coward? I'll see thee damned ere
I call thee coward, but I would give a thousand
pound I could run as fast as thou canst. You are
straight enough in the shoulders you care not who
sees your back. Call you that backing of your     155
friends? A plague upon such backing! Give me them
that will face me.—Give me a cup of sack.—I am a
rogue if I drunk today.

PRINCE   O villain, thy lips are scarce wiped since thou
drunk'st last.     160

FALSTAFF   All is one for that. (*He drinketh.*) A plague of
all cowards, still say I.

PRINCE   What's the matter?

FALSTAFF   What's the matter? There be four of us here
have ta'en a thousand pound this day morning.     165

PRINCE   Where is it, Jack, where is it?

FALSTAFF   Where is it? Taken from us it is. A hundred
upon poor four of us.

PRINCE   What, a hundred, man?

FALSTAFF   I am a rogue if I were not at half-sword     170
with a dozen of them two hours together. I have
'scaped by miracle. I am eight times thrust through
the doublet, four through the hose, my buckler
cut through and through, my sword hacked like
a handsaw. *Ecce signum!* I never dealt better since     175
I was a man. All would not do. A plague of
all cowards! Let them speak. ⌐*Pointing to Gadshill, Bardolph, and Peto.*¬ If they speak more or
less than truth, they are villains, and the sons of
darkness.     180

⌐PRINCE¬   Speak, sirs, how was it?

⌐BARDOLPH¬   We four set upon some dozen.

FALSTAFF   Sixteen at least, my lord.

⌐BARDOLPH¬   And bound them.

191. **other:** others

200, 201. **peppered, paid:** killed

203. **call me horse:** i.e., feel free to insult me

203–4. **my old ward:** i.e., the stance I take in defending myself

204. **Here . . . point:** i.e., this is how I stood, and this is how I held my sword

209. **afront:** abreast; **mainly:** vigorously, violently

210. **I . . . ado:** i.e., I delayed no longer **made me:** i.e., made **ado:** ceremony, fuss

211. **target:** shield, buckler

215. **by these hilts:** i.e., by my sword (a common oath)

219. **mark:** pay attention to

PETO   No, no, they were not bound.                                          185

FALSTAFF   You rogue, they were bound, every man of
   them, or I am a Jew else, an Ebrew Jew.

⌈BARDOLPH⌉   As we were sharing, some six or seven
   fresh men set upon us.

FALSTAFF   And unbound the rest, and then come in the      190
   other.

PRINCE   What, fought you with them all?

FALSTAFF   All? I know not what you call all, but if I
   fought not with fifty of them I am a bunch of
   radish. If there were not two- or three-and-fifty      195
   upon poor old Jack, then am I no two-legged
   creature.

PRINCE   Pray God you have not murdered some of
   them.

FALSTAFF   Nay, that's past praying for. I have peppered     200
   two of them. Two I am sure I have paid, two rogues
   in buckram suits. I tell thee what, Hal, if I tell thee a
   lie, spit in my face, call me horse. Thou knowest my
   old ward. Here I lay, and thus I bore my point. Four
   rogues in buckram let drive at me.                        205

PRINCE   What, four? Thou said'st but two even now.

FALSTAFF   Four, Hal, I told thee four.

POINS   Ay, ay, he said four.

FALSTAFF   These four came all afront, and mainly
   thrust at me. I made me no more ado, but took all     210
   their seven points in my target, thus.

PRINCE   Seven? Why there were but four even now.

FALSTAFF   In buckram?

POINS   Ay, four in buckram suits.

FALSTAFF   Seven by these hilts, or I am a villain else.     215

PRINCE, ⌈*to Poins*⌉   Prithee, let him alone. We shall have
   more anon.

FALSTAFF   Dost thou hear me, Hal?

PRINCE   Ay, and mark thee too, Jack.

224. **Down . . . hose:** Poins plays on a second meaning of **points,** i.e., the laces that hold up a man's breeches.

225. **followed me:** i.e., followed

226. **with a thought:** i.e., as quick as a thought

231. **Kendal green:** coarse woolen cloth

236. **knotty-pated:** blockheaded

237. **tallow-catch:** perhaps, tallow-keech (a rolled-up lump of fat sent by the butcher to the candle-maker); or, perhaps, the pan used to collect drippings from roasting meat

246. **at the strappado:** i.e., being tortured by being hauled up with ropes (See page 88.); **racks:** instruments of torture on which a victim's limbs were torn apart (See page 90.)

251. **this sin:** i.e., of hiding the truth

251–52. **sanguine:** (1) red-cheeked; (2) courageous; (3) confident, hopeful

254. **'Sblood:** an oath by Christ's blood

255. **dried . . . stockfish:** All of these suggest emaciation. **neat's:** cow's or ox's; **pizzle:** penis (dried to make a whip); **stockfish:** dried cod

FALSTAFF  Do so, for it is worth the listening to. These  220
nine in buckram that I told thee of—
PRINCE  So, two more already.
FALSTAFF  Their points being broken—
POINS  Down fell their hose.
FALSTAFF  Began to give me ground, but I followed me  225
close, came in foot and hand, and, with a thought,
seven of the eleven I paid.
PRINCE  O monstrous! Eleven buckram men grown out
of two!
FALSTAFF  But as the devil would have it, three misbe-  230
gotten knaves in Kendal green came at my back,
and let drive at me, for it was so dark, Hal, that thou
couldst not see thy hand.
PRINCE  These lies are like their father that begets
them, gross as a mountain, open, palpable. Why,  235
thou claybrained guts, thou knotty-pated fool, thou
whoreson, obscene, greasy tallow-catch—
FALSTAFF  What, art thou mad? Art thou mad? Is not
the truth the truth?
PRINCE  Why, how couldst thou know these men in  240
Kendal green when it was so dark thou couldst not
see thy hand? Come, tell us your reason. What sayest
thou to this?
POINS  Come, your reason, Jack, your reason.
FALSTAFF  What, upon compulsion? Zounds, an I were  245
at the strappado or all the racks in the world, I
would not tell you on compulsion. Give you a
reason on compulsion? If reasons were as plentiful
as blackberries, I would give no man a reason upon
compulsion, I.  250
PRINCE  I'll be no longer guilty of this sin. This sanguine coward, this bed-presser, this horse-back-
breaker, this huge hill of flesh—
FALSTAFF  'Sblood, you starveling, you elfskin, you
dried neat's tongue, you bull's pizzle, you stockfish!  255

257. **yard:** yardstick

258. **tuck:** rapier

266–67. **outfaced . . . prize:** i.e., forced your booty from you

273. **starting-hole:** escape hole (a hunting term)

275. **apparent:** obvious, visible

282. **Hercules:** in Greek mythology, a hero of extraordinary strength and courage

282–83. **The lion . . . prince:** an accepted belief

288. **clap to:** slam shut

288–89. **Watch . . . tomorrow:** Falstaff plays on Jesus' words to the disciples in the Garden of Gethsemane: "Watch and pray that you enter not into temptation" (Matthew 26.41). **watch:** (1) keep prayerful vigil; (2) stay awake and revel   **pray:** (1) address prayers to God; (2) prey on innocent victims

291–92. **play extempore:** an impromptu play

"At the strappado." (2.4.246)
From Girolamo Maggi, *De tintinnabulis liber* . . . (1689).

88

O, for breath to utter what is like thee! You tailor's yard, you sheath, you bowcase, you vile standing tuck—

PRINCE   Well, breathe awhile, and then to it again, and when thou hast tired thyself in base comparisons, 260 hear me speak but this.

POINS   Mark, Jack.

PRINCE   We two saw you four set on four, and bound them and were masters of their wealth. Mark now how a plain tale shall put you down. Then did we 265 two set on you four and, with a word, outfaced you from your prize, and have it, yea, and can show it you here in the house. And, Falstaff, you carried your guts away as nimbly, with as quick dexterity, and roared for mercy, and still run and roared, as 270 ever I heard bull-calf. What a slave art thou to hack thy sword as thou hast done, and then say it was in fight! What trick, what device, what starting-hole canst thou now find out to hide thee from this open and apparent shame? 275

POINS   Come, let's hear, Jack. What trick hast thou now?

FALSTAFF   By the Lord, I knew you as well as he that made you. Why, hear you, my masters, was it for me to kill the heir apparent? Should I turn upon the 280 true prince? Why, thou knowest I am as valiant as Hercules, but beware instinct. The lion will not touch the true prince. Instinct is a great matter. I was now a coward on instinct. I shall think the better of myself, and thee, during my life— 285 I for a valiant lion, and thou for a true prince. But, by the Lord, lads, I am glad you have the money.—Hostess, clap to the doors.—Watch to-night, pray tomorrow. Gallants, lads, boys, hearts of gold, all the titles of good fellowship come to 290 you. What, shall we be merry? Shall we have a play extempore?

293. **Content:** i.e., I am content, I agree; **argument:** plot, story

300. **at door:** i.e., at the door

302–3. **royal man:** A **royal** (a coin worth 10 shillings) exceeded a **noble** (a coin worth about 7 shillings); Hal here makes the usual pun (see line 299).

304. **manner:** kind

306. **Gravity:** a grave (serious) old man

322. **beslubber:** soil, daub

324. **did . . . before:** i.e., did something I had not done in the past seven years

Victims tortured on a rack. (2.4.246)
From Girolamo Maggi, *De tintinnabulis liber . . .* (1689).

PRINCE   Content, and the argument shall be thy running away.

FALSTAFF   Ah, no more of that, Hal, an thou lovest me.   295

*Enter Hostess.*

HOSTESS   O Jesu, my lord the Prince—

PRINCE   How now, my lady the hostess, what sayst thou to me?

HOSTESS   Marry, my lord, there is a nobleman of the court at door would speak with you. He says he   300 comes from your father.

PRINCE   Give him as much as will make him a royal man and send him back again to my mother.

FALSTAFF   What manner of man is he?

HOSTESS   An old man.   305

FALSTAFF   What doth Gravity out of his bed at midnight? Shall I give him his answer?

PRINCE   Prithee do, Jack.

FALSTAFF   Faith, and I'll send him packing.   *He exits.*

PRINCE   Now, sirs. ⌜*To Gadshill.*⌝ By 'r Lady, you fought   310 fair.—So did you, Peto.—So did you, Bardolph.— You are lions too. You ran away upon instinct. You will not touch the true prince. No, fie!

BARDOLPH   Faith, I ran when I saw others run.

PRINCE   Faith, tell me now in earnest, how came Falstaff's sword so hacked?   315

PETO   Why, he hacked it with his dagger and said he would swear truth out of England but he would make you believe it was done in fight, and persuaded us to do the like.   320

BARDOLPH   Yea, and to tickle our noses with speargrass to make them bleed, and then to beslubber our garments with it, and swear it was the blood of true men. I did that I did not this seven year before: I blushed to hear his monstrous devices.   325

PRINCE   O villain, thou stolest a cup of sack eighteen

327. **taken . . . manner:** i.e., captured with the stolen goods on you

328. **extempore:** i.e., on any and every occasion (This reference to Bardolph's red face and nose is elaborated on in the word **fire** and in lines 331–32—with the reference to **these meteors, these exhalations**—and again at 3.3.25–54.)

334. **portend:** i.e., predict, herald (**Meteors** were thought to be **exhalations** and were thought to appear as omens.)

335. **Hot livers:** the result, it was thought, of much drinking; **cold:** i.e., empty

336. **Choler:** anger; **rightly taken:** i.e., correctly understood (Hal responds as if the phrase meant "lawfully arrested.")

337. **halter:** i.e., hanging (with a pun on collar/choler)

339. **bombast:** (1) cotton padding or stuffing; (2) inflated language

343. **thumb-ring:** a signet ring worn on the thumb

347–48. **That same . . . Percy:** i.e., Hotspur

348. **Amamon:** the name of a demon

349. **bastinado:** beating on the feet; **Lucifer:** i.e., the devil (whose horns suggest the image of the **cuckold**)

349–50. **swore . . . liegeman:** i.e., made the devil swear to serve him

351. **Welsh hook:** a heavy weapon with a hooked end

359. **hit it:** i.e., got it exactly right (Hal responds to the literal meaning.)

years ago, and wert taken with the manner, and ever
since thou hast blushed extempore. Thou hadst fire
and sword on thy side, and yet thou ran'st away.
What instinct hadst thou for it?       330

BARDOLPH  My lord, do you see these meteors? Do you
behold these exhalations?

PRINCE  I do.

BARDOLPH  What think you they portend?

PRINCE  Hot livers and cold purses.      335

BARDOLPH  Choler, my lord, if rightly taken.

PRINCE  No. If rightly taken, halter.

*Enter Falstaff.*

Here comes lean Jack. Here comes bare-bone.—
How now, my sweet creature of bombast? How long
is 't ago, Jack, since thou sawest thine own knee?    340

FALSTAFF  My own knee? When I was about thy years,
Hal, I was not an eagle's talon in the waist. I could
have crept into any alderman's thumb-ring. A
plague of sighing and grief! It blows a man up like a
bladder. There's villainous news abroad. Here was  345
Sir John Bracy from your father. You must to the
court in the morning. That same mad fellow of the
north, Percy, and he of Wales that gave Amamon the
bastinado, and made Lucifer cuckold, and swore
the devil his true liegeman upon the cross of a  350
Welsh hook—what a plague call you him?

POINS  ⌜Owen⌝ Glendower.

FALSTAFF  Owen, Owen, the same, and his son-in-law
Mortimer, and old Northumberland, and that
sprightly Scot of Scots, Douglas, that runs a-horse-  355
back up a hill perpendicular—

PRINCE  He that rides at high speed, and with his pistol
kills a sparrow flying.

FALSTAFF  You have hit it.

PRINCE  So did he never the sparrow.    360

361. **mettle:** spirit, courage

369. **blue-caps:** Scots soldiers (who wore "blue bonnets")

373. **like:** i.e., likely

374. **buffeting:** strife

374–75. **buy maidenheads:** Rape was, and is, common in wartime.

378. **horrible afeard:** i.e., horribly afraid

384. **chid:** chided, scolded

385. **If . . . me:** i.e., I beg you

387. **stand for:** i.e., play the role of

390. **state:** chair of state, throne

392. **taken for:** understood to be; **joined stool:** a stool made of parts fitted together

396. **moved:** emotionally stirred

"The earth shaked like a coward." (3.1.16-17)
From Conrad Lycosthenes, *Prodigiorum* (1557).

FALSTAFF   Well, that rascal hath good mettle in him. He
will not run.

PRINCE   Why, what a rascal art thou then to praise him
so for running?

FALSTAFF   A-horseback, you cuckoo, but afoot he will     365
not budge a foot.

PRINCE   Yes, Jack, upon instinct.

FALSTAFF   I grant you, upon instinct. Well, he is there
too, and one Mordake, and a thousand blue-caps
more. Worcester is stolen away tonight. Thy father's     370
beard is turned white with the news. You may buy
land now as cheap as stinking mackerel.

PRINCE   Why then, it is like if there come a hot June,
and this civil buffeting hold, we shall buy maidenheads as they buy hobnails, by the hundreds.            375

FALSTAFF   By the Mass, thou sayest true. It is like we
shall have good trading that way. But tell me, Hal,
art not thou horrible afeard? Thou being heir
apparent, could the world pick thee out three such
enemies again as that fiend Douglas, that spirit        380
Percy, and that devil Glendower? Art thou not
horribly afraid? Doth not thy blood thrill at it?

PRINCE   Not a whit, i' faith. I lack some of thy instinct.

FALSTAFF   Well, thou wilt be horribly chid tomorrow
when thou comest to thy father. If thou love me,       385
practice an answer.

PRINCE   Do thou stand for my father and examine me
upon the particulars of my life.

FALSTAFF   Shall I? Content. ⌈*He sits down.*⌉ This chair
shall be my state, this dagger my scepter, and this     390
cushion my crown.

PRINCE   Thy state is taken for a joined stool, thy golden
scepter for a leaden dagger, and thy precious rich
crown for a pitiful bald crown.

FALSTAFF   Well, an the fire of grace be not quite out of    395
thee, now shalt thou be moved.—Give me a cup of

398. **in passion:** passionately, emotionally

399. **King Cambyses' vein:** i.e., a highly ornate style (*Cambyses, King of Persia* was a tragedy from the 1560s.)

400. **leg:** i.e., elaborate bow

404. **vain:** in vain, useless

405. **holds his countenance:** i.e., keeps a straight face

406. **convey:** lead away; **tristful:** unhappy

408–9. **harlotry players:** rascally actors

410–11. **tickle-brain:** a slang term for liquor

412–13. **how . . . accompanied:** i.e., who you spend time with

413–15. **though . . . wears:** an echo of John Lyly's *Euphues* (1578), once very popular for its highly mannered style: "Though the camomile, the more it is trodden and pressed down, the more it spreadeth, yet the violet the oftener it is handled and touched, the sooner it withereth and decayeth."

414. **so:** Most editions follow Q3 here and print "yet." Though this makes more sense of the passage, it may be funnier with **so.**

415. **wasted:** decayed, worn; **wears:** decays, is ruined

418. **trick:** trait, characteristic

419. **nether:** lower; **warrant me:** furnish me with a guarantee

421. **pointed at:** i.e., mocked

422. **micher:** truant

427–28. **This pitch . . . defile:** Biblical: "He that toucheth pitch shall be defiled" (Ecclesiasticus 13.1).

sack to make my eyes look red, that it may be
thought I have wept, for I must speak in passion,
and I will do it in King Cambyses' vein.

PRINCE, ⌐*bowing*⌐  Well, here is my leg.                    400

FALSTAFF  And here is my speech. ⌐*As King.*⌐ Stand
aside, nobility.

HOSTESS  O Jesu, this is excellent sport, i' faith!

FALSTAFF, ⌐*as King*⌐
Weep not, sweet queen, for trickling tears are vain.

HOSTESS  O the Father, how he holds his countenance!    405

FALSTAFF, ⌐*as King*⌐
For God's sake, lords, convey my ⌐tristful⌐ queen,
For tears do stop the floodgates of her eyes.

HOSTESS  O Jesu, he doth it as like one of these harlotry
players as ever I see.

FALSTAFF  Peace, good pint-pot. Peace, good tickle-    410
brain.—⌐*As King.*⌐ Harry, I do not only marvel
where thou spendest thy time, but also how thou
art accompanied. For though the camomile, the
more it is trodden on, the faster it grows, so youth,
the more it is wasted, the sooner it wears. That    415
thou art my son I have partly thy mother's word,
partly my own opinion, but chiefly a villainous
trick of thine eye and a foolish hanging of thy
nether lip that doth warrant me. If then thou be
son to me, here lies the point: why, being son to    420
me, art thou so pointed at? Shall the blessed sun of
heaven prove a micher and eat blackberries? A
question not to be asked. Shall the son of England
prove a thief and take purses? A question to be
asked. There is a thing, Harry, which thou hast    425
often heard of, and it is known to many in our land
by the name of pitch. This pitch, as ancient writers
do report, doth defile; so doth the company thou
keepest. For, Harry, now I do not speak to thee in
drink, but in tears; not in pleasure, but in passion;    430

434. **an it like:** i.e., if it please

435. **goodly:** (1) handsome; (2) large; **portly:** (1) stately; (2) fat

436. **corpulent:** (1) full-bodied; (2) very fat

437. **carriage:** bearing

440. **lewdly given:** i.e., inclined to wicked living

441–42. **tree . . . fruit:** Biblical: "The tree is known by his fruit" (Matthew 12.33).

444. **him keep with:** i.e., keep him with you; stay with him

445. **naughty varlet:** bad boy

449. **dost it:** i.e., play the part of king

451. **rabbit-sucker:** baby rabbit (not yet weaned)

452. **poulter's hare:** dead rabbit hung up for sale **poulter:** poultry dealer

460. **tickle . . . prince:** i.e., amuse you in my role as prince (probably addressed to the others onstage)

461. **Ungracious:** irreverent, without grace

463. **grace:** virtue; God's grace

464. **tun:** (1) large barrel; (2) ton

465. **converse:** associate

466. **trunk:** (1) body; (2) large container; **humors:** bodily fluids; diseases; **bolting-hutch:** sifting bin

not in words only, but in woes also. And yet there is
a virtuous man whom I have often noted in thy
company, but I know not his name.

PRINCE   What manner of man, an it like your Majesty?

FALSTAFF, ⌜*as King*⌝   A goodly portly man, i' faith, and a     435
corpulent; of a cheerful look, a pleasing eye, and a
most noble carriage, and, as I think, his age some
fifty, or, by 'r Lady, inclining to threescore; and now
I remember me, his name is Falstaff. If that man
should be lewdly given, he deceiveth me, for, Harry,     440
I see virtue in his looks. If then the tree may be
known by the fruit, as the fruit by the tree, then
peremptorily I speak it: there is virtue in that
Falstaff; him keep with, the rest banish. And tell me
now, thou naughty varlet, tell me where hast thou     445
been this month?

PRINCE   Dost thou speak like a king? Do thou stand for
me, and I'll play my father.

FALSTAFF, ⌜*rising*⌝   Depose me? If thou dost it half so
gravely, so majestically, both in word and matter,     450
hang me up by the heels for a rabbit-sucker or a
poulter's hare.

PRINCE, ⌜*sitting down*⌝   Well, here I am set.

FALSTAFF   And here I stand.—Judge, my masters.

PRINCE, ⌜*as King*⌝   Now, Harry, whence come you?     455

FALSTAFF, ⌜*as Prince*⌝   My noble lord, from Eastcheap.

PRINCE, ⌜*as King*⌝   The complaints I hear of thee are
grievous.

FALSTAFF, ⌜*as Prince*⌝   'Sblood, my lord, they are false.
—Nay, I'll tickle you for a young prince, i' faith.     460

PRINCE, ⌜*as King*⌝   Swearest thou? Ungracious boy,
henceforth ne'er look on me. Thou art violently
carried away from grace. There is a devil haunts
thee in the likeness of an old fat man. A tun of man
is thy companion. Why dost thou converse with that     465
trunk of humors, that bolting-hutch of beastliness,

467. **bombard:** leather wine jug

468. **cloakbag:** i.e., suitcase

468–69. **roasted . . . belly:** i.e., roast stuffed ox (It is unclear why ox roasts are here associated with Manningtree, a town in Essex.)

470–71. **that . . . years:** Each of these terms includes a paradox: **reverend, gray, father,** and **years** refer to Falstaff's age and the behavior that should go with it; **Vice, iniquity, ruffian,** and **vanity** describe his actual immoral behavior. The **Vice** was a character in earlier drama who, among other things, led the hero astray.

473. **cunning:** learned, skillful

474. **craft:** deceit, fraud

477–78. **take . . . you:** i.e., help me understand what you mean

486. **saving your reverence:** a conventional request to be excused for being about to use an indecent word

487. **sack and sugar:** i.e., drinking sugared wine

489. **host:** innkeeper

490–91. **Pharaoh's lean kine:** In the Bible (Genesis 41) the **lean kine** (cattle) in Pharaoh's dream predict famine.

that swollen parcel of dropsies, that huge bombard
of sack, that stuffed cloakbag of guts, that roasted
Manningtree ox with the pudding in his belly, that
reverend Vice, that gray iniquity, that father ruffian,      470
that vanity in years? Wherein is he good, but to taste
sack and drink it? Wherein neat and cleanly but to
carve a capon and eat it? Wherein cunning but in
craft? Wherein crafty but in villainy? Wherein villainous but in all things? Wherein worthy but in      475
nothing?

FALSTAFF, ⌜*as Prince*⌝  I would your Grace would take
me with you. Whom means your Grace?

PRINCE, ⌜*as King*⌝  That villainous abominable mislead-
er of youth, Falstaff, that old white-bearded Satan.      480

FALSTAFF, ⌜*as Prince*⌝  My lord, the man I know.

PRINCE, ⌜*as King*⌝  I know thou dost.

FALSTAFF, ⌜*as Prince*⌝  But to say I know more harm in
him than in myself were to say more than I know.
That he is old, the more the pity; his white hairs do      485
witness it. But that he is, saving your reverence, a
whoremaster, that I utterly deny. If sack and sugar
be a fault, God help the wicked. If to be old and
merry be a sin, then many an old host that I know is
damned. If to be fat be to be hated, then Pharaoh's      490
⌜lean⌝ kine are to be loved. No, my good lord,
banish Peto, banish Bardolph, banish Poins, but for
sweet Jack Falstaff, kind Jack Falstaff, true Jack
Falstaff, valiant Jack Falstaff, and therefore more
valiant being as he is old Jack Falstaff, banish not      495
him thy Harry's company, banish not him thy
Harry's company. Banish plump Jack, and banish
all the world.

PRINCE  I do, I will.
                ⌜*A loud knocking, and Bardolph, Hostess, and*
                                *Francis exit.*⌝

501. **watch:** group of officers

505–6. **the devil . . . fiddlestick:** i.e., what a to-do

510–12. **Never . . . so:** These lines have been interpreted in many different ways. One possible way is as follows: "I am virtuous and brave, though I seem otherwise. You are a true prince, though you seem otherwise."

514. **major:** i.e., major premise (The syllogism that Falstaff denies is, perhaps: all men who run are cowards; Falstaff ran; therefore, Falstaff is a coward. Falstaff has argued that some men run for other reasons than cowardice—e.g., out of instinctive recognition of "the true prince.")

515–16. **become not a cart:** i.e., am not as fit to be carted (i.e., dragged through the streets in a cart on my way to be hanged) See page 106.

518. **halter:** hangman's noose

519. **arras:** a hanging screen of tapestry fabric

520. **walk up above:** i.e., go upstairs; **true:** innocent, honest

522. **their date is out:** i.e., their lease has run out

*Enter Bardolph running.*

BARDOLPH   O my lord, my lord, the Sheriff with a most     500
much monstrous watch is at the door.
FALSTAFF   Out, you rogue.—Play out the play. I have
much to say in the behalf of that Falstaff.

*Enter the Hostess.*

HOSTESS   O Jesu, my lord, my lord—
PRINCE   Heigh, heigh, the devil rides upon a fiddle-     505
stick. What's the matter?
HOSTESS   The Sheriff and all the watch are at the door.
They are come to search the house. Shall I let them
in?
FALSTAFF   Dost thou hear, Hal? Never call a true piece     510
of gold a counterfeit. Thou art essentially made
without seeming so.
PRINCE   And thou a natural coward without instinct.
FALSTAFF   I deny your major. If you will deny the
Sheriff, so; if not, let him enter. If I become not a     515
cart as well as another man, a plague on my
bringing up. I hope I shall as soon be strangled with
a halter as another.
PRINCE, ⌜*standing*⌝   Go hide thee behind the arras. The
rest walk up above.—Now, my masters, for a true     520
face and good conscience.
FALSTAFF   Both which I have had, but their date is out;
and therefore I'll hide me.          ⌜*He hides.*⌝
PRINCE   Call in the Sheriff.
          ⌜*All but the Prince and Peto exit.*⌝

*Enter Sheriff and the Carrier.*

PRINCE
Now, Master Sheriff, what is your will with me?     525
SHERIFF
First pardon me, my lord. A hue and cry
Hath followed certain men unto this house.

537. **withal:** i.e., with

544. **morrow:** morning

546. **Paul's:** i.e., St. Paul's Cathedral

555. **Item:** likewise (from Latin *ita*, meaning "so," used to introduce each article in a list or inventory); **s.:** shilling(s); **d.:** denarius, penny or pennies

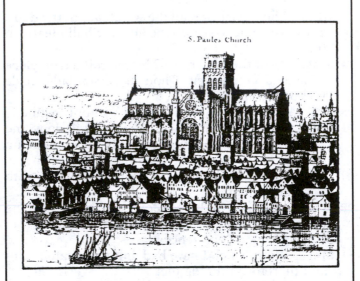

St. Paul's Cathedral. (2.4.546)
From Claes Jansz Visscher, *Londinum Florentissima Britanniae Urbs* . . . (1625).

PRINCE   What men?

SHERIFF
One of them is well known, my gracious lord.
A gross fat man.                                          530

CARRIER                 As fat as butter.

PRINCE
The man I do assure you is not here,
For I myself at this time have employed him.
And, sheriff, I will engage my word to thee
That I will by tomorrow dinner time                      535
Send him to answer thee or any man
For anything he shall be charged withal.
And so let me entreat you leave the house.

SHERIFF
I will, my lord. There are two gentlemen
Have in this robbery lost three hundred marks.           540

PRINCE
It may be so. If he have robbed these men,
He shall be answerable; and so farewell.

SHERIFF   Good night, my noble lord.

PRINCE
I think it is good morrow, is it not?

SHERIFF
Indeed, my lord, I think it be two o'clock.              545
                    *He exits ⌐with the Carrier.⌐*

PRINCE   This oily rascal is known as well as Paul's. Go
call him forth.

PETO   Falstaff!—Fast asleep behind the arras, and
snorting like a horse.

PRINCE   Hark, how hard he fetches breath. Search his     550
pockets. (*He searcheth his pocket, and findeth certain
papers.*) What hast thou found?

PETO   Nothing but papers, my lord.

PRINCE   Let's see what they be. Read them.

⌐PETO *reads*⌐

   *Item, a capon, . . . 2s. 2d.*                         555

559. **ob.:** obolus, halfpenny
561. **deal:** quantity
562. **close:** secret, hidden; **at . . . advantage:** at a more favorable time
566. **charge of foot:** i.e., command of an infantry troop
567. **twelve score:** i.e., 240 yards
568. **advantage:** i.e., interest; **betimes:** early

A prisoner drawn on a cart to execution. (2.4.515-16)
From John Geninges, *The life and death of Mr. Edmund Geninges priest* (1614).

*Item, sauce, . . . 4d.*
*Item, sack, two gallons, . . . 5s. 8d.*
*Item, anchovies and sack after supper, . . . 2s. 6d.*
*Item, bread, . . . ob.*

⌈PRINCE⌉ O monstrous! But one halfpennyworth of     560
bread to this intolerable deal of sack? What there is
else, keep close. We'll read it at more advantage.
There let him sleep till day. I'll to the court in the
morning. We must all to the wars, and thy place
shall be honorable. I'll procure this fat rogue a     565
charge of foot, and I know his death will be a march
of twelve score. The money shall be paid back again
with advantage. Be with me betimes in the morning, and so good morrow, Peto.

PETO   Good morrow, good my lord.                     570

*They exit.*

*The History of*

# HENRY IV
## Part 1

ACT 3

**3.1** Hotspur, Worcester, Mortimer, and the leader of the Welsh rebels, Glendower, meet in Wales to make final the terms of their plot against King Henry and to determine how they will divide up the conquered kingdom. Hotspur ridicules Glendower to his face and is criticized by Mortimer and Worcester for doing so. Glendower brings in the wives of Hotspur and Mortimer to take leave of their husbands.

---

1. **promises:** i.e., the commitment of the **parties** allied with Hotspur, Glendower, and Mortimer in rebellion against King Henry

2. **induction:** initial steps; **prosperous hope:** i.e., hope of prospering

8. **Lancaster:** King Henry, formerly duke of Lancaster

14. **front:** forehead (See page 180.)

15. **burning cressets:** i.e., stars or comets, which, according to a belief that goes back to classical antiquity, are omens of a newborn's greatness (Literally, **cressets** are fire baskets, iron vessels containing combustibles and mounted on poles or suspended from roofs.)

# ⌐ACT 3⌐

## ⌐Scene 1⌐

*Enter Hotspur, Worcester, Lord Mortimer, ⌐and⌐ Owen
Glendower.*

MORTIMER
  These promises are fair, the parties sure,
  And our induction full of prosperous hope.
HOTSPUR
  Lord Mortimer and cousin Glendower,
  Will you sit down? And uncle Worcester—
  A plague upon it, I have forgot the map.                    5
GLENDOWER
  No, here it is. Sit, cousin Percy,
  Sit, good cousin Hotspur, for by that name
  As oft as Lancaster doth speak of you
  His cheek looks pale, and with a rising sigh
  He wisheth you in heaven.                                   10
HOTSPUR                              And you in hell,
  As oft as he hears Owen Glendower spoke of.
GLENDOWER
  I cannot blame him. At my nativity
  The front of heaven was full of fiery shapes,
  Of burning cressets, and at my birth                        15
  The frame and huge foundation of the earth
  Shaked like a coward.
HOTSPUR                          Why, so it would have done

111

28. **Diseasèd:** (1) disordered; (2) sick (Hotspur's explanation [in lines 29–36] of earthquakes as wind erupting from within the earth goes back to classical antiquity.)

29. **teeming:** prolific, fertile

32. **which . . . striving:** i.e., the wind struggling to be released

33. **beldam:** grandmother

35. **distemp'rature:** disorder, ailment

36. **passion:** pain

38. **these crossings:** this opposition, contradiction

44. **courses:** proceedings

45. **in the roll:** i.e., in the list or catalog

46. **he:** i.e., any person; **clipped in with:** embraced or surrounded by

47. **chides:** i.e., crashes against (literally, loudly and vehemently rebukes)

48. **Which:** i.e., who; **read to me;** i.e., given me lessons

50. **trace:** keep up with; **art:** magic

51. **hold me pace:** i.e., keep pace with me

At the same season if your mother's cat
Had but kittened, though yourself had never been          20
   born.
GLENDOWER
   I say the earth did shake when I was born.
HOTSPUR
   And I say the earth was not of my mind,
   If you suppose as fearing you it shook.
GLENDOWER
   The heavens were all on fire; the earth did tremble.          25
HOTSPUR
   O, then the earth shook to see the heavens on fire,
   And not in fear of your nativity.
   Diseasèd nature oftentimes breaks forth
   In strange eruptions; oft the teeming earth
   Is with a kind of colic pinched and vexed          30
   By the imprisoning of unruly wind
   Within her womb, which, for enlargement striving,
   Shakes the old beldam earth and topples down
   Steeples and moss-grown towers. At your birth
   Our grandam earth, having this distemp'rature,          35
   In passion shook.
GLENDOWER          Cousin, of many men
   I do not bear these crossings. Give me leave
   To tell you once again that at my birth
   The front of heaven was full of fiery shapes,          40
   The goats ran from the mountains, and the herds
   Were strangely clamorous to the frighted fields.
   These signs have marked me extraordinary,
   And all the courses of my life do show
   I am not in the roll of common men.          45
   Where is he living, clipped in with the sea
   That chides the banks of England, Scotland, Wales,
   Which calls me pupil or hath read to me?
   And bring him out that is but woman's son
   Can trace me in the tedious ways of art          50
   And hold me pace in deep experiments.

54. **mad:** insane (with fury)

55. **vasty deep:** perhaps, ocean, or, perhaps, abyss

60. **coz:** i.e., cousin (This familiar form, and Hotspur's shift to the familiar **thee** and **thou**, could suggest disrespect.)

61. **Tell . . . devil:** proverbial

67. **made head:** led an army

68. **power:** armed forces

68, 69. **Wye, Severn:** rivers near the English-Welsh border

70. **Bootless:** unsuccessful

72. **agues:** chills and fevers

73. **right:** territory

74. **our threefold order ta'en:** i.e., the document recording our pact (**Threefold** may refer to the plan to divide the island into three parts, or to the fact that the document is being prepared in triplicate. See lines 83–84.)

75. **Archdeacon:** i.e., the archdeacon of Bangor, at whose home, according to the chronicles, the plan was made for dividing the realm

76. **limits:** territories, regions

HOTSPUR
I think there's no man speaks better Welsh.
I'll to dinner.

MORTIMER
Peace, cousin Percy. You will make him mad.

GLENDOWER
I can call spirits from the vasty deep.                    55

HOTSPUR
Why, so can I, or so can any man,
But will they come when you do call for them?

GLENDOWER
Why, I can teach you, cousin, to command the
    devil.

HOTSPUR
And I can teach thee, coz, to shame the devil      60
By telling truth. Tell truth and shame the devil.
If thou have power to raise him, bring him hither,
And I'll be sworn I have power to shame him
    hence.
O, while you live, tell truth and shame the devil!      65

MORTIMER
Come, come, no more of this unprofitable chat.

GLENDOWER
Three times hath Henry Bolingbroke made head
Against my power; thrice from the banks of Wye
And sandy-bottomed Severn have I sent him
Bootless home and weather-beaten back.            70

HOTSPUR
Home without boots, and in foul weather too!
How 'scapes he agues, in the devil's name?

GLENDOWER
Come, here is the map. Shall we divide our right
According to our threefold order ta'en?

MORTIMER
The Archdeacon hath divided it                        75
Into three limits very equally:

77–78. **England . . . east:** i.e., all England south-east of the Trent and Severn rivers

80. **that bound;** i.e., these boundaries

82. **lying off from:** i.e., starting from

83. **indentures . . . drawn:** i.e., the document re-cording our pact is drawn up in triplicate

84. **sealèd interchangeably:** i.e., each copy bear-ing the seals of the three nobles

85. **this . . . execute:** i.e., can be done tonight

90. **father:** i.e., father-in-law

96. **conduct:** escort, safe-conduct

100. **moiety:** share

101. **not one:** i.e., neither

102. **comes me:** i.e., comes; **cranking:** twisting

103. **cuts me:** i.e., cuts, removes

104. **cantle:** slice

106. **smug:** smooth

107. **fair and evenly:** i.e., straight

109. **bottom:** bottom land, lowland, river valley

A griffin. (3.1.156)
From Giulio Cesare Capaccio, *Delle imprese trattato* . . . (1592).

England, from Trent and Severn hitherto,
By south and east is to my part assigned;
All westward, Wales beyond the Severn shore,
And all the fertile land within that bound                    80
To Owen Glendower; and, dear coz, to you
The remnant northward lying off from Trent.
And our indentures tripartite are drawn,
Which being sealèd interchangeably—
A business that this night may execute—                      85
Tomorrow, cousin Percy, you and I
And my good Lord of Worcester will set forth
To meet your father and the Scottish power,
As is appointed us, at Shrewsbury.
My father Glendower is not ready yet,                         90
Nor shall we need his help these fourteen days.
⌜*To Glendower.*⌝ Within that space you may have
      drawn together
Your tenants, friends, and neighboring gentlemen.
GLENDOWER
A shorter time shall send me to you, lords,                   95
And in my conduct shall your ladies come,
From whom you now must steal and take no leave,
For there will be a world of water shed
Upon the parting of your wives and you.
HOTSPUR, ⌜*looking at the map*⌝
Methinks my moiety, north from Burton here,                  100
In quantity equals not one of yours.
See how this river comes me cranking in
And cuts me from the best of all my land
A huge half-moon, a monstrous ⌜cantle⌝ out.
I'll have the current in this place dammed up,               105
And here the smug and silver Trent shall run
In a new channel, fair and evenly.
It shall not wind with such a deep indent
To rob me of so rich a bottom here.

111–15. **Yea . . . you:** i.e., see how the Trent winds and turns up in the same way on the other side, cutting from its opposite bank just as much as it takes from your side   **he:** i.e., the river Trent   **runs me up:** i.e., turns up   **like:** similar   **continent:** bank (literally, container)

116. **charge:** expense; **trench him:** i.e., divert it into a newly dug course

128. **framèd to:** adapted to, arranged for

130. **the tongue:** i.e., the English language

131. **virtue:** accomplishment

132. **Marry:** a mild oath

134. **meter balladmongers:** hawkers of metrical ballads (whom Hotspur here equates with courtly composers)

135. **brazen can'stick:** brass candlestick; **turned:** i.e., turned on a lathe (to smooth and polish it)

136. **dry:** unlubricated

137. **nothing an:** i.e., not nearly as much on

139. **forced gait:** jerky steps; **shuffling nag:** hobbled horse (Note the jerky rhythm of the line itself.)

GLENDOWER
  Not wind? It shall, it must. You see it doth.          110
MORTIMER, ⌜*to Hotspur*⌝
  Yea, but mark how he bears his course, and runs
    me up
  With like advantage on the other side,
  Gelding the opposèd continent as much
  As on the other side it takes from you.          115
WORCESTER
  Yea, but a little charge will trench him here
  And on this north side win this cape of land,
  And then he runs straight and even.
HOTSPUR
  I'll have it so. A little charge will do it.
GLENDOWER   I'll not have it altered.          120
HOTSPUR   Will not you?
GLENDOWER   No, nor you shall not.
HOTSPUR   Who shall say me nay?
GLENDOWER   Why, that will I.
HOTSPUR
  Let me not understand you, then; speak it in Welsh.          125
GLENDOWER
  I can speak English, lord, as well as you,
  For I was trained up in the English court,
  Where being but young I framèd to the harp
  Many an English ditty lovely well
  And gave the tongue a helpful ornament—          130
  A virtue that was never seen in you.
HOTSPUR
  Marry, and I am glad of it with all my heart.
  I had rather be a kitten and cry "mew"
  Than one of these same ⌜meter⌝ balladmongers.
  I had rather hear a brazen can'stick turned,          135
  Or a dry wheel grate on the axletree,
  And that would set my teeth nothing an edge,
  Nothing so much as mincing poetry.
  'Tis like the forced gait of a shuffling nag.

143. **bargain:** i.e., driving a bargain
144. **cavil on:** quibble about
147. **writer:** scribe; **withal:** at the same time
148. **Break with:** tell, advise
151. **cross:** oppose, contradict
152. **choose:** i.e., choose to do otherwise
153. **moldwarp:** mole
154. **Merlin:** the magician in Arthurian legend
156. **griffin:** a mythological creature with the wings and head of the eagle and the body of the lion (See page 116.); **moulten:** i.e., moulted
157. **A couching . . . cat:** This line parodies the heraldic language in which the crests of noble houses are described. It plays with "couchant"—which refers to an animal depicted on a crest as lying down with its head raised—and with "rampant"—which refers to an animal reared up on its hind legs—and it includes among heraldic beasts the ordinary **cat.** (See page 212.)
158. **skimble-skamble stuff:** i.e., nonsense
159. **puts . . . faith:** i.e., makes it impossible for me to believe in anything, even my Christian faith
160. **held me:** i.e., held me in conversation
161. **several:** various
162–63. **go to:** an expression, perhaps, of impatience or, perhaps, of skepticism
164. **marked him not a word:** paid no attention to a word he said
166–67. **rather live . . . far:** i.e., far rather . . . live
168. **cates:** delicacies
169. **summer house:** house in the country, built for pleasure and recreation

GLENDOWER   Come, you shall have Trent turned.     140
HOTSPUR
  I do not care. I'll give thrice so much land
  To any well-deserving friend;
  But in the way of bargain, mark you me,
  I'll cavil on the ninth part of a hair.
  Are the indentures drawn? Shall we be gone?     145
GLENDOWER
  The moon shines fair. You may away by night.
  I'll haste the writer, and withal
  Break with your wives of your departure hence.
  I am afraid my daughter will run mad,
  So much she doteth on her Mortimer.    *He exits.*   150
MORTIMER
  Fie, cousin Percy, how you cross my father!
HOTSPUR
  I cannot choose. Sometime he angers me
  With telling me of the moldwarp and the ant,
  Of the dreamer Merlin and his prophecies,
  And of a dragon and a finless fish,     155
  A clip-winged griffin and a moulten raven,
  A couching lion and a ramping cat,
  And such a deal of skimble-skamble stuff
  As puts me from my faith. I tell you what—
  He held me last night at least nine hours     160
  In reckoning up the several devils' names
  That were his lackeys. I cried "Hum," and "Well, go
    to,"
  But marked him not a word. O, he is as tedious
  As a tired horse, a railing wife,     165
  Worse than a smoky house. I had rather live
  With cheese and garlic in a windmill, far,
  Than feed on cates and have him talk to me
  In any summer house in Christendom.
MORTIMER
  In faith, he is a worthy gentleman,     170

171–72. **profited . . . concealments:** advanced in secret knowledge

174. **mines of India:** i.e., the gold mines of the Indies

175. **temper:** temperament, character

177. **come . . . humor:** oppose his temper, or mood

179. **Might:** i.e., who could

181. **use it:** i.e., take advantage of Glendower's forbearance

182. **willful-blame:** i.e., blameworthy for your willfulness

184. **besides:** out of

187. **blood:** mettle, spirit

188. **dearest grace:** most honorable credit

189. **present:** show

190. **want of government:** lack of discretion

191. **opinion:** conceit, arrogance

192. **haunting:** i.e., habitually associated with (with the sense also of infesting and of supernatural visitation)

193. **Loseth:** i.e., causes him to lose

194. **parts:** qualities; accomplishments

195. **Beguiling:** cheating

196. **schooled:** instructed; **be your speed:** i.e., bring you success

198. **spite:** annoyance, irritation

Exceedingly well read and profited
In strange concealments, valiant as a lion,
And wondrous affable, and as bountiful
As mines of India. Shall I tell you, cousin?
He holds your temper in a high respect                    175
And curbs himself even of his natural scope
When you come cross his humor. Faith, he does.
I warrant you that man is not alive
Might so have tempted him as you have done
Without the taste of danger and reproof.                  180
But do not use it oft, let me entreat you.
WORCESTER, ⌜to Hotspur⌝
In faith, my lord, you are too willful-blame,
And, since your coming hither, have done enough
To put him quite besides his patience.
You must needs learn, lord, to amend this fault.          185
Though sometimes it show greatness, courage,
  blood—
And that's the dearest grace it renders you—
Yet oftentimes it doth present harsh rage,
Defect of manners, want of government,                    190
Pride, haughtiness, opinion, and disdain,
The least of which, haunting a nobleman,
Loseth men's hearts and leaves behind a stain
Upon the beauty of all parts besides,
Beguiling them of commendation.                           195
HOTSPUR
Well, I am schooled. Good manners be your speed!
Here come our wives, and let us take our leave.

*Enter Glendower with the Ladies.*

MORTIMER
This is the deadly spite that angers me:
My wife can speak no English, I no Welsh.
GLENDOWER
My daughter weeps; she'll not part with you.             200
She'll be a soldier too, she'll to the wars.

202. **my aunt Percy:** i.e., Hotspur's wife (See note to 1.3.82–87 for information about the Mortimer-Percy family tie.)

204. **peevish:** obstinate; **harlotry:** good-for-nothing (most often with reference to a harlot, or whore)

206. **That pretty Welsh:** i.e., your tears

209. **perfect in:** conversant with

209–10. **but for shame . . . thee:** i.e., if I were not ashamed to appear unmanly, I'd weep with you **parley:** speech

212. **feeling disputation:** A **disputation** was a debate, an exchange of speeches among academics sustaining, attacking, and defending a thesis. The word **feeling** carries several meanings, suggesting the exchange of feelings through touch and the emotional intensity of the exchange.

215. **highly penned:** written in a high style

217. **division:** a rapid, melodious passage of music

220. **wanton:** luxuriant; **rushes:** i.e., green rushes, commonly strewn on floors of houses

223. **crown . . . sleep:** i.e., make sleep the supreme ruler

224. **heaviness:** sleepiness

MORTIMER
Good father, tell her that she and my aunt Percy
Shall follow in your conduct speedily.
> *Glendower speaks to her in Welsh,*
> *and she answers him in the same.*

GLENDOWER
She is desperate here, a peevish self-willed harlotry,
One that no persuasion can do good upon.     205
> *The Lady speaks in Welsh.*

MORTIMER
I understand thy looks. That pretty Welsh
Which thou pourest down from these swelling
   heavens
I am too perfect in, and but for shame
In such a parley should I answer thee.     210
> *The Lady ⌜speaks⌝ again in Welsh. ⌜They kiss.⌝*
I understand thy kisses, and thou mine,
And that's a feeling disputation;
But I will never be a truant, love,
Till I have learned thy language; for thy tongue
Makes Welsh as sweet as ditties highly penned,     215
Sung by a fair queen in a summer's bower,
With ravishing division, to her lute.

GLENDOWER
Nay, if you melt, then will she run mad.
> *The Lady speaks again in Welsh.*

MORTIMER
O, I am ignorance itself in this!

GLENDOWER
She bids you on the wanton rushes lay you down     220
And rest your gentle head upon her lap,
And she will sing the song that pleaseth you,
And on your eyelids crown the god of sleep,
Charming your blood with pleasing heaviness,
Making such difference 'twixt wake and sleep     225
As is the difference betwixt day and night

227. **heavenly harnessed team:** in mythology, the team of horses that draws the sun's chariot

228. **progress:** royal journey

230. **book . . . drawn:** indentures . . . drawn up (See note to line 83.)

233. **straight:** straightway, immediately

234. **perfect:** expert

239. **he:** i.e., since he; or, that he; **humorous:** capricious, flighty

244. **brach:** bitch hound

246. **broken:** i.e., cut

249. **Neither:** i.e., I won't be quiet either; **a woman's fault:** According to Elizabethan conduct books, women were to be chaste, silent, and obedient.

255. **in good sooth:** a very mild oath   **sooth:** truth

256. **Heart:** i.e., Christ's heart

SOL

"The heavenly harnessed team." (3.1.227)
From Hyginus, *Fabularum liber* (1549).

The hour before the heavenly harnessed team
Begins his golden progress in the east.

MORTIMER
With all my heart I'll sit and hear her sing.
By that time will our book, I think, be drawn.    230

GLENDOWER
Do so, and those musicians that shall play to you
Hang in the air a thousand leagues from hence,
And straight they shall be here. Sit and attend.

HOTSPUR
Come, Kate, thou art perfect in lying down.
Come, quick, quick, that I may lay my head in thy    235
lap.

LADY PERCY    Go, you giddy goose.

*The music plays.*

HOTSPUR
Now I perceive the devil understands Welsh,
And 'tis no marvel he is so humorous.
By 'r Lady, he is a good musician.    240

LADY PERCY    Then should you be nothing but musical,
for you are altogether governed by humors. Lie
still, you thief, and hear the lady sing in Welsh.

HOTSPUR    I had rather hear Lady, my brach, howl in
Irish.    245

LADY PERCY    Wouldst thou have thy head broken?

HOTSPUR    No.

LADY PERCY    Then be still.

HOTSPUR    Neither; 'tis a woman's fault.

LADY PERCY    Now God help thee!    250

HOTSPUR    To the Welsh lady's bed.

LADY PERCY    What's that?

HOTSPUR    Peace, she sings.

*Here the Lady sings a Welsh song.*

HOTSPUR    Come, Kate, I'll have your song too.

LADY PERCY    Not mine, in good sooth.    255

HOTSPUR    Not yours, in good sooth! Heart, you swear

257. **comfit-maker's wife:** Hotspur insists that his wife, a noblewoman or **lady** (line 262), use strong oaths to set herself off from the prim wives of ordinary London citizens like the **comfit-maker** or confectioner, who never go further than **Finsbury** (line 261), a playing field just north of the city.

257–59. **"Not you . . . day":** Hotspur's catalog of very mild oaths   **mend:** amend, free from sin

260. **sarcenet:** soft, insubstantial (literally, a thin, soft silk material)

264. **pepper-gingerbread:** a coarse, hot-spicy comfit or confection

265. **velvet-guards . . . citizens:** i.e., citizens in Sunday clothes trimmed (guarded) with velvet

268. **'Tis . . . way:** i.e., singing is the quickest way

268–69. **to turn . . . teacher:** i.e., to turn into a tailor (since tailors, like weavers, were said to sing at their work) or to become a bird's singing teacher

270. **away:** i.e., go away, leave

274. **this:** i.e., now; **but:** just

**3.2** Prince Hal reconciles himself with his father by swearing to fight the rebels and to defeat Hotspur.

————————

1. **give us leave:** a polite request for privacy

5–19. **I know . . . heart:** King Henry suggests that the only way of explaining Hal's attraction to the tavern is as divine punishment of Hal and himself: Hal is God's **scourge, the rod of heaven,** i.e., the instrument through whom God punishes King Henry for his transgressions.

*(continued)*

like a comfit-maker's wife! "Not you, in good
sooth," and "as true as I live," and "as God shall
mend me," and "as sure as day"—
And givest such sarcenet surety for thy oaths          260
As if thou never walk'st further than Finsbury.
Swear me, Kate, like a lady as thou art,
A good mouth-filling oath, and leave "in sooth,"
And such protest of pepper-gingerbread
To velvet-guards and Sunday citizens.                  265
Come, sing.

LADY PERCY   I will not sing.

HOTSPUR   'Tis the next way to turn tailor, or be red-
breast teacher. An the indentures be drawn, I'll
away within these two hours, and so come in when      270
you will.                                       *He exits.*

GLENDOWER
Come, come, Lord Mortimer, you are as slow
As hot Lord Percy is on fire to go.
By this our book is drawn. We'll but seal,
And then to horse immediately.                         275

MORTIMER   With all my heart.
                                          *They exit.*


⌜Scene 2⌝
*Enter the King, Prince of Wales, and others.*

KING
Lords, give us leave; the Prince of Wales and I
Must have some private conference, but be near at
    hand,
For we shall presently have need of you.
                                          *Lords exit.*

I know not whether God will have it so                   5
For some displeasing service I have done,
That, in His secret doom, out of my blood

7. **doom:** judgment; **blood:** offspring
9. **thy . . . life:** i.e., the way you live your life
10–11. **marked/For:** i.e., destined to be
12. **else:** i.e., if such is not the case
14. **lewd:** poor, sorry, vulgar
15. **attempts:** endeavors, efforts
16. **rude society:** unrefined company
18. **blood:** i.e., royal blood
19. **hold their:** i.e., be on a
20. **So . . . Majesty:** a polite request to speak
21. **Quit:** prove myself innocent of
24–30. **Yet . . . submission:** Hal offers to refute the charges against him, and to provide an accurate account (**true submission**) of how he has strayed (**wandered**), for which conduct he begs pardon.
25. **in reproof:** upon disproof or refutation
26. **ear of greatness:** i.e., ears of great persons such as King Henry
27. **pickthanks:** those who seek favor by telling tales; **newsmongers:** retailers of news
28–29. **wherein . . . irregular:** i.e., in which my youth has gone astray and transgressed rules (*Regula* is Latin for "rules.")
32. **affections:** inclinations
33. **from:** away from
34. **rudely:** i.e., through violence (The chronicles say that Hal was banished from the council for striking the lord chief justice.)
38. **hope . . . time:** i.e., the hopes that people had for what you could achieve in your time
40. **forethink:** anticipate

He'll breed revengement and a scourge for me.
But thou dost in thy passages of life
Make me believe that thou art only marked                    10
For the hot vengeance and the rod of heaven
To punish my mistreadings. Tell me else,
Could such inordinate and low desires,
Such poor, such bare, such lewd, such mean
    attempts,                                                15
Such barren pleasures, rude society
As thou art matched withal, and grafted to,
Accompany the greatness of thy blood,
And hold their level with thy princely heart?
PRINCE
So please your Majesty, I would I could                      20
Quit all offenses with as clear excuse
As well as I am doubtless I can purge
Myself of many I am charged withal.
Yet such extenuation let me beg
As, in reproof of many tales devised,                        25
Which oft the ear of greatness needs must hear,
By smiling pickthanks and base newsmongers,
I may for some things true, wherein my youth
Hath faulty wandered and irregular,
Find pardon on my true submission.                           30
KING
God pardon thee. Yet let me wonder, Harry,
At thy affections, which do hold a wing
Quite from the flight of all thy ancestors.
Thy place in council thou hast rudely lost,
Which by thy younger brother is supplied,                    35
And art almost an alien to the hearts
Of all the court and princes of my blood.
The hope and expectation of thy time
Is ruined, and the soul of every man
Prophetically do forethink thy fall.                         40
Had I so lavish of my presence been,

42. **common-hackneyed:** i.e., common (A hackney was a horse available to anyone for hire.)

44. **Opinion:** probably not modern "public opinion," but the views of the ruling class (See Leggatt's "Modern Perspective.")

45. **loyal to possession:** i.e., loyal to Richard II, then in possession of the crown

46. **reputeless:** inglorious

47. **of no . . . likelihood:** i.e., undistinguished by any promise of greatness

52. **stole . . . heaven:** i.e., put on a saintlike demeanor

58. **pontifical:** belonging to a bishop or archbishop, for example

59. **my state:** i.e., the splendor accompanying my public appearance

60. **Seldom:** i.e., seldom seen; **feast:** religious festival or feast day

61. **solemnity:** dignity, awful grandeur, as befitting a ceremony

62. **skipping:** flighty, frivolous

63. **rash bavin:** i.e., flashy (Literally, **bavin** is brushwood used as kindling.)

64. **carded:** debased (literally, adulterated by mixing with inferior matter); **state:** position, status

66. **their scorns:** i.e., scorn for the **fools** with whom he **mingled**

67. **countenance:** (1) approval; (2) face; **against his name:** i.e., to the dishonor of his reputation

68–69. **stand . . . comparative:** i.e., engage in (verbal) combat with empty young satirists (quick to make comparisons)

71. **Enfeoffed . . . popularity:** i.e., surrendered himself entirely to the pursuit of popular approval

So common-hackneyed in the eyes of men,
So stale and cheap to vulgar company,
Opinion, that did help me to the crown,
Had still kept loyal to possession      45
And left me in reputeless banishment,
A fellow of no mark nor likelihood.
By being seldom seen, I could not stir
But like a comet I was wondered at,
That men would tell their children "This is he."      50
Others would say "Where? Which is Bolingbroke?"
And then I stole all courtesy from heaven,
And dressed myself in such humility
That I did pluck allegiance from men's hearts,
Loud shouts and salutations from their mouths,      55
Even in the presence of the crownèd king.
Thus did I keep my person fresh and new,
My presence, like a robe pontifical,
Ne'er seen but wondered at, and so my state,
Seldom but sumptuous, showed like a feast      60
And won by rareness such solemnity.
The skipping king, he ambled up and down
With shallow jesters and rash bavin wits,
Soon kindled and soon burnt; carded his state,
Mingled his royalty with cap'ring fools,      65
Had his great name profanèd with their scorns,
And gave his countenance, against his name,
To laugh at gibing boys and stand the push
Of every beardless vain comparative;
Grew a companion to the common streets,      70
Enfeoffed himself to popularity,
That, being daily swallowed by men's eyes,
They surfeited with honey and began
To loathe the taste of sweetness, whereof a little
More than a little is by much too much.      75
So, when he had occasion to be seen,

77–78. **cuckoo . . . regarded:** Proverbial: No one regards the June cuckoo's song. (Cuckoos were abundant in June.)

79. **community:** i.e., familiarity

84. **rendered such aspect:** i.e., gave him such looks

85. **cloudy:** frowning

87. **line:** rank, category

89. **participation:** (1) fellowship, association; (2) partaking (in common activities)

92. **that:** i.e., that which

93. **foolish tenderness:** i.e., weeping

97. **to:** i.e., at

100. **to boot:** as well, in addition

101–2. **He . . . succession:** i.e., Percy has a stronger claim to the throne based on merit (**worthy interest to the state**) than you, because your claim is a shadowy one based only on heredity and not supported by merit

103. **of . . . like to right:** i.e., without any right to the throne, or even anything like such a right

104. **harness:** armor, and, by extension, armed men

105. **Turns head:** directs an army; **lion's:** i.e., king's

106. **no . . . years:** i.e., no older

108. **arms:** i.e., war

110. **high:** i.e., great

He was but as the cuckoo is in June,
Heard, not regarded; seen, but with such eyes
As, sick and blunted with community,
Afford no extraordinary gaze     80
Such as is bent on sunlike majesty
When it shines seldom in admiring eyes,
But rather drowsed and hung their eyelids down,
Slept in his face, and rendered such aspect
As cloudy men use to their adversaries,   85
Being with his presence glutted, gorged, and full.
And in that very line, Harry, standest thou,
For thou hast lost thy princely privilege
With vile participation. Not an eye
But is aweary of thy common sight,    90
Save mine, which hath desired to see thee more,
Which now doth that I would not have it do,
Make blind itself with foolish tenderness.

PRINCE
I shall hereafter, my thrice gracious lord,
Be more myself.        95

KING For all the world
As thou art to this hour was Richard then
When I from France set foot at Ravenspurgh,
And even as I was then is Percy now.
Now, by my scepter, and my soul to boot,  100
He hath more worthy interest to the state
Than thou, the shadow of succession.
For of no right, nor color like to right,
He doth fill fields with harness in the realm,
Turns head against the lion's armèd jaws,  105
And, being no more in debt to years than thou,
Leads ancient lords and reverend bishops on
To bloody battles and to bruising arms.
What never-dying honor hath he got
Against renownèd Douglas, whose high deeds, 110
Whose hot incursions and great name in arms,

112–13. **Holds . . . capital:** i.e., is regarded by all soldiers as preeminent and worthy of the highest military title

115. **Mars:** the god of war

118. **Discomfited:** defeated; **ta'en:** captured

119. **Enlargèd:** released

125. **Capitulate:** draw up articles of agreement; **up:** i.e., up in arms

126. **wherefore:** why

128. **dearest:** (1) most loved; (2) direst

129. **like:** i.e., likely; **vassal:** abject

130. **start of spleen:** outburst of bad temper or of whimsy, caprice

137. **on Percy's head:** i.e., to Percy's cost

141. **favors:** facial features (The word could also refer to the scarves, sleeves, and other ornaments or insignia worn into battle by knights.)

143. **lights:** dawns

146. **unthought-of:** disrespected

Holds from all soldiers chief majority
And military title capital
Through all the kingdoms that acknowledge Christ.
Thrice hath this Hotspur, Mars in swaddling          115
   clothes,
This infant warrior, in his enterprises
Discomfited great Douglas, ta'en him once,
Enlargèd him, and made a friend of him,
To fill the mouth of deep defiance up                120
And shake the peace and safety of our throne.
And what say you to this? Percy, Northumberland,
The Archbishop's Grace of York, Douglas,
   Mortimer,
Capitulate against us and are up.                    125
But wherefore do I tell these news to thee?
Why, Harry, do I tell thee of my foes,
Which art my nearest and dearest enemy?
Thou that art like enough, through vassal fear,
Base inclination, and the start of spleen,           130
To fight against me under Percy's pay,
To dog his heels, and curtsy at his frowns,
To show how much thou art degenerate.
PRINCE
Do not think so. You shall not find it so.
And God forgive them that so much have swayed        135
Your Majesty's good thoughts away from me.
I will redeem all this on Percy's head,
And, in the closing of some glorious day,
Be bold to tell you that I am your son,
When I will wear a garment all of blood              140
And stain my favors in a bloody mask,
Which, washed away, shall scour my shame with it.
And that shall be the day, whene'er it lights,
That this same child of honor and renown,
This gallant Hotspur, this all-praisèd knight,       145
And your unthought-of Harry chance to meet.

147. **every honor:** i.e., every **glorious deed** that has brought him honor (Hal images them as insignia worn on Hotspur's helmet, and contrasts them with the **shames** worn on his own.)

152. **factor:** agent

153. **engross up:** buy up in great quantity, monopolize

154–57. **And . . . heart:** i.e., "Hotspur will either yield to me and confess that all the glory is mine, or I will capture the glory by killing him"

156. **worship of his time:** honor won in his lifetime

157. **reckoning:** account

160. **salve:** i.e., put a salve on, and thereby heal

161. **intemperance:** excesses

162. **bands:** bonds, debts

164. **parcel:** part

165. **in this:** i.e., through this vow; or, through the action you have promised

166. **charge:** command (of soldiers); **sovereign trust:** (1) the highest responsibility; (2) responsibility delegated from the sovereign himself

169. **Mortimer of Scotland:** not the English ally of Percy and Glendower; probably an error for the Scottish earl of March

172. **head:** army

177. **advertisement:** intelligence (pronounced **advèrtisement**)

For every honor sitting on his helm,
Would they were multitudes, and on my head
My shames redoubled! For the time will come
That I shall make this northern youth exchange          150
His glorious deeds for my indignities.
Percy is but my factor, good my lord,
To engross up glorious deeds on my behalf.
And I will call him to so strict account
That he shall render every glory up,          155
Yea, even the slightest worship of his time,
Or I will tear the reckoning from his heart.
This in the name of God I promise here,
The which if He be pleased I shall perform,
I do beseech your Majesty may salve          160
The long-grown wounds of my intemperance.
If not, the end of life cancels all bands,
And I will die a hundred thousand deaths
Ere break the smallest parcel of this vow.

KING
A hundred thousand rebels die in this.          165
Thou shalt have charge and sovereign trust herein.

*Enter Blunt.*

How now, good Blunt? Thy looks are full of speed.

BLUNT
So hath the business that I come to speak of.
Lord Mortimer of Scotland hath sent word
That Douglas and the English rebels met          170
The eleventh of this month at Shrewsbury.
A mighty and a fearful head they are,
If promises be kept on every hand,
As ever offered foul play in a state.

KING
The Earl of Westmoreland set forth today,          175
With him my son, Lord John of Lancaster,
For this advertisement is five days old.—

179. **we ourselves:** i.e., I; **meeting:** i.e., meeting place

180. **Bridgenorth:** a town on the Severn, twenty miles from the eventual battleground near Shrewsbury

181–82. **by which . . . valuèd:** i.e., according to this calculation, as I have estimated the time we need for what we have to do

185. **Advantage:** perhaps, (1) opportunity (to rebel); or, perhaps, (2) the superior position (of the rebels) (It is possible that the whole line simply adapts the proverb "Delay breeds danger."); **him:** i.e., itself


**3.3** Falstaff tries to swindle the Hostess of his inn. Prince Hal offers Falstaff a command in the infantry.

---

1. **am I not fallen away:** i.e., haven't I shrunk

2. **bate:** abate, grow thin

4. **applejohn:** an old apple with a shriveled skin

5–6. **am in some liking:** (1) am so inclined; (2) have some flesh on me

6. **out of heart:** (1) dispirited; (2) in poor condition

9. **peppercorn, brewer's horse:** Both look old and shriveled. (Decrepit horses were sold to brewers to pull their carts.)

15. **given:** inclined

20. **good compass:** within the bounds of moderation (**Compass** also means "girth," the sense in which Bardolph immediately uses it.)

On Wednesday next, Harry, you shall set forward.
On Thursday we ourselves will march. Our meeting
Is Bridgenorth. And, Harry, you shall march                    180
Through Gloucestershire; by which account,
Our business valuèd, some twelve days hence
Our general forces at Bridgenorth shall meet.
Our hands are full of business. Let's away.
Advantage feeds him fat while men delay.                       185

*They exit.*

⌜Scene 3⌝
*Enter Falstaff and Bardolph.*

FALSTAFF  Bardolph, am I not fallen away vilely since
this last action? Do I not bate? Do I not dwindle?
Why, my skin hangs about me like an old lady's
loose gown. I am withered like an old applejohn.
Well, I'll repent, and that suddenly, while I am in        5
some liking. I shall be out of heart shortly, and then
I shall have no strength to repent. An I have not
forgotten what the inside of a church is made of, I
am a peppercorn, a brewer's horse. The inside of a
church! Company, villainous company, hath been            10
the spoil of me.

BARDOLPH  Sir John, you are so fretful you cannot live
long.

FALSTAFF  Why, there is it. Come, sing me a bawdy
song, make me merry. I was as virtuously given as a        15
gentleman need to be, virtuous enough: swore
little; diced not above seven times—a week; went to
a bawdy house not above once in a quarter—of an
hour; paid money that I borrowed—three or four
times; lived well and in good compass; and now I           20
live out of all order, out of all compass.

BARDOLPH  Why, you are so fat, Sir John, that you must

25. **amend:** (1) improve; (2) reform

26. **admiral:** flagship (which led the fleet, at night, by means of a lantern)

27. **nose:** another reference to Bardolph's drink-reddened nose

31–32. **death's . . . mori:** i.e., a skull or an image of a skull (kept as a reminder of one's mortality)

33. **Dives . . . purple:** See Luke 16.19–31, for the story of the rich man (called "Dives" in the Latin Vulgate) who dressed in purple and who, after death, burned in hell.

36. **God's angel:** There are several references in the Bible to angels appearing as fire: Exodus 3.2, Psalms 104.4, and Hebrews 1.7.

37. **given over:** i.e., to evil

38. **son . . . darkness:** This biblical reference combines language from Matthew 8.12 and 1 Thessalonians 5.5.

40–41. **ignis fatuus, ball of wildfire:** a phosphorescent light that hovers over swampy ground at night, a will-o'-the-wisp (A **ball of wildfire** was also a kind of firework, and **wildfire** can refer to a skin disease.)

42. **triumph:** i.e., illuminated public festivity

44. **links:** small torches

46. **drunk me:** i.e., drunk (at my expense)

47. **good cheap:** cheaply; **dearest chandler's:** most expensive candlemaker's

48. **salamander:** literally, a lizard thought to live in fire (See page 146.)

51–52. **I . . . belly:** Proverbial (as a retort to an insult): "I wish it were in your belly."

55. **Dame Partlet the hen:** Pertilote (or Partlet) is Chauntecleer's favorite (but nagging) hen in Chaucer's "Nun's Priest's Tale."

needs be out of all compass, out of all reasonable
compass, Sir John.

FALSTAFF  Do thou amend thy face, and I'll amend my  25
life. Thou art our admiral, thou bearest the lantern
in the poop, but 'tis in the nose of thee. Thou art the
Knight of the Burning Lamp.

BARDOLPH  Why, Sir John, my face does you no harm.

FALSTAFF  No, I'll be sworn, I make as good use of it as  30
many a man doth of a death's-head or a *memento
mori*. I never see thy face but I think upon hellfire
and Dives that lived in purple, for there he is in his
robes, burning, burning. If thou wert any way given
to virtue, I would swear by thy face. My oath should  35
be "By this fire, ⌈that's⌉ God's angel." But thou art
altogether given over, and wert indeed, but for the
light in thy face, the son of utter darkness. When
thou ran'st up Gad's Hill in the night to catch my
horse, if I did not think thou hadst been an *ignis*  40
*fatuus*, or a ball of wildfire, there's no purchase in
money. O, thou art a perpetual triumph, an everlast-
ing bonfire-light. Thou hast saved me a thousand
marks in links and torches, walking with thee in the
night betwixt tavern and tavern, but the sack that  45
thou hast drunk me would have bought me lights as
good cheap at the dearest chandler's in Europe. I
have maintained that salamander of yours with fire
any time this two-and-thirty years, God reward me
for it.  50

BARDOLPH  'Sblood, I would my face were in your
belly!

FALSTAFF  Godamercy, so should I be sure to be heart-
burned!

*Enter Hostess.*

How now, Dame Partlet the hen, have you enquired  55
yet who picked my pocket?

61. **tithe:** tenth part
72. **to your back:** i.e., for you
73. **Dowlas:** coarse linen
74. **bolters:** sieves
76. **holland:** fine linen; **of:** i.e., at
77. **ell:** a yard and a quarter
78. **diet:** meals; **by-drinkings:** drinks between meals
84–5. **Let . . . cheeks:** a suggestion that Bardolph's red nose and cheeks could be (like rubies and carbuncles) sold or otherwise converted to cash
85. **denier:** coin of very small value
86. **younker:** youngster, novice
88. **seal ring:** a ring bearing a seal or signet
92. **jack:** silly, saucy fellow; **sneak-up:** sneak

A memento mori. (3.3.31-32)
From the Folger Library collection (c. 1640).

144

HOSTESS   Why, Sir John, what do you think, Sir John, do you think I keep thieves in my house? I have searched, I have enquired, so has my husband, man by man, boy by boy, servant by servant. The ⌜tithe⌝ of a hair was never lost in my house before.

FALSTAFF   You lie, hostess. Bardolph was shaved and lost many a hair, and I'll be sworn my pocket was picked. Go to, you are a woman, go.

HOSTESS   Who, I? No, I defy thee! God's light, I was never called so in mine own house before.

FALSTAFF   Go to, I know you well enough.

HOSTESS   No, Sir John, you do not know me, Sir John. I know you, Sir John. You owe me money, Sir John, and now you pick a quarrel to beguile me of it. I bought you a dozen of shirts to your back.

FALSTAFF   Dowlas, filthy dowlas. I have given them away to bakers' wives; they have made bolters of them.

HOSTESS   Now, as I am a true woman, holland of eight shillings an ell. You owe money here besides, Sir John, for your diet and by-drinkings and money lent you, four-and-twenty pound.

FALSTAFF, ⌜*pointing to Bardolph*⌝   He had his part of it. Let him pay.

HOSTESS   He? Alas, he is poor. He hath nothing.

FALSTAFF   How, poor? Look upon his face. What call you rich? Let them coin his nose. Let them coin his cheeks. I'll not pay a denier. What, will you make a younker of me? Shall I not take mine ease in mine inn but I shall have my pocket picked? I have lost a seal ring of my grandfather's worth forty mark.

HOSTESS, ⌜*to Bardolph*⌝   O Jesu, I have heard the Prince tell him, I know not how oft, that that ring was copper.

FALSTAFF   How? The Prince is a jack, a sneak-up.

94 SD. **truncheon:** officer's short staff

95. **is . . . door:** i.e., is that how things are?

97. **Newgate fashion:** i.e., two by two, like an officer leading a prisoner to Newgate prison

100. **honest:** honorable

111. **eightpenny:** i.e., paltry

120. **stewed prune:** Stewed prunes were served in houses of prostitution—perhaps in the misplaced belief that they prevented venereal disease.

121. **drawn fox:** i.e., a fox driven out of its lair by hunters and forced to escape through trickery

121–22. **Maid . . . ward: Maid Marian** was an unsavory character in morris dances and May games, often played by a man; the deputy of the ward was its most responsible citizen, and his **wife** would thus have to be the model of respectability.

122. **to thee:** in comparison to you

A salamander. (3.3.48)
From Gilles Sadeler, *Symbola diuina & humana pontificum* (1600).

'Sblood, an he were here, I would cudgel him like a
dog if he would say so.

*Enter the Prince marching,* ⌈*with Peto,*⌉ *and Falstaff
meets him playing upon his truncheon like a fife.*

How now, lad, is the wind in that door, i' faith? Must          95
we all march?

BARDOLPH   Yea, two and two, Newgate fashion.

HOSTESS, ⌈*to Prince*⌉   My lord, I pray you, hear me.

PRINCE   What say'st thou, Mistress Quickly? How doth
thy husband? I love him well; he is an honest man.          100

HOSTESS   Good my lord, hear me.

FALSTAFF   Prithee, let her alone, and list to me.

PRINCE   What say'st thou, Jack?

FALSTAFF   The other night I fell asleep here, behind the
arras, and had my pocket picked. This house is          105
turned bawdy house; they pick pockets.

PRINCE   What didst thou lose, Jack?

FALSTAFF   Wilt thou believe me, Hal, three or four
bonds of forty pound apiece, and a seal ring of my
grandfather's.          110

PRINCE   A trifle, some eightpenny matter.

HOSTESS   So I told him, my lord, and I said I heard
your Grace say so. And, my lord, he speaks most
vilely of you, like a foul-mouthed man, as he is, and
said he would cudgel you.          115

PRINCE   What, he did not!

HOSTESS   There's neither faith, truth, nor womanhood
in me else.

FALSTAFF   There's no more faith in thee than in a
stewed prune, nor no more truth in thee than in a          120
drawn fox, and for womanhood, Maid Marian may
be the deputy's wife of the ward to thee. Go, you
thing, go.

HOSTESS   Say, what thing, what thing?

FALSTAFF   What thing? Why, a thing to thank God on.          125

128. **setting . . . aside:** i.e., your knighthood excepted

135. **neither fish nor flesh:** a reference, perhaps, to uncertainty then about whether an otter is a **fish** or an animal (**flesh**)

142. **this:** i.e., the

160. **girdle:** belt from which the sword hangs

A seventeenth-century view of Falstaff and the Hostess.
From *The wits, or Sport against sport* (1662).

HOSTESS   I am no thing to thank God on, I would thou
shouldst know it! I am an honest man's wife, and,
setting thy knighthood aside, thou art a knave to
call me so.

FALSTAFF   Setting thy womanhood aside, thou art a 130
beast to say otherwise.

HOSTESS   Say, what beast, thou knave, thou?

FALSTAFF   What beast? Why, an otter.

PRINCE   An otter, Sir John. Why an otter?

FALSTAFF   Why, she's neither fish nor flesh; a man 135
knows not where to have her.

HOSTESS   Thou art an unjust man in saying so. Thou or
any man knows where to have me, thou knave,
thou.

PRINCE   Thou sayst true, hostess, and he slanders thee 140
most grossly.

HOSTESS   So he doth you, my lord, and said this other
day you owed him a thousand pound.

PRINCE   Sirrah, do I owe you a thousand pound?

FALSTAFF   A thousand pound, Hal? A million. Thy love is 145
worth a million; thou owest me thy love.

HOSTESS   Nay, my lord, he called you "jack," and said
he would cudgel you.

FALSTAFF   Did I, Bardolph?

BARDOLPH   Indeed, Sir John, you said so. 150

FALSTAFF   Yea, if he said my ring was copper.

PRINCE   I say 'tis copper. Darest thou be as good as thy
word now?

FALSTAFF   Why, Hal, thou knowest, as thou art but
man, I dare, but as thou art prince, I fear thee as I 155
fear the roaring of the lion's whelp.

PRINCE   And why not as the lion?

FALSTAFF   The King himself is to be feared as the lion.
Dost thou think I'll fear thee as I fear thy father?
Nay, an I do, I pray God my girdle break. 160

PRINCE   O, if it should, how would thy guts fall about

163. **bosom:** probably referring to both the chest and belly

164. **midriff:** diaphragm

166. **embossed:** (1) bulging, swollen; (2) foaming at the mouth from exhaustion, like a hunted deer; **rascal:** (1) villain; (2) young deer

167. **reckonings:** bills

168. **memorandums:** souvenirs

169–70. **long-winded:** Fighting cocks were given sugar to prolong their breath.

171. **injuries:** i.e., things whose loss would be an injury

172. **stand to it:** i.e., persevere in it, insist on it; **pocket up:** quietly put up with (with a pun on **pocket**)

176–78. **I . . . frailty:** a variation on the proverb "Flesh is frail"

184. **still:** always

186. **For:** i.e., as for

187. **answered:** justified; taken care of

194. **me:** i.e., for me

195. **with unwashed hands:** immediately and without ceremony

197. **charge of foot:** command of a company of infantry

thy knees! But, sirrah, there's no room for faith,
truth, nor honesty in this bosom of thine. It is all
filled up with guts and midriff. Charge an honest
woman with picking thy pocket? Why, thou whore-     165
son, impudent, embossed rascal, if there were
anything in thy pocket but tavern reckonings,
memorandums of bawdy houses, and one poor
pennyworth of sugar candy to make thee long-
winded, if thy pocket were enriched with any other     170
injuries but these, I am a villain. And yet you will
stand to it! You will not pocket up wrong! Art thou
not ashamed?

FALSTAFF   Dost thou hear, Hal? Thou knowest in the
state of innocency Adam fell, and what should poor     175
Jack Falstaff do in the days of villainy? Thou seest I
have more flesh than another man and therefore
more frailty. You confess, then, you picked my
pocket.

PRINCE   It appears so by the story.     180

FALSTAFF   Hostess, I forgive thee. Go make ready
breakfast, love thy husband, look to thy servants,
cherish thy ⌜guests.⌝ Thou shalt find me tractable
to any honest reason. Thou seest I am pacified still.
Nay, prithee, begone. (*Hostess exits.*) Now, Hal, to     185
the news at court. For the robbery, lad, how is that
answered?

PRINCE   O, my sweet beef, I must still be good angel to
thee. The money is paid back again.

FALSTAFF   O, I do not like that paying back. 'Tis a double     190
labor.

PRINCE   I am good friends with my father and may do
anything.

FALSTAFF   Rob me the Exchequer the first thing thou
dost, and do it with unwashed hands too.     195

BARDOLPH   Do, my lord.

PRINCE   I have procured thee, Jack, a charge of foot.

198. **of horse:** i.e., cavalry
199. **one:** i.e., a man, someone
201. **unprovided:** unprepared; ill-equipped
211. **Temple hall:** i.e., Inner Temple hall of the Inns at Court (the legal community) in London
214. **furniture:** equipment
217. **brave:** splendid

FALSTAFF   I would it had been of horse. Where shall I
find one that can steal well? O, for a fine thief of
the age of two-and-twenty or thereabouts! I am hei-     200
nously unprovided. Well, God be thanked for these
rebels. They offend none but the virtuous. I laud
them; I praise them.

PRINCE   Bardolph.

BARDOLPH   My lord.     205

PRINCE, ⌈*handing Bardolph papers*⌉
Go, bear this letter to Lord John of Lancaster,
To my brother John; this to my Lord of
Westmoreland.               ⌈*Bardolph exits.*⌉
Go, Peto, to horse, to horse, for thou and I
Have thirty miles to ride yet ere dinner time.     210
                      ⌈*Peto exits.*⌉
Jack, meet me tomorrow in the Temple hall
At two o'clock in the afternoon;
There shalt thou know thy charge, and there receive
Money and order for their furniture.
The land is burning. Percy stands on high,     215
And either we or they must lower lie.     ⌈*He exits.*⌉

FALSTAFF
Rare words, brave world!—Hostess, my breakfast,
come.—
O, I could wish this tavern were my drum.
                      ⌈*He exits.*⌉

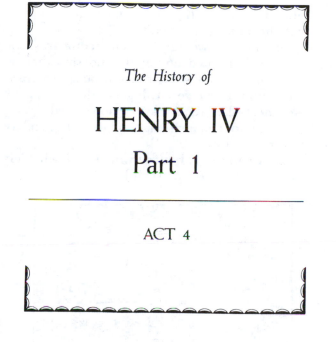

*The History of*

# HENRY IV
## Part 1

### ACT 4

**4.1** Hotspur, Worcester, and Douglas learn that Hotspur's father, Northumberland, is too sick to join them in the coming battle. They also learn that King Henry is approaching with a great army, including the splendidly armed Prince Hal, and that Glendower and his forces have been delayed.

---

2. **fine:** (1) refined; (2) cunning, crafty

3. **attribution:** name, credit

4–5. **As not . . . world:** Hotspur compares soldiers to newly minted currency, and says that no soldier minted in this season would be so generally accepted and praised. **general:** generally

7. **soothers:** flatterers; **braver:** more worthy

9. **task me to:** i.e., challenge me to be as good as; **approve me:** test me

11–12. **No man . . . beard him:** i.e., I will defy anyone, no matter how powerful

Helmet with beaver down. (4.1.110)
From Henry Peacham, *Minerua Britanna* (1612).

# ⌜ACT 4⌝

---

## ⌜Scene 1⌝
⌜*Enter Hotspur, Worcester, and Douglas.*⌝

HOTSPUR
　Well said, my noble Scot. If speaking truth
　In this fine age were not thought flattery,
　Such attribution should the Douglas have
　As not a soldier of this season's stamp
　Should go so general current through the world.　　5
　By God, I cannot flatter. I do defy
　The tongues of soothers. But a braver place
　In my heart's love hath no man than yourself.
　Nay, task me to my word; approve me, lord.
DOUGLAS　Thou art the king of honor.　　10
　No man so potent breathes upon the ground
　But I will beard him.
HOTSPUR　　　　　　　Do so, and 'tis well.

　　*Enter ⌜a Messenger⌝ with letters.*

　What letters hast thou there? ⌜*To Douglas.*⌝ I can but
　　thank you.　　15
MESSENGER　These letters come from your father.
HOTSPUR
　Letters from him! Why comes he not himself?
MESSENGER
　He cannot come, my lord. He is grievous sick.

**157**

19. **Zounds:** i.e., by Christ's wounds, a strong oath
20. **justling:** jostling, colliding; **power:** army
21. **government:** command
22. **letters:** i.e., letter
26. **feared:** i.e., feared for
27. **the state of time:** i.e., this juncture in our affairs
29. **better worth:** of greater value
34. **by deputation:** by his deputies
35. **drawn:** drawn up, mobilized
36. **meet:** appropriate, fitting
38. **On . . . own:** i.e., on anybody but himself
39. **bold advertisement:** (1) warning to be bold; (2) fearless instruction (pronounced **advèrtisement**)
40. **conjunction:** joint force; **on:** i.e., proceed
43–44. **possessed . . . purposes:** i.e., aware of all our plans

A knight dressed in mail armor. (4.1.122)
From Henry Peacham, *Minerua Britanna* (1612).

HOTSPUR

    Zounds, how has he the leisure to be sick

    In such a justling time? Who leads his power?    20

    Under whose government come they along?

MESSENGER, ⌜*handing letter to Hotspur, who begins*

    *reading it*⌝

    His letters bears his mind, not I, my ⌜lord.⌝

WORCESTER

    I prithee, tell me, doth he keep his bed?

MESSENGER

    He did, my lord, four days ere I set forth,

    And, at the time of my departure thence,    25

    He was much feared by his physicians.

WORCESTER

    I would the state of time had first been whole

    Ere he by sickness had been visited.

    His health was never better worth than now.

HOTSPUR

    Sick now? Droop now? This sickness doth infect    30

    The very lifeblood of our enterprise.

    'Tis catching hither, even to our camp.

    He writes me here that inward sickness—

    And that his friends by deputation

    Could not so soon be drawn, nor did he think it    35

      meet

    To lay so dangerous and dear a trust

    On any soul removed but on his own;

    Yet doth he give us bold advertisement

    That with our small conjunction we should on    40

    To see how fortune is disposed to us,

    For, as he writes, there is no quailing now,

    Because the King is certainly possessed

    Of all our purposes. What say you to it?

WORCESTER

    Your father's sickness is a maim to us.    45

47–48. **His . . . it:** i.e., his absence seems to us at the present moment a greater difficulty than it will actually turn out to be

48. **Were it:** i.e., would it be

49–50. **To . . . cast:** i.e., to risk all that we have on one throw (of the dice)   **exact:** i.e., total, complete (pronounced **èxact**)   **states:** estates

50. **main:** (1) stake, bet; (2) army

51. **nice hazard:** delicately balanced chance; i.e., risky venture

54. **list:** limit, boundary

57. **A sweet reversion:** i.e., comforting hopes (A **reversion** is literally property that will one day revert to you.)

59. **A comfort of retirement:** i.e., some support for a possible retreat

61. **big:** threateningly

62. **maidenhead:** first stage or trial

64. **hair:** nature

65. **Brooks:** can tolerate

67. **loyalty:** i.e., to King Henry

69. **apprehension:** (1) idea; (2) fear

71. **question in:** i.e., doubt about

72. **off'ring side:** i.e., the party that has started the war

73. **strict arbitrament:** rigorous judgment of an impartial arbitrator

74. **loop:** i.e., loophole

76. **draws:** i.e., draws back, opens

**HOTSPUR**
A perilous gash, a very limb lopped off!
And yet, in faith, it is not. His present want
Seems more than we shall find it. Were it good
To set the exact wealth of all our states
All at one cast? To set so rich a main 50
On the nice hazard of one doubtful hour?
It were not good, for therein should we read
The very bottom and the soul of hope,
The very list, the very utmost bound
Of all our fortunes. 55

**DOUGLAS**
Faith, and so we should, where now remains
A sweet reversion. We may boldly spend
Upon the hope of what ⌜is⌝ to come in.
A comfort of retirement lives in this.

**HOTSPUR**
A rendezvous, a home to fly unto, 60
If that the devil and mischance look big
Upon the maidenhead of our affairs.

**WORCESTER**
But yet I would your father had been here.
The quality and hair of our attempt
Brooks no division. It will be thought 65
By some that know not why he is away
That wisdom, loyalty, and mere dislike
Of our proceedings kept the Earl from hence.
And think how such an apprehension
May turn the tide of fearful faction 70
And breed a kind of question in our cause.
For well you know, we of the off'ring side
Must keep aloof from strict arbitrament,
And stop all sight-holes, every loop from whence
The eye of reason may pry in upon us. 75
This absence of your father's draws a curtain

79. **strain too far:** i.e., exaggerate the way his absence will be perceived

81. **opinion:** reputation

82. **dare:** daring

84. **make a head:** lead an army

87. **Yet:** i.e., as yet

97. **hitherwards intended:** i.e., intends to come here

101. **daffed:** doffed, thrust

103. **furnished:** equipped

104–5. **All . . . bathed:** The extreme compression of the figures of speech in this passage has made editors suspect that a line may have dropped out after "wind." **plumed:** i.e., with feathers atop their helmets **estridges:** (1) ostriches; (2) goshawks **Bated:** beat their wings

Pegasus. (4.1.115)
From August Casimir Redel, *Apophtegmata symbolica* (n.d.).

That shows the ignorant a kind of fear
Before not dreamt of.

HOTSPUR                    You strain too far.
I rather of his absence make this use:                        80
It lends a luster and more great opinion,
A larger dare, to our great enterprise
Than if the Earl were here, for men must think
If we without his help can make a head
To push against a kingdom, with his help                     85
We shall o'erturn it topsy-turvy down.
Yet all goes well; yet all our joints are whole.

DOUGLAS
As heart can think. There is not such a word
Spoke of in Scotland as this term of fear.

*Enter Sir Richard Vernon.*

HOTSPUR
My cousin Vernon, welcome, by my soul.                       90

VERNON
Pray God my news be worth a welcome, lord.
The Earl of Westmoreland, seven thousand strong,
Is marching hitherwards, with him Prince John.

HOTSPUR
No harm, what more?

VERNON                    And further I have learned          95
The King himself in person is set forth,
Or hitherwards intended speedily,
With strong and mighty preparation.

HOTSPUR
He shall be welcome too. Where is his son,
The nimble-footed madcap Prince of Wales,                    100
And his comrades, that daffed the world aside
And bid it pass?

VERNON                    All furnished, all in arms,
All plumed like estridges that with the wind
Bated like eagles having lately bathed,                      105

106. **images:** gilded effigies of entombed warriors

109. **Wanton:** frisky

110. **beaver:** i.e., helmet (literally, the face guard on a helmet) See page 156.

111. **cuisses:** thigh armor

112. **feathered Mercury: Mercury,** the messenger of the gods, is often pictured with wings on his helmet and heels.

113. **seat:** i.e., saddle

114. **As if:** i.e., as if he were

115. **wind:** wheel about; **Pegasus:** the mythological winged horse (See page 162.)

116. **witch:** i.e., bewitch

118. **agues:** chills and fevers

119. **sacrifices in their trim:** i.e., animals adorned to be offered as blood sacrifices

120. **maid . . . war:** perhaps, Bellona, Roman goddess of war

122. **mailèd:** i.e., dressed in mail armor (See page 158.)

124. **reprisal:** prize; **nigh:** near

125. **taste:** test, try

129. **corse:** i.e., corpse

132. **Worcester:** a city on the Severn, just south of Shrewsbury

133. **draw:** i.e., muster; **power:** army

136. **battle:** army; **reach unto:** i.e., amount to

Glittering in golden coats like images,
As full of spirit as the month of May,
And gorgeous as the sun at midsummer,
Wanton as youthful goats, wild as young bulls.
I saw young Harry with his beaver on,                110
His cuisses on his thighs, gallantly armed,
Rise from the ground like feathered Mercury
And vaulted with such ease into his seat
As if an angel ⌜dropped⌝ down from the clouds,
To turn and wind a fiery Pegasus                     115
And witch the world with noble horsemanship.
HOTSPUR
No more, no more! Worse than the sun in March
This praise doth nourish agues. Let them come.
They come like sacrifices in their trim,
And to the fire-eyed maid of smoky war               120
All hot and bleeding will we offer them.
The mailèd Mars shall on his ⌜altar⌝ sit
Up to the ears in blood. I am on fire
To hear this rich reprisal is so nigh
And yet not ours. Come, let me taste my horse,       125
Who is to bear me like a thunderbolt
Against the bosom of the Prince of Wales.
Harry to Harry shall, hot horse to horse,
Meet and ne'er part till one drop down a corse.
O, that Glendower were come!                         130
VERNON                            There is more news.
I learned in Worcester, as I rode along,
He ⌜cannot⌝ draw his power this fourteen days.
DOUGLAS
That's the worst tidings that I hear of ⌜yet.⌝
WORCESTER
Ay, by my faith, that bears a frosty sound.          135
HOTSPUR
What may the King's whole battle reach unto?

140. **powers of us:** i.e., our armies

**4.2** Falstaff discloses to the audience how he has misused his commission as an officer to take money from men eager to avoid serving as soldiers, and how he has filled the ranks instead with beggars and prisoners. Prince Hal and Westmoreland overtake him and urge him to hasten to the impending battle.

---

5. **Lay out:** i.e., pay for it yourself

6. **makes an angel:** i.e., brings your debt to me to **an angel** (a coin worth several shillings)

7. **An . . . labor:** Falstaff's answer takes literally Bardolph's statement (that the bottle "makes an angel"), and he tells Bardolph to take for himself the coin that the bottle "makes."

8. **answer:** i.e., take legal responsibility for; **coinage:** counterfeiting (of the coins)

12. **soused gurnet:** small pickled fish; **press:** authority to conscript or impress soldiers

15. **press me:** conscript; **good:** well-off; **yeomen's:** landowners'

16. **contracted:** engaged

16–17. **such . . . banns:** i.e., who were just about to be married (literally, who had already had their intentions to marry read out in church on two successive Sundays)

17–18. **commodity:** lot, stock

18. **warm slaves:** i.e., well-off cowards; **as had as lief:** as would rather

19. **drum:** The **drum** in Shakespeare's plays often symbolizes military action or zeal. **caliver:** light musket

*166*

**VERNON**
To thirty thousand.
**HOTSPUR**                    Forty let it be.
My father and Glendower being both away,
The powers of us may serve so great a day.          140
Come, let us take a muster speedily.
Doomsday is near. Die all, die merrily.
**DOUGLAS**
Talk not of dying. I am out of fear
Of death or death's hand for this one half year.

                                        *They exit.*

⌜Scene 2⌝
*Enter Falstaff ⌜and⌝ Bardolph.*

**FALSTAFF**   Bardolph, get thee before to Coventry. Fill
me a bottle of sack. Our soldiers shall march
through. We'll to Sutton ⌜Coldfield⌝ tonight.
**BARDOLPH**   Will you give me money, captain?
**FALSTAFF**   Lay out, lay out.                                    5
**BARDOLPH**   This bottle makes an angel.
**FALSTAFF**   An if it do, take it for thy labor. An if it make
twenty, take them all. I'll answer the coinage. Bid
my lieutenant Peto meet me at town's end.
**BARDOLPH**   I will, captain. Farewell.          *He exits.*   10
**FALSTAFF**   If I be not ashamed of my soldiers, I am a
soused gurnet. I have misused the King's press
damnably. I have got, in exchange of a hundred
and fifty soldiers, three hundred and odd pounds. I
press me none but good householders, ⌜yeomen's⌝   15
sons, inquire me out contracted bachelors, such as
had been asked twice on the banns—such a commodity of warm slaves as had as ⌜lief⌝ hear the devil
as a drum, such as fear the report of a caliver worse

20. **struck:** wounded

21. **toasts-and-butter:** soft citizens; **hearts:** considered the seat of courage

23. **bought . . . services:** i.e., bribed Falstaff to be released from military service

23–24. **my . . . charge:** company under my command

24. **ancients:** ensigns, standard-bearers

25. **gentlemen of companies:** those of a rank between privates and officers

25–27. **Lazarus . . . sores:** Falstaff again refers to Luke's story (16.19–31) of the beggar (Lazarus) and the rich man, here called a **glutton** (see 3.3.33). He pictures the story in terms of a cheap wall hanging (**painted cloth**) upon which this biblical scene has been painted—rather than woven, as in more expensive tapestries. (See page 182.)

28. **discarded:** dismissed; **unjust:** dishonest

28–29. **younger . . . brothers:** i.e., young men with no hope of an inheritance, since, according to the custom of primogeniture then in force, the eldest son inherited all of the family property

29. **revolted:** runaway

30. **tradefallen:** whose jobs have disappeared; **cankers of:** cankerworms that are abundant in

31. **dishonorable-ragged:** i.e., dishonorable in their raggedness

32. **feazed ancient:** frayed flag (ensign)

33. **rooms of them as have:** places of those who have

35–36. **prodigals . . . husks:** In Luke 15.11–32, the prodigal son is given a job feeding swine, and, in his hunger, envies them the **draff** (swill, refuse) and **husks** he feeds them. *(continued)*

than a struck fowl or a hurt wild duck. I pressed me 20
none but such toasts-and-butter, with hearts in their
bellies no bigger than pins' heads, and they have
bought out their services, and now my whole
charge consists of ancients, corporals, lieutenants,
gentlemen of companies—slaves as ragged as Laza- 25
rus in the painted cloth, where the glutton's dogs
licked his sores; and such as indeed were never
soldiers, but discarded, unjust servingmen, younger
sons to younger brothers, revolted tapsters, and
ostlers tradefallen, the cankers of a calm world and 30
a long peace, ten times more dishonorable-ragged
than an old feazed ancient; and such have I to fill up
the rooms of them as have bought out their services,
that you would think that I had a hundred and fifty
tattered prodigals lately come from swine-keeping, 35
from eating draff and husks. A mad fellow met me
on the way and told me I had unloaded all the
gibbets and pressed the dead bodies. No eye hath
seen such scarecrows. I'll not march through Coventry with them, that's flat. Nay, and the villains 40
march wide betwixt the legs as if they had gyves on,
for indeed I had the most of them out of prison.
There's not a shirt and a half in all my company,
and the half shirt is two napkins tacked together
and thrown over the shoulders like a herald's coat 45
without sleeves; and the shirt, to say the truth,
stolen from my host at Saint Albans or the red-nose
innkeeper of Daventry. But that's all one; they'll find
linen enough on every hedge.

*Enter the Prince ⌜and the⌝ Lord of Westmoreland.*

PRINCE   How now, blown Jack? How now, quilt?       50
FALSTAFF   What, Hal, how now, mad wag? What a devil
   dost thou in Warwickshire?—My good Lord of

38. **pressed:** conscripted

41. **gyves:** ankle fetters (See page 198.)

45–46. **herald's . . . sleeves:** i.e., tabard, the herald's sleeveless coat

47. **my host:** i.e., the innkeeper

48. **all one:** i.e., no matter

49. **on every hedge:** i.e., where it is hung to dry after being washed

50. **blown:** (1) swollen; (2) winded; **quilt:** i.e., well-padded (with a pun on **Jack,** which is a quilted soldier's jacket)

53. **I . . . mercy:** i.e., I beg your pardon

56. **powers:** forces

57. **looks for:** expects

58. **away . . . night:** i.e., travel all night

59. **fear:** doubt

62. **butter:** i.e., fat

66. **toss:** i.e., toss on a pike

66–67. **powder:** i.e., gunpowder

67. **pit:** grave

70. **bare:** i.e., threadbare, ragged

71. **for:** as for

74. **three fingers:** i.e., fat that is as thick as the breadth of three fingers

76. **field:** i.e., battlefield

81–83. **To . . . guest:** Proverbial: "It is better coming to the beginning of a feast than the end of a fray."

Westmoreland, I cry you mercy. I thought your
Honor had already been at Shrewsbury.

WESTMORELAND   Faith, Sir John, 'tis more than time          55
that I were there and you too, but my powers are
there already. The King, I can tell you, looks for us
all. We must away all night.

FALSTAFF   Tut, never fear me. I am as vigilant as a cat to
steal cream.                                                 60

PRINCE   I think to steal cream indeed, for thy theft hath
already made thee butter. But tell me, Jack, whose
fellows are these that come after?

FALSTAFF   Mine, Hal, mine.

PRINCE   I did never see such pitiful rascals.               65

FALSTAFF   Tut, tut, good enough to toss; food for powder, food for powder. They'll fill a pit as well as
better. Tush, man, mortal men, mortal men.

WESTMORELAND   Ay, but, Sir John, methinks they are
exceeding poor and bare, too beggarly.                       70

FALSTAFF   Faith, for their poverty, I know not where
they had that, and for their bareness, I am sure they
never learned that of me.

PRINCE   No, I'll be sworn, unless you call three fingers
in the ribs bare. But, sirrah, make haste. Percy is          75
already in the field.                         *He exits.*

FALSTAFF   What, is the King encamped?

WESTMORELAND   He is, Sir John. I fear we shall stay too
long.                                   ⌜*He exits.*⌝

FALSTAFF   Well,                                             80
To the latter end of a fray and the beginning of a
   feast
Fits a dull fighter and a keen guest.
                                     ⌜*He*⌝ *exits.*

**4.3**  As Hotspur argues with his fellow commanders about when to fight, they are visited by Sir Walter Blunt, who brings them a request from the king that they state their grievances and a promise that, if the grievances are just, they will be answered and the rebels pardoned. After listing their grievances, Hotspur promises to send Worcester the next morning to continue discussions with the king.

---

1. **him:** i.e., King Henry
5. **supply:** reinforcements
14. **well-respected:** i.e., reasonably considered, not rash; **bid me on:** i.e., urge me to act
23. **leading:** generalship
25. **Drag . . . expedition:** slow or prevent speedy action; **horse:** cavalry

⌜Scene 3⌝

*Enter Hotspur, Worcester, Douglas, ⌜and⌝ Vernon.*

HOTSPUR
We'll fight with him tonight.

WORCESTER                              It may not be.

DOUGLAS
You give him then advantage.

VERNON                              Not a whit.

HOTSPUR
Why say you so? Looks he not for supply?                5

VERNON   So do we.

HOTSPUR   His is certain; ours is doubtful.

WORCESTER
Good cousin, be advised. Stir not tonight.

VERNON, ⌜*to Hotspur*⌝
Do not, my lord.

DOUGLAS               You do not counsel well.         10
You speak it out of fear and cold heart.

VERNON
Do me no slander, Douglas. By my life
(And I dare well maintain it with my life),
If well-respected honor bid me on,
I hold as little counsel with weak fear             15
As you, my lord, or any Scot that this day lives.
Let it be seen tomorrow in the battle
Which of us fears.

DOUGLAS   Yea, or tonight.

VERNON   Content.                                    20

HOTSPUR   Tonight, say I.

VERNON
Come, come, it may not be. I wonder much,
Being men of such great leading as you are,
That you foresee not what impediments
Drag back our expedition. Certain horse            25
Of my cousin Vernon's are not yet come up.

28. **pride and mettle:** spirit

32. **journey-bated:** exhausted, or abated, by travel; **brought low:** dispirited

35 SD. **parley:** a trumpet call indicating the approach of a delegation from the opposing army for the purpose of discussion

37. **respect:** attention

39. **determination:** opinion, persuasion

42. **quality:** party, side

44. **defend:** forbid; **still:** always

45. **limit:** bounds (perhaps of allegiance, or of duty)

47. **my charge:** the duty given me to carry out

48. **griefs:** grievances

53. **Which:** i.e., your **deserts,** your good deeds

Your uncle Worcester's ⌐horse⌐ came but today,
And now their pride and mettle is asleep,
Their courage with hard labor tame and dull,
That not a horse is half the half of himself.                    30

HOTSPUR
So are the horses of the enemy
In general journey-bated and brought low.
The better part of ours are full of rest.

WORCESTER
The number of the King exceedeth ⌐ours.⌐
For God's sake, cousin, stay till all come in.                   35
                              *The trumpet sounds a parley.*

                *Enter Sir Walter Blunt.*

BLUNT
I come with gracious offers from the King,
If you vouchsafe me hearing and respect.

HOTSPUR
Welcome, Sir Walter Blunt, and would to God
You were of our determination.
Some of us love you well, and even those some          40
Envy your great deservings and good name
Because you are not of our quality
But stand against us like an enemy.

BLUNT
And God defend but still I should stand so,
So long as out of limit and true rule                            45
You stand against anointed majesty.
But to my charge. The King hath sent to know
The nature of your griefs, and whereupon
You conjure from the breast of civil peace
Such bold hostility, teaching his duteous land            50
Audacious cruelty. If that the King
Have any way your good deserts forgot,
Which he confesseth to be manifold,
He bids you name your griefs, and with all speed

57. **suggestion:** prompting, enticement

62. **not . . . strong:** i.e., when he had fewer than twenty-six followers

64. **unminded:** unnoticed, unregarded

68. **sue his livery:** to recover his inheritance, which, upon the death of his father, John of Gaunt, had been seized by Richard II; **beg his peace:** i.e., be reconciled with Richard

74. **The more . . . knee:** i.e., all the lords and barons, the greater and lesser, did him homage, removing their caps and kneeling

76. **stood in lanes:** i.e., lined the road

79. **golden:** (1) propitious (for Henry's future); (2) splendidly dressed

80. **as . . . itself:** i.e., since the great come to recognize their own power

81. **Steps me:** i.e., steps

82. **while his blood was poor:** i.e., while he was still being meek in temper

84. **forsooth:** a mild oath; **takes on him:** i.e., takes it upon himself

85. **strait:** strict

87. **Cries out upon:** vehemently objects to

88–89. **this face,/This seeming brow:** i.e., this pretense

You shall have your desires with interest                    55
And pardon absolute for yourself and these
Herein misled by your suggestion.
HOTSPUR
  The King is kind, and well we know the King
  Knows at what time to promise, when to pay.
  My father and my uncle and myself                          60
  Did give him that same royalty he wears,
  And when he was not six-and-twenty strong,
  Sick in the world's regard, wretched and low,
  A poor unminded outlaw sneaking home,
  My father gave him welcome to the shore;                   65
  And when he heard him swear and vow to God
  He came but to be Duke of Lancaster,
  To sue his livery, and beg his peace
  With tears of innocency and terms of zeal,
  My father, in kind heart and pity moved,                   70
  Swore him assistance and performed it too.
  Now when the lords and barons of the realm
  Perceived Northumberland did lean to him,
  The more and less came in with cap and knee,
  Met him in boroughs, cities, villages,                     75
  Attended him on bridges, stood in lanes,
  Laid gifts before him, proffered him their oaths,
  Gave him their heirs as pages, followed him
  Even at the heels in golden multitudes.
  He presently, as greatness knows itself,                   80
  Steps me a little higher than his vow
  Made to my father while his blood was poor
  Upon the naked shore at Ravenspurgh,
  And now forsooth takes on him to reform
  Some certain edicts and some strait decrees                85
  That lie too heavy on the commonwealth,
  Cries out upon abuses, seems to weep
  Over his ⌜country's⌝ wrongs, and by this face,
  This seeming brow of justice, did he win
  The hearts of all that he did angle for,                   90

91. **cut me off:** i.e., cut off
93. **In deputation:** i.e., as deputies
94. **personal:** i.e., personally engaged
99. **in . . . that:** i.e., right after that; **tasked:** taxed
100. **March:** i.e., Mortimer
101. **if every . . . placed:** i.e., if everyone were in his rightful position
102. **his king:** i.e., king over Henry IV; **engaged:** involved, entangled
103. **forfeited:** i.e., abandoned
104. **happy:** fortunate
105. **intelligence:** spies
106. **Rated . . . from:** drove away by scolding; **board:** table
110. **head of safety:** i.e., army raised to ensure our own safety; **withal:** i.e., in addition
112. **indirect:** not descending in a direct line of succession
115–16. **let . . . again:** i.e., leave some hostage with us to guarantee Worcester's safe return to us
118. **our purposes:** i.e., what we propose
119. **grace:** mercy

Proceeded further—cut me off the heads
Of all the favorites that the absent king
In deputation left behind him here
When he was personal in the Irish war.

BLUNT
Tut, I came not to hear this.                                    95

HOTSPUR                          Then to the point.
In short time after, he deposed the King,
Soon after that deprived him of his life
And, in the neck of that, tasked the whole state.
To make that worse, suffered his kinsman March         100
(Who is, if every owner were well placed,
Indeed his king) to be engaged in Wales,
There without ransom to lie forfeited,
Disgraced me in my happy victories,
Sought to entrap me by intelligence,                      105
Rated mine uncle from the council board,
In rage dismissed my father from the court,
Broke oath on oath, committed wrong on wrong,
And in conclusion drove us to seek out
This head of safety, and withal to pry                    110
Into his title, the which we find
Too indirect for long continuance.

BLUNT
Shall I return this answer to the King?

HOTSPUR
Not so, Sir Walter. We'll withdraw awhile.
Go to the King, and let there be impawned                 115
Some surety for a safe return again,
And in the morning early shall mine uncle
Bring him our purposes. And so farewell.

BLUNT
I would you would accept of grace and love.

HOTSPUR
And maybe so we shall.                                    120

BLUNT                          Pray God you do.
                                    ⌜*They exit.*⌝

**4.4** The archbishop of York and Sir Michael, who sympathize with Hotspur, debate the chances of his success against the king's greater force.

---

0 SD. **Sir Michael:** perhaps a priest, or perhaps a knight, since "sir" was the title of courtesy for both

1. **brief:** letter

4. **To whom:** i.e., to those to whom

5. **How . . . import:** i.e., how important they are

10. **bide the touch:** be put to the test (as in the testing of gold for purity)

15. **Whose . . . proportion:** i.e., whose army was the largest

17. **a rated sinew:** i.e., accounted most strong

18. **o'erruled:** dissuaded

25. **head:** army

"The front of heaven . . . full of fiery shapes." (3.1.14)
From Conrad Lycosthenes, *Prodigiorum* (1557).

⌜Scene 4⌝

*Enter Archbishop of York ⌜and⌝ Sir Michael.*

ARCHBISHOP, ⌜*handing papers*⌝
Hie, good Sir Michael, bear this sealèd brief
With wingèd haste to the Lord Marshal,
This to my cousin Scroop, and all the rest
To whom they are directed. If you knew
How much they do import, you would make haste.    5

SIR MICHAEL
My good lord, I guess their tenor.

ARCHBISHOP    Like enough you do.
Tomorrow, good Sir Michael, is a day
Wherein the fortune of ten thousand men
Must bide the touch. For, sir, at Shrewsbury,    10
As I am truly given to understand,
The King with mighty and quick-raisèd power
Meets with Lord Harry. And I fear, Sir Michael,
What with the sickness of Northumberland,
Whose power was in the first proportion,    15
And what with Owen Glendower's absence thence,
Who with them was a rated sinew too
And comes not in, o'erruled by prophecies,
I fear the power of Percy is too weak
To wage an instant trial with the King.    20

SIR MICHAEL
Why, my good lord, you need not fear.
There is Douglas and Lord Mortimer.

ARCHBISHOP    No, Mortimer is not there.

SIR MICHAEL
But there is Mordake, Vernon, Lord Harry Percy,
And there is my Lord of Worcester, and a head    25
Of gallant warriors, noble gentlemen.

ARCHBISHOP
And so there is. But yet the King hath drawn
The special head of all the land together:

31. **corrivals:** partners, associates

31–32. **dear . . . arms:** i.e., men of great reputation as military commanders

"Lazarus . . . where the . . . dogs licked his sores."
(4.2.25-27)
From Guillaume Guérault, *Figures de la Bible* (1565-70).

The Prince of Wales, Lord John of Lancaster,
The noble Westmoreland, and warlike Blunt,          30
And many more corrivals and dear men
Of estimation and command in arms.

SIR MICHAEL
Doubt not, my lord, they shall be well opposed.

ARCHBISHOP
I hope no less, yet needful 'tis to fear;
And to prevent the worst, Sir Michael, speed.       35
For if Lord Percy thrive not, ere the King
Dismiss his power he means to visit us,
For he hath heard of our confederacy,
And 'tis but wisdom to make strong against him.
Therefore make haste. I must go write again         40
To other friends. And so farewell, Sir Michael.

*They exit.*

*The History of*

# HENRY IV
## Part 1

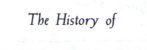

ACT 5

**5.1** Worcester and Vernon visit the king's camp, where Worcester repeats the grievances that he says have led to the rebellion. Prince Hal offers to oppose Hotspur in single combat, and King Henry promises pardon and reconciliation to the rebels if they yield.

———————

3. **his distemp'rature:** i.e., the sun's sickness
5. **play . . . purposes:** i.e., act as the herald signaling the sun's meanings
8. **sympathize:** harmonize
13. **easy:** comfortable

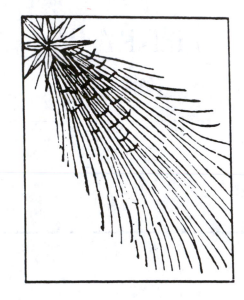

"Like a comet I was wondered at." (3.2.49)
From Hartmann Schedel, *Liber chronicorum* (1493).

# ⌜ACT 5⌝

⌜Scene 1⌝

*Enter the King, Prince of Wales, Lord John of Lancaster,*
*Sir Walter Blunt, ⌜and⌝ Falstaff.*

KING
How bloodily the sun begins to peer
Above yon bulky hill. The day looks pale
At his distemp'rature.

PRINCE              The southern wind
Doth play the trumpet to his purposes,          5
And by his hollow whistling in the leaves
Foretells a tempest and a blust'ring day.

KING
Then with the losers let it sympathize,
For nothing can seem foul to those that win.

*The trumpet sounds.*

*Enter Worcester ⌜and Vernon.⌝*

How now, my Lord of Worcester? 'Tis not well     10
That you and I should meet upon such terms
As now we meet. You have deceived our trust
And made us doff our easy robes of peace
To crush our old limbs in ungentle steel.
This is not well, my lord; this is not well.      15
What say you to it? Will you again unknit
This churlish knot of all-abhorrèd war

187

18–22. **And . . . times:** i.e., return to your proper subordinate position (Henry compares the formerly obedient Worcester to a star or planet that moved properly around the earth in its sphere [**orb**] in Ptolemaic cosmology. Henry then likens the present rebellious Worcester to a meteor drawn up [i.e., **exhaled**] as a fiery gas, and thought to be a fearful portent [**prodigy of fear**] of evil that has been broken open [**broached**] to afflict the future [**unborn times**].)

25. **entertain:** occupy, fill up; **lag end:** latter part

27. **dislike:** i.e., hostility

30. **chewet:** (1) chough, jackdaw (hence a chatterer); (2) mincemeat pie

32. **from:** i.e., away from; **house:** i.e., family

33. **remember:** remind

36. **posted:** rode post-haste

38. **place:** political and social position; **account:** reputation

39. **Nothing:** not at all

45. **new-fall'n:** newly inherited

51. **injuries:** wrongs; **wanton:** lawless, violent

And move in that obedient orb again
Where you did give a fair and natural light,
And be no more an exhaled meteor,                              20
A prodigy of fear, and a portent
Of broachèd mischief to the unborn times?
WORCESTER   Hear me, my liege:
For mine own part I could be well content
To entertain the lag end of my life                           25
With quiet hours. For I protest
I have not sought the day of this dislike.
KING
You have not sought it. How comes it then?
FALSTAFF   Rebellion lay in his way, and he found it.
PRINCE   Peace, chewet, peace.                                 30
WORCESTER
It pleased your Majesty to turn your looks
Of favor from myself and all our house;
And yet I must remember you, my lord,
We were the first and dearest of your friends.
For you my staff of office did I break                        35
In Richard's time, and posted day and night
To meet you on the way and kiss your hand
When yet you were in place and in account
Nothing so strong and fortunate as I.
It was myself, my brother, and his son                        40
That brought you home and boldly did outdare
The dangers of the time. You swore to us,
And you did swear that oath at Doncaster,
That you did nothing purpose 'gainst the state,
Nor claim no further than your new-fall'n right,              45
The seat of Gaunt, dukedom of Lancaster.
To this we swore our aid. But in short space
It rained down fortune show'ring on your head,
And such a flood of greatness fell on you—
What with our help, what with the absent king,                50
What with the injuries of a wanton time,

52. **seeming sufferances:** apparent sufferings

58. **gripe . . . hand:** i.e., grasp control of the king-dom

61. **gull:** nestling, young bird; **cuckoo's bird:** The cuckoo lays its egg in the nest of a bird such as the **sparrow,** who, when the egg hatches, feeds the fledgling until it grows so large as to be threatening.

64. **our love:** i.e., those of us who love you

65. **swallowing:** i.e., being swallowed

66. **safety:** i.e., safety's

68. **by such means:** i.e., on such grounds

70. **dangerous countenance:** threatening behav-ior

71. **troth:** sworn word

73. **articulate:** i.e., articulated, itemized article by article

75. **face:** trim, or cover with another layer of cloth

76. **color:** (1) hue; (2) pretext, fiction

77. **changelings:** turncoats, renegades; **poor dis-contents:** the discontented impoverished

78. **rub the elbow:** a gesture of satisfaction (like rubbing one's hands together)

79. **hurlyburly innovation:** i.e., chaotic change

80. **want:** lack

81. **water colors:** i.e., thin fictions; **impaint:** de-pict; or, beautify; **his:** i.e., its

82. **moody:** angry, sullen

85. **Shall:** i.e., who shall; **full:** very

The seeming sufferances that you had borne,
And the contrarious winds that held the King
So long in his unlucky Irish wars
That all in England did repute him dead—                    55
And from this swarm of fair advantages
You took occasion to be quickly wooed
To gripe the general sway into your hand,
Forgot your oath to us at Doncaster;
And being fed by us, you used us so                         60
As that ungentle gull, the cuckoo's bird,
Useth the sparrow—did oppress our nest,
Grew by our feeding to so great a bulk
That even our love durst not come near your sight
For fear of swallowing; but with nimble wing               65
We were enforced for safety sake to fly
Out of your sight and raise this present head,
Whereby we stand opposèd by such means
As you yourself have forged against yourself
By unkind usage, dangerous countenance,                    70
And violation of all faith and troth
Sworn to us in your younger enterprise.

KING
These things indeed you have articulate,
Proclaimed at market crosses, read in churches,
To face the garment of rebellion                           75
With some fine color that may please the eye
Of fickle changelings and poor discontents,
Which gape and rub the elbow at the news
Of hurlyburly innovation.
And never yet did insurrection want                        80
Such water colors to impaint his cause,
Nor moody beggars starving for a time
Of pellmell havoc and confusion.

PRINCE
In both your armies there is many a soul
Shall pay full dearly for this encounter                   85

88. **hopes:** i.e., hope for salvation

89. **This . . . head:** i.e., this current rebellion not charged against his reputation

90. **braver:** nobler

93. **latter:** i.e., present

95. **chivalry:** the code governing the action of knights

97. **this:** i.e., I say this

98. **he:** Hotspur; **take the odds:** have the advantage

99. **estimation:** reputation

100. **either side:** i.e., both sides

103. **Albeit:** although

106. **cousin's:** kinsman's

112. **wait on us:** are in our service

113. **office:** duty

115. **it:** i.e., our offer

The Colossus. (5.1.124)
From Henry Peacham, *Minerua Britanna* (1612).

If once they join in trial. Tell your nephew,
The Prince of Wales doth join with all the world
In praise of Henry Percy. By my hopes,
This present enterprise set off his head,
I do not think a braver gentleman,                              90
More active-valiant, or more valiant-young,
More daring or more bold, is now alive
To grace this latter age with noble deeds.
For my part, I may speak it to my shame,
I have a truant been to chivalry,                               95
And so I hear he doth account me too.
Yet this before my father's majesty:
I am content that he shall take the odds
Of his great name and estimation,
And will, to save the blood on either side,                    100
Try fortune with him in a single fight.

KING
And, Prince of Wales, so dare we venture thee,
Albeit considerations infinite
Do make against it.—No, good Worcester, no.
We love our people well, even those we love                    105
That are misled upon your cousin's part.
And, will they take the offer of our grace,
Both he and they and you, yea, every man
Shall be my friend again, and I'll be his.
So tell your cousin, and bring me word                         110
What he will do. But if he will not yield,
Rebuke and dread correction wait on us,
And they shall do their office. So begone.
We will not now be troubled with reply.
We offer fair. Take it advisedly.                              115

*Worcester exits ⌜with Vernon.⌝*

PRINCE
It will not be accepted, on my life.
The Douglas and the Hotspur both together
Are confident against the world in arms.

119. **charge:** command

120. **on their:** i.e., as soon as we have their

124. **colossus:** a gigantic statue in human form whose legs, according to legend, spanned the harbor at Rhodes (See page 192.)

127. **thou . . . death:** proverbial

131. **pricks:** spurs

131–32. **prick me off:** mark me for death

132–33. **set to a leg:** set a broken leg

133. **grief:** pain

136–37. **A trim reckoning:** a fine balance sheet or total

138. **insensible:** not perceptible by the senses

140. **suffer:** allow

141. **scutcheon:** i.e., funerary device (literally, a piece of metal, cloth, or paper painted with the deceased's coat of arms or other emblem, to be displayed in funeral processions and subsequently hung up in churches)

142. **catechism:** instructive questions and answers (literally, a book teaching basic religious principles through a series of questions and answers) See page xxxi.

**5.2** Worcester lies to Hotspur, telling him that the king made no offer of pardon and is ready to begin the battle. Hotspur sends his own defiance to the king by Douglas. On Douglas's return, Hotspur and his men prepare for battle.

———

KING
> Hence, therefore, every leader to his charge,
> For on their answer will we set on them, 120
> And God befriend us as our cause is just.

*They exit. Prince and Falstaff remain.*

FALSTAFF   Hal, if thou see me down in the battle and bestride me, so; 'tis a point of friendship.

PRINCE   Nothing but a colossus can do thee that friendship. Say thy prayers, and farewell. 125

FALSTAFF   I would 'twere bedtime, Hal, and all well.

PRINCE   Why, thou owest God a death.    ⌈*He exits.*⌉

FALSTAFF   'Tis not due yet. I would be loath to pay Him before His day. What need I be so forward with Him that calls not on me? Well, 'tis no matter. 130 Honor pricks me on. Yea, but how if honor prick me off when I come on? How then? Can honor set to a leg? No. Or an arm? No. Or take away the grief of a wound? No. Honor hath no skill in surgery, then? No. What is honor? A word. What is in that word 135 "honor"? What is that "honor"? Air. A trim reckoning. Who hath it? He that died o' Wednesday. Doth he feel it? No. Doth he hear it? No. 'Tis insensible, then? Yea, to the dead. But will ⌈it⌉ not live with the living? No. Why? Detraction will not suffer it. There- 140 fore, I'll none of it. Honor is a mere scutcheon. And so ends my catechism.

*He exits.*

⌈Scene 2⌉

*Enter Worcester* ⌈*and*⌉ *Sir Richard Vernon.*

WORCESTER
> O no, my nephew must not know, Sir Richard,
> The liberal and kind offer of the King.

4. **undone:** destroyed, ruined

7. **still:** always

8. **in:** i.e., when punishing

13. **a wild trick:** i.e., the characteristic wildness

14. **Look . . . can:** i.e., no matter how we appear; **or . . . or:** i.e., either . . . or

15. **misquote:** incorrectly observe; misinterpret

20. **an adopted . . . privilege:** i.e., a nickname (Hotspur) that gives him the privilege of being impulsive

21. **spleen:** sudden impulse, whim

23. **train:** entice, allure

24. **ta'en:** caught, contracted (as if a disease)

25. **spring:** source

28. **Deliver:** i.e., report

31. **Deliver up:** release (This line indicates that Westmoreland served as the hostage from the king's side, held by Hotspur to ensure Worcester's safe return from the parley with the king. See note to 4.3.115–16.)

**VERNON**
  'Twere best he did.
**WORCESTER**        Then are we all ⌈undone.⌉
  It is not possible, it cannot be                    5
  The King should keep his word in loving us.
  He will suspect us still and find a time
  To punish this offense in other faults.
  ⌈Suspicion⌉ all our lives shall be stuck full of
    eyes,                                   10
  For treason is but trusted like the fox,
  Who, never so tame, so cherished and locked up,
  Will have a wild trick of his ancestors.
  Look how we can, or sad or merrily,
  Interpretation will misquote our looks,        15
  And we shall feed like oxen at a stall,
  The better cherished still the nearer death.
  My nephew's trespass may be well forgot;
  It hath the excuse of youth and heat of blood,
  And an adopted name of privilege—        20
  A harebrained Hotspur governed by a spleen.
  All his offenses live upon my head
  And on his father's. We did train him on,
  And his corruption being ta'en from us,
  We as the spring of all shall pay for all.      25
  Therefore, good cousin, let not Harry know
  In any case the offer of the King.
**VERNON**
  Deliver what you will; I'll say 'tis so.

        *Enter ⌈Hotspur, Douglas, and their army.⌉*

  Here comes your cousin.
HOTSPUR, ⌈*to Douglas*⌉  My uncle is returned.    30
  Deliver up my Lord of Westmoreland.—
  Uncle, what news?
**WORCESTER**
  The King will bid you battle presently.

34. **Defy . . . Westmoreland:** i.e., tell Westmoreland to take our reply of defiance back to the king

36. **shall:** i.e., I shall

37. **seeming:** i.e., semblance of

41. **forswearing . . . forsworn:** denying with a false oath that he had ever sworn falsely (or that he had ever broken his oath)

45. **brave:** proud

46. **engaged:** held hostage

47. **cannot . . . him:** i.e., must of necessity bring King Henry

52. **Harry Monmouth:** i.e., Prince Hal, called **Monmouth** after his birthplace in Wales

53. **showed his tasking:** i.e., did his challenge appear as he delivered it

55. **urged:** put forward

57. **gentle . . . arms:** gentlemanly practice and test of military skill

Man in gyves. (4.2.41)
From Cesare Vecellio, *Degli habiti antichi et moderni* (1590).

DOUGLAS, ⌜*to Hotspur*⌝
Defy him by the Lord of Westmoreland.

HOTSPUR
Lord Douglas, go you and tell him so.                    35

DOUGLAS
Marry, and shall, and very willingly.      *Douglas exits.*

WORCESTER
There is no seeming mercy in the King.

HOTSPUR
Did you beg any? God forbid!

WORCESTER
I told him gently of our grievances,
Of his oath-breaking, which he mended thus          40
By now forswearing that he is forsworn.
He calls us "rebels," "traitors," and will scourge
With haughty arms this hateful name in us.

                    *Enter Douglas.*

DOUGLAS
Arm, gentlemen, to arms. For I have thrown
A brave defiance in King Henry's teeth,                  45
And Westmoreland, that was engaged, did bear it,
Which cannot choose but bring him quickly on.

WORCESTER
The Prince of Wales stepped forth before the King,
And, nephew, challenged you to single fight.

HOTSPUR
O, would the quarrel lay upon our heads,                 50
And that no man might draw short breath today
But I and Harry Monmouth! Tell me, tell me,
How showed his tasking? Seemed it in contempt?

VERNON
No, by my soul. I never in my life
Did hear a challenge urged more modestly,                55
Unless a brother should a brother dare
To gentle exercise and proof of arms.

58. **gave . . . man:** i.e., credited you with all manly qualities

59. **Trimmed up . . . praises:** adorned his praise of you

62. **dispraising . . . you:** i.e., disparaging his praise as unequal to your merits

64. **cital:** recital, account

68. **pause:** cease, stop

69. **envy:** malice, hostility

70. **owe:** own, possess

71. **misconstrued . . . wantonness:** i.e., misunderstood in his unruliness and extravagant behavior

73. **On:** i.e., of

74. **so . . . liberty:** so unrestrained in his conduct

80–82. **Better . . . persuasion:** i.e., you can better arouse yourselves for battle by thinking about how you will fight than by listening to me, since I have no talent for rousing oratory

86–88. **To spend . . . hour:** i.e., even if life were only an hour long, it would be too long a time if spent in ignoble action    **dial's point:** the hand of a clock or sundial    **Still:** always

90. **brave:** splendid, glorious

He gave you all the duties of a man,
Trimmed up your praises with a princely tongue,
Spoke your deservings like a chronicle,                    60
Making you ever better than his praise
By still dispraising praise valued with you,
And, which became him like a prince indeed,
He made a blushing cital of himself,
And chid his truant youth with such a grace               65
As if he mastered there a double spirit
Of teaching and of learning instantly.
There did he pause, but let me tell the world:
If he outlive the envy of this day,
England did never owe so sweet a hope                     70
So much misconstrued in his wantonness.

HOTSPUR
Cousin, I think thou art enamorèd
On his follies. Never did I hear
Of any prince so wild a liberty.
But be he as he will, yet once ere night                  75
I will embrace him with a soldier's arm
That he shall shrink under my courtesy. —
Arm, arm with speed, and, fellows, soldiers,
    friends,
Better consider what you have to do                       80
Than I that have not well the gift of tongue
Can lift your blood up with persuasion.

*Enter a Messenger.*

MESSENGER   My lord, here are letters for you.
HOTSPUR   I cannot read them now. —
O gentlemen, the time of life is short;                   85
To spend that shortness basely were too long
If life did ride upon a dial's point,
Still ending at the arrival of an hour.
An if we live, we live to tread on kings;
If die, brave death, when princes die with us.            90

91. **for:** i.e., as for; **fair:** just
92. **intent of bearing:** object for which we bear them
94. **cuts . . . tale:** i.e., stops me from talking
97. **temper:** i.e., tempered steel
98. **withal:** i.e., with
99. **adventure of:** what chances to happen on
100. **Esperance, Percy:** the battle cries of the Percy clan
103. **heaven to earth:** i.e., as sure as heaven is greater than earth


**5.3** The battle begins. Douglas kills Blunt, who is disguised as King Henry. Falstaff enters alone to disclose to the audience that he has led his men to their massacre. When Prince Hal enters and asks Falstaff to lend him a sword, Falstaff instead gives him a bottle of sack.

------------

0 SD. **Alarum:** trumpet call

Now, for our consciences, the arms are fair
When the intent of bearing them is just.

*Enter another ⌜Messenger.⌝*

⌜SECOND⌝ MESSENGER
  My lord, prepare. The King comes on apace.
HOTSPUR
  I thank him that he cuts me from my tale,
  For I profess not talking. Only this:          95
  Let each man do his best. And here draw I a sword,
  Whose temper I intend to stain
  With the best blood that I can meet withal
  In the adventure of this perilous day.
  Now, Esperance! Percy! And set on.          100
  Sound all the lofty instruments of war,
  And by that music let us all embrace,
  For, heaven to earth, some of us never shall
  A second time do such a courtesy.
        *Here they embrace. The trumpets sound.*
                    ⌜*They exit.*⌝


### ⌜Scene 3⌝

*The King enters with his power, ⌜crosses the stage and exits.⌝ Alarum to the battle. Then enter Douglas, and Sir Walter Blunt, ⌜disguised as the King.⌝*

BLUNT, ⌜*as King*⌝
  What is thy name that in ⌜the⌝ battle thus
  Thou crossest me? What honor dost thou seek
  Upon my head?
DOUGLAS        Know then my name is Douglas,
  And I do haunt thee in the battle thus     5
  Because some tell me that thou art a king.
BLUNT, ⌜*as King*⌝  They tell thee true.

8. **dear:** dearly, at great cost

8–9. **bought / Thy likeness:** paid for resembling you

20. **full:** very

22. **Semblably . . . himself:** i.e., dressed and equipped to look like the king

23. **whither:** wherever

26. **coats:** perhaps, tunics emblazoned with the king's coat of arms and worn over armor

31. **stand . . . day:** i.e., are in a position to win

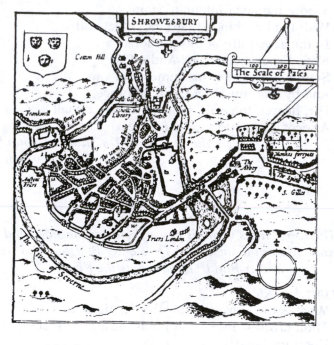

A bird's-eye view of the city of Shrewsbury.
From John Speed, *A prospect of the most famous part of the world* (1631).

DOUGLAS
The Lord of Stafford dear today hath bought
Thy likeness, for instead of thee, King Harry,
This sword hath ended him. So shall it thee,                    10
Unless thou yield thee as my prisoner.
BLUNT, ⌜*as King*⌝
I was not born a yielder, thou proud Scot,
And thou shalt find a king that will revenge
Lord Stafford's death.

> *They fight. Douglas kills Blunt.*

> *Then enter Hotspur.*

HOTSPUR
O Douglas, hadst thou fought at Holmedon thus,             15
I never had triumphed upon a Scot.
DOUGLAS
All's done, all's won; here breathless lies the King.
HOTSPUR   Where?
DOUGLAS   Here.
HOTSPUR
This, Douglas? No, I know this face full well.              20
A gallant knight he was; his name was Blunt,
Semblably furnished like the King himself.
DOUGLAS, ⌜*addressing Blunt's corpse*⌝
⌜A⌝ fool go with thy soul whither it goes!
A borrowed title hast thou bought too dear.
Why didst thou tell me that thou wert a king?              25
HOTSPUR
The King hath many marching in his coats.
DOUGLAS
Now, by my sword, I will kill all his coats.
I'll murder all his wardrobe, piece by piece,
Until I meet the King.
HOTSPUR                         Up and away!                 30
Our soldiers stand full fairly for the day.

> ⌜*They exit.*⌝

31 SD. **Alarm:** i.e., alarum, trumpet call

32. **shot-free:** i.e., free from paying his shot, or bill, at the tavern

33. **shot:** arrows or bullets; **scoring:** (1) cutting (with weapons on the battlefield); (2) chalking up or notching on a tally the number of drinks a customer has had in a tavern

34. **Soft:** i.e., wait a minute

35. **Here's no vanity:** perhaps a reference to Falstaff's earlier speech about the emptiness and futility of honor

39. **peppered:** destroyed

40. **for the town's end:** i.e., destined to loiter at the city gates (See page 218.)

43. **stark:** rigid

47. **breathe:** rest, pause

48. **Turk Gregory:** The **Turk** was considered a merciless fighter, and **Gregory** probably referred either to Pope Gregory VII (11th century) or Pope Gregory XIII (16th century), both of whom were accused of violence by Protestant writers.

49. **paid:** i.e., killed

50. **made him sure:** killed him (In the next line, the prince's reply uses the meaning of **sure** as "safe, secure.")

57. **that:** that which

*Alarm. Enter Falstaff alone.*

FALSTAFF   Though I could 'scape shot-free at London,
  I fear the shot here. Here's no scoring but upon
  the pate.—Soft, who are you? Sir Walter Blunt.
  There's honor for you. Here's no vanity. I am as hot      35
  as molten lead, and as heavy too. God keep lead out
  of me; I need no more weight than mine own
  bowels. I have led my ragamuffins where they are
  peppered. There's not three of my hundred and fifty
  left alive, and they are for the town's end, to beg      40
  during life. But who comes here?

*Enter the Prince.*

PRINCE
  What, stand'st thou idle here? Lend me thy sword.
  Many a nobleman lies stark and stiff
  Under the hoofs of vaunting enemies,
  Whose deaths are yet unrevenged. I prithee      45
  Lend me thy sword.
FALSTAFF   O Hal, I prithee give me leave to breathe
  awhile. Turk Gregory never did such deeds in arms
  as I have done this day. I have paid Percy; I have
  made him sure.      50
PRINCE
  He is indeed, and living to kill thee.
  I prithee, lend me thy sword.
FALSTAFF   Nay, before God, Hal, if Percy be alive, thou
  gett'st not my sword; but take my pistol, if thou
  wilt.      55
PRINCE
  Give it me. What, is it in the case?
FALSTAFF   Ay, Hal, 'tis hot, 'tis hot. There's that will
  sack a city.

*The Prince draws it out, and finds it
to be a bottle of sack.*

59. **dally:** (1) chat; (2) delay; (3) mock

62. **carbonado:** meat that is cut crosswise and grilled

63. **grinning honor:** a reference to the death agony visible on Blunt's face

**5.4** Prince Hal saves King Henry from death at the hands of Douglas. Hal then meets Hotspur. While they are fighting, Falstaff and Douglas enter; they fight, Falstaff falls down as if he were dead, and Douglas exits. Hal kills Hotspur. Finding Falstaff's body, Hal briefly mourns his death. When Hal leaves, Falstaff rises, sees the slain Percy, stabs him in the thigh, and picks up the body, planning to claim the credit for killing him. When Prince Hal reenters with his brother and meets Falstaff, Hal agrees to give his support to Falstaff's lie.

---

0 SD. **excursions:** i.e., soldiers issuing across the stage as if moving against the enemy

1. **bleedest:** In the chronicles, Prince Hal is described as having been badly cut on the face.

5. **make up:** bring up your troops (into the battle)

6. **retirement:** retreat; **amaze:** fill with sudden fear and panic

13. **stained:** i.e., (1) with blood and dirt; (2) with defeat

PRINCE
What, is it a time to jest and dally now?
　　　　　　　*He throws the bottle at him ⌜and⌝ exits.*
FALSTAFF　Well, if Percy be alive, I'll pierce him. If he do　60
come in my way, so; if he do not, if I come in his
willingly, let him make a carbonado of me. I like not
such grinning honor as Sir Walter hath. Give me
life, which, if I can save, so: if not, honor comes
unlooked for, and there's an end.　　　　　　　　　65
　　　　　　　　　　　　　　⌜*He exits.*⌝


　　　　　　　　　⌜Scene 4⌝
*Alarm, excursions. Enter the King, the Prince, Lord John
of Lancaster, ⌜and the⌝ Earl of Westmoreland.*

KING
I prithee, Harry, withdraw thyself. Thou bleedest
too much.
Lord John of Lancaster, go you with him.
LANCASTER
Not I, my lord, unless I did bleed too.
PRINCE
I beseech your Majesty, make up,　　　　　　　　5
Lest your retirement do amaze your friends.
KING
I will do so.—My Lord of Westmoreland,
Lead him to his tent.
WESTMORELAND
Come, my lord, I'll lead you to your tent.
PRINCE
Lead me, my lord? I do not need your help,　　　10
And God forbid a shallow scratch should drive
The Prince of Wales from such a field as this,
Where stained nobility lies trodden on,
And rebels' arms triumph in massacres.

15. **breathe:** pause
20. **as my soul:** i.e., as if you were my soul
21–22. **at . . . maintenance:** at sword's point with more courageous and active bearing
23. **ungrown:** i.e., youthful
25. **Hydra's heads:** The mythical Hydra grew two heads for every one that was cut off.
27. **colors:** i.e., coats emblazoned with the king's arms
30. **his shadows:** those disguised as the king
31. **very king:** i.e., the king himself
32. **Seek:** i.e., who seek
34. **assay:** fight with
37. **mine:** i.e., my conquest

Hydra. (5.4.25)
From Jacob Typot, *Symbola diuina . . .* (1652).

LANCASTER
We breathe too long. Come, cousin Westmoreland,	15
Our duty this way lies. For God's sake, come.
⌐*Lancaster and Westmoreland exit.*⌐

PRINCE
By God, thou hast deceived me, Lancaster.
I did not think thee lord of such a spirit.
Before, I loved thee as a brother, John,
But now I do respect thee as my soul.	20

KING
I saw him hold Lord Percy at the point
With lustier maintenance than I did look for
Of such an ungrown warrior.

PRINCE
O, this boy lends mettle to us all.	*He exits.*

⌐*Enter Douglas.*⌐

DOUGLAS
Another king! They grow like Hydra's heads.—	25
I am the Douglas, fatal to all those
That wear those colors on them. What art thou
That counterfeit'st the person of a king?

KING
The King himself, who, Douglas, grieves at heart,
So many of his shadows thou hast met	30
And not the very king. I have two boys
Seek Percy and thyself about the field,
But, seeing thou fall'st on me so luckily,
I will assay thee. And defend thyself.

DOUGLAS
I fear thou art another counterfeit,	35
And yet, in faith, thou bearest thee like a king.
But mine I am sure thou art, whoe'er thou be,
And thus I win thee.

*They fight. The King being in danger,*
*enter Prince of Wales.*

39. **like:** i.e., likely
45. **succor:** help, relief
46. **straight:** i.e., straightway, immediately
48. **opinion:** reputation
49. **mak'st . . . tender of:** have some loving regard for
52. **hearkened for:** desired to hear of
54. **insulting:** triumphing
55. **in your end:** i.e., in bringing about your end

A heraldic lion. (3.1.157)
From Conrad Lycosthenes, *Prodigiorum* (1557).

212

PRINCE
   Hold up thy head, vile Scot, or thou art like
   Never to hold it up again. The spirits                    40
   Of valiant Shirley, Stafford, Blunt are in my arms.
   It is the Prince of Wales that threatens thee,
   Who never promiseth but he means to pay.
                              *They fight. Douglas flieth.*
   ⌜*To King.*⌝   Cheerly, my lord. How fares your Grace?
   Sir Nicholas Gawsey hath for succor sent,                 45
   And so hath Clifton. I'll to Clifton straight.
KING   Stay and breathe awhile.
   Thou hast redeemed thy lost opinion
   And showed thou mak'st some tender of my life
   In this fair rescue thou hast brought to me.              50
PRINCE
   O God, they did me too much injury
   That ever said I hearkened for your death.
   If it were so, I might have let alone
   The insulting hand of Douglas over you,
   Which would have been as speedy in your end               55
   As all the poisonous potions in the world,
   And saved the treacherous labor of your son.
KING
   Make up to Clifton. I'll to Sir Nicholas Gawsey.
                              *King exits.*

                    *Enter Hotspur.*

HOTSPUR
   If I mistake not, thou art Harry Monmouth.
PRINCE
   Thou speak'st as if I would deny my name.                 60
HOTSPUR
   My name is Harry Percy.
PRINCE                        Why then I see
   A very valiant rebel of the name.
   I am the Prince of Wales; and think not, Percy,

66. **Two . . . sphere:** proverbial (In Ptolemaic cosmology, each star moved in its own sphere. See the note to 5.1.18–22.)

67. **brook:** tolerate, endure

71. **name in arms:** i.e., reputation as a fighter

73. **budding honors:** See note to 3.2.147.

75. **vanities:** boasts; inanities

80. **Than:** i.e., than of

85. **a stop:** an end

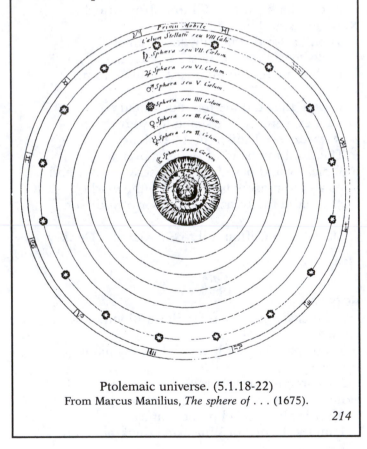

Ptolemaic universe. (5.1.18-22)
From Marcus Manilius, *The sphere of . . .* (1675).

To share with me in glory any more.                          65
Two stars keep not their motion in one sphere,
Nor can one England brook a double reign
Of Harry Percy and the Prince of Wales.

HOTSPUR
⌐Nor⌐ shall it, Harry, for the hour is come
To end the one of us, and would to God                       70
Thy name in arms were now as great as mine.

PRINCE
I'll make it greater ere I part from thee,
And all the budding honors on thy crest
I'll crop to make a garland for my head.

HOTSPUR
I can no longer brook thy vanities.          *They fight.*    75

*Enter Falstaff.*

FALSTAFF    Well said, Hal! To it, Hal! Nay, you shall find
no boys' play here, I can tell you.

*Enter Douglas. He fighteth with Falstaff, ⌐who⌐ falls
down as if he were dead. ⌐Douglas exits.⌐ The Prince
killeth Percy.*

HOTSPUR
O Harry, thou hast robbed me of my youth.
I better brook the loss of brittle life
Than those proud titles thou hast won of me.                 80
They wound my thoughts worse than thy sword my
    flesh.
But thoughts, the slaves of life, and life, time's fool,
And time, that takes survey of all the world,
Must have a stop. O, I could prophesy,                       85
But that the earthy and cold hand of death
Lies on my tongue. No, Percy, thou art dust,
And food for—                              ⌐*He dies.*⌐

PRINCE
For worms, brave Percy. Fare thee well, great heart.

92. **bound:** territory

95. **stout:** formidable; brave

96. **sensible:** i.e., aware

97. **dear a show:** great an expression

98. **favors:** ornaments or insignia worn into battle

101. **Adieu:** good-bye

107. **heavy:** (1) sorrowful; (2) weighty

108. **vanity:** idle or unprofitable conduct

111. **Emboweled:** disemboweled (in preparation for embalming); **by and by:** soon

112. **in blood:** in your own blood (It is possible that Hal continues the metaphor of Falstaff as a **deer;** if so, **in blood** would also mean "in full vigor.")

114. **leave . . . eat me:** i.e., permission to pickle me in salt and eat me (like a slain deer after it has been disemboweled)

116. **termagant:** savage (**Termagant** was a fictional Muslim god, shown in early drama as noisy and unrestrained.); **paid me scot and lot:** (1) paid me in full; (2) killed me

122. **The better . . . discretion:** proverbial before Shakespeare

Ill-weaved ambition, how much art thou shrunk!     90
When that this body did contain a spirit,
A kingdom for it was too small a bound,
But now two paces of the vilest earth
Is room enough. This earth that bears thee dead
Bears not alive so stout a gentleman.              95
If thou wert sensible of courtesy,
I should not make so dear a show of zeal.
But let my favors hide thy mangled face;
                    ⌜*He covers Hotspur's face.*⌝
And even in thy behalf I'll thank myself
For doing these fair rites of tenderness.          100
Adieu, and take thy praise with thee to heaven.
Thy ignominy sleep with thee in the grave,
But not remembered in thy epitaph.
                    *He spieth Falstaff on the ground.*
What, old acquaintance, could not all this flesh
Keep in a little life? Poor Jack, farewell.        105
I could have better spared a better man.
O, I should have a heavy miss of thee
If I were much in love with vanity.
Death hath not struck so fat a deer today,
Though many dearer in this bloody fray.            110
Emboweled will I see thee by and by;
Till then in blood by noble Percy lie.     *He exits.*
                    *Falstaff riseth up.*
FALSTAFF   Emboweled? If thou embowel me today, I'll
give you leave to powder me and eat me too
tomorrow. 'Sblood, 'twas time to counterfeit, or   115
that hot termagant Scot had paid me scot and lot
too. Counterfeit? I lie. I am no counterfeit. To die is
to be a counterfeit, for he is but the counterfeit of a
man who hath not the life of a man; but to counterfeit dying when a man thereby liveth is to be no      120
counterfeit, but the true and perfect image of life
indeed. The better part of valor is discretion, in the

129. **Nothing . . . eyes:** i.e., nothing but an eyewitness could refute my story

132. **fleshed:** used for the first time

139. **fantasy:** imagination

142. **a double man:** (1) two men in one (with Hotspur on his back); (2) an apparition

143. **jack:** knave

145–46. **I look . . . duke:** i.e., I expect to be given a title (for this)

"For the town's end, to beg during life." (5.3.40-41)
From August Casimir Redel, *Apophtegmata symbolica* (n.d.).

which better part I have saved my life. Zounds, I am afraid of this gunpowder Percy, though he be dead. How if he should counterfeit too, and rise? By my faith, I am afraid he would prove the better counterfeit. Therefore I'll make him sure, yea, and I'll swear I killed him. Why may not he rise as well as I? Nothing confutes me but eyes, and nobody sees me. Therefore, sirrah, ⌜*stabbing him*⌝ with a new wound in your thigh, come you along with me.

*He takes up Hotspur on his back.*

*Enter Prince* ⌜*and*⌝ *John of Lancaster.*

PRINCE
Come, brother John. Full bravely hast thou fleshed
Thy maiden sword.

LANCASTER                    But soft, whom have we here?
Did you not tell me this fat man was dead?

PRINCE  I did; I saw him dead,
Breathless and bleeding on the ground.—Art thou alive?
Or is it fantasy that plays upon our eyesight?
I prithee, speak. We will not trust our eyes
Without our ears. Thou art not what thou seem'st.

FALSTAFF   No, that's certain. I am not a double man. But if I be not Jack Falstaff, then am I a jack. There is Percy. If your father will do me any honor, so; if not, let him kill the next Percy himself. I look to be either earl or duke, I can assure you.

PRINCE
Why, Percy I killed myself, and saw thee dead.

FALSTAFF   Didst thou? Lord, Lord, how this world is given to lying. I grant you, I was down and out of breath, and so was he, but we rose both at an instant and fought a long hour by Shrewsbury clock. If I may be believed, so; if not, let them that should reward valor bear the sin upon their own heads. I'll

154. **take . . . death:** i.e., swear an oath at the moment of my death (when the eternal life of my soul is at risk)

156–57. **eat . . . sword:** a comic variation on the cliché "eat his words"

160. **luggage:** i.e., that which you are lugging

161. **do thee grace:** bring you into favor (with the king)

162. **happiest:** most fitting; most favorable

164. **highest:** i.e., perhaps, highest ground (from which the battlefield may be surveyed)

167. **grow great:** i.e., be made a **duke** or **earl**

168. **purge:** (1) lose weight through purging; (2) repent


**5.5** The king's forces having won, King Henry condemns Worcester and Vernon to death, and the king and his supporters prepare to march against the remaining rebels.

———————

1. **rebuke:** (1) shame, disgrace; (2) reproof
5. **tenor:** nature
6. **upon our party:** on our side

take it upon my death, I gave him this wound in
the thigh. If the man were alive and would deny          155
it, zounds, I would make him eat a piece of my
sword.

LANCASTER
This is the strangest tale that ever I heard.

PRINCE
This is the strangest fellow, brother John. —
Come bring your luggage nobly on your back.          160
For my part, if a lie may do thee grace,
I'll gild it with the happiest terms I have.
                                        *A retreat is sounded.*
The trumpet sounds retreat; the day is ⌈ours.⌉
Come, brother, let us to the highest of the field
To see what friends are living, who are dead.          165
                                        *They exit.*

FALSTAFF     I'll follow, as they say, for reward. He that
rewards me, God reward him. If I do grow great,
I'll grow less, for I'll purge and leave sack and live
cleanly as a nobleman should do.
                        *He exits* ⌈*carrying Hotspur's body.*⌉


                        ⌈Scene 5⌉
*The trumpets sound. Enter the King, Prince of Wales,*
*Lord John of Lancaster, Earl of Westmoreland, with*
*Worcester and Vernon prisoners,* ⌈*and Soldiers.*⌉

KING
Thus ever did rebellion find rebuke. —
Ill-spirited Worcester, did not we send grace,
Pardon, and terms of love to all of you?
And wouldst thou turn our offers contrary,
Misuse the tenor of thy kinsman's trust?          5
Three knights upon our party slain today,
A noble earl, and many a creature else

10. **intelligence:** information
12. **patiently:** calmly
20. **Upon . . . fear:** i.e., in terrified retreat
27. **honorable bounty:** i.e., the honor of this kindness or generosity

Had been alive this hour
If, like a Christian, thou hadst truly borne
Betwixt our armies true intelligence.                10
WORCESTER
What I have done my safety urged me to.
And I embrace this fortune patiently,
Since not to be avoided it falls on me.
KING
Bear Worcester to the death, and Vernon too.
Other offenders we will pause upon.                15
⌐*Worcester and Vernon exit, under guard.*⌐
How goes the field?
PRINCE
The noble Scot, Lord Douglas, when he saw
The fortune of the day quite turned from him,
The noble Percy slain, and all his men
Upon the foot of fear, fled with the rest,                20
And, falling from a hill, he was so bruised
That the pursuers took him. At my tent
The Douglas is, and I beseech your Grace
I may dispose of him.
KING                                   With all my heart.          25
PRINCE
Then, brother John of Lancaster, to you
This honorable bounty shall belong.
Go to the Douglas and deliver him
Up to his pleasure, ransomless and free.
His valors shown upon our crests today                30
Have taught us how to cherish such high deeds,
Even in the bosom of our adversaries.
LANCASTER
I thank your Grace for this high courtesy,
Which I shall give away immediately.
KING
Then this remains, that we divide our power.                35
You, son John, and my cousin Westmoreland,

37. **bend you:** turn; **dearest:** greatest
43. **his:** its
44. **such another day:** i.e., another day such as this one
46. **leave:** stop (fighting)

Towards York shall bend you with your dearest
   speed
To meet Northumberland and the prelate Scroop,
Who, as we hear, are busily in arms.                    40
Myself and you, son Harry, will towards Wales
To fight with Glendower and the Earl of March.
Rebellion in this land shall lose his sway,
Meeting the check of such another day.
And since this business so fair is done,                45
Let us not leave till all our own be won.

                                  *They exit.*

# Textual Notes

The reading of the present text appears to the left of the square bracket. This edition is based on the earliest extant printings of the play: the fragmentary earliest quarto preserved at the Folger Library (**Q0,** 1598) is our source for 1.3.206–2.2.117; the first surviving complete printed version (**Q1,** also 1598) is our source for the rest of the play. Q1 survives in three copies: the Devonshire copy (**Dev.**) at the Huntington Library, San Marino, California; the Cambridge copy (**Cam.**) at Trinity College, Cambridge University, England; the British Library copy (**BL**) in London, England. The earliest sources of readings not in Q0 or Q1 are indicated as follows: **Q2** is the second quarto of 1599; **Q3** is the third quarto of 1604; **Q4** is the fourth quarto of 1608; **Q5** is the fifth quarto of 1613; **Q6** is the sixth quarto of 1622; **F** is the Shakespeare First Folio of 1623, in which *1 Henry IV* is a slightly edited reprint of Q5. **Ed.** is an earlier editor of Shakespeare, from the editor(s) of the Second Folio of 1632 to the present. No sources are given for emendations of punctuation or for corrections of obvious typographical errors, such as turned letters that produce no known word. **SD** means stage direction; **SP** means speech prefix; ~ refers to a word already quoted; ⌃ indicates the omission of a punctuation mark.

1.1.        22. levy] Q1 (leauy)
                30. Therefor] Q1 (Therefore)
                39. Herefordshire] Herdforshire Q1
                49. lord] Q1 (L.)
                53. Archibald] Archibold Q1

62. a] Q5; *omit* Q1
69. blood, did] ~. ~ Q1
76. WESTMORELAND In . . . is ˄ a] Ed.; In . . .
is. | *West.* A Q1
93. use ˄ . . . keeps,] ~, . . . ~ ˄ Q1

1.2.
18. art king] Q2; art a king Q1
35. proof ˄ now:] ~. ~ ˄ Q1
84. similes] Q5; smiles Q1
112. Poins!] ~ ˄ Q1
119–20. Sir John Sack-and-Sugar? Jack,] Ed.; ~ ~
~, ~ ˄ ~~? Q1
144. Who,] ~ ˄ Q1
165. thou] Ed.; the Q1
169. Peto, Bardolph] Ed.; Haruey, Rossill Q1

1.3.
9. ne'er] Q1 (neare)
21. SD *Worcester*] Q1 (*Wor.*)
35. reaped] F (rept)
53. what—] ~ ˄ Q1
97. war.] ~, Q1
98. tongue ˄] ~: Q1
100. sedgy] Q1 (siedgie)
132. SD *Worcester*] Q1 (*Wor.*)
200. west,] ~. Q1
206. *The Q0 fragment begins.*
206. SP HOTSPUR] Q5; *omit* Q0
224. You ˄] ~, Q0
247. whipped] Q1; whip Q0
253. kept,] ~ ˄ Q0
274. granted.—You, my lord,] Ed.; ~ ˄ ~ ˄
~~. Q0
304. course.] ~ ˄ Q0
306. Lord] Q0 (Lo:)
309. our] Q1; out Q0

2.1.
36. FIRST] Ed.; *omit* Q0
43. when,] ~ ˄ Q0

51. SD-52. SD *Carriers exit. . . . Chamberlain.*] Ed.; *Enter Chamberlaine. Exeunt.* | *Gad.* What ho: Chamberlaine. Q0

69. Saint] Saine Q0

82. in,] ~ ˄ Q0

2.2.    0. SD *Bardolph, and Peto*] Ed.; *and Peto, &c.* Q0

4. hanged! Poins] ~ ˄ ~ Q0

13. square] Q0 (squire)

37. my] mine Q1

43, 69, 75. SP FALSTAFF] *Fast.* Q0

54. SP BARDOLPH] Ed.; Bardoll (*as a word in Poins's speech*) Q0

55. SP GADSHILL] Ed.; *Bar.* Q0

81. SP FIRST TRAVELER] Ed.; *Trauel.* Q0

85. SP TRAVELERS] Ed.; *Trauel.* Q0

90. SP TRAVELERS] Ed.; *Tra.* Q0

117. fat] *omit* Q1

117. *Q0 fragment ends.*

2.3.    1. SP HOTSPUR] Ed.; *omit* Q1

4. In respect] F; in the respect Q1

39 *and hereafter.* SP LADY PERCY] *Lady* Q1

50. thee murmur ˄] the murmur, Q1

52. Courage!] ~ ˄ Q1

59. sleep] sleeepe Q1

73. horse? A roan] Q3; horse, Roane Q1

2.4.    34. precedent] F; present Q1

37. SP POINS] Q4; *Prin.* Q1

88. SD *1 line later in* Q1

181. SP PRINCE] F; *Gad.* Q1

182, 184, 188. SP BARDOLPH] Ed.; *Ross.* Q1

296. lord] Q1 (Lo.)

312. lions too. You] Q1 Dev. (lions to, you); lions, to you Q1 Cam., BL

337. SD *1 line earlier in* Q1

352. Owen] Ed.; O Q1

406. tristful] Ed.; trustfull Q1
429. For, Harry, now] Q1 Dev. (for Harrie,
     now); for Harrie now Q1 Cam., BL
456. My] Mv Q1
491. lean] Q2; lane Q1
552. What] Ed.; *Pr.* What Q1
555, 560. SPP F; *omit* Q1
558. anchovies] anchaues Q1

3.1.
49. son ⌄] sonne, Q1 BL; sonne? Q1 Dev.,
    Cam.
81. coz] Q1 (coose)
104. cantle] F; scantle Q1
105. dammed] Q1 (damnd)
110. wind?] ~ ⌄ Q1
134. meter] Ed.; miter Q1
136. axletree] Q1 (exle tree)
146. night.] ~ ⌄ Q1
148. your wives] ~, ~ Q1
157. lion] Q1 (Leon)
196. schooled.] ~ ⌄ Q1
203. SD *Glendower*] *Glondower* Q1
211. I] Ed.; *Mor.* I Q1
213. truant,] F; ~ ⌄ Q1
273. hot] F; Hot. Q1

3.2.
4. SD *exit*] *Exennt* Q1
61. won] Q1 (wan)
80. gaze ⌄] ~. Q1
86. gorged] gordge Q1
113. capital ⌄] ~. Q1
119. Enlargèd] Enlargd Q1
166. SD *1 line later in* Q1

3.3.
36. that's] Ed.; that Q1
54. SD *1 line later in* Q1 (*as* "Enter host.")
61. tithe] Ed.; tight Q1
95. How] Ed.; *Falst.* How Q1

121. womanhood] womandood Q1
143. owed] Q1 (ought)
183. guests] F; ghesse Q1
188. beef] Q1 (beoffe)

4.1.
  0. SD Q2; *omit* Q1
  1 *and hereafter to 94.* SP HOTSPUR] Ed.;
    *Per.* Q1
  5. world.] ~ ˏ Q1
  13. SD *a Messenger*] F; *one* Q1, *in which SD*
    *is 1 line earlier*
  22. lord] Ed.; mind Q1
  58. is] F; tis Q1
  89. SD *Richard*] *Ri.* Q1
  114. dropped] Q2; drop Q1
  122. altar] Q4; altars Q1
  129. ne'er] Q1 (neare)
  133. cannot] Q5; can Q1
  134. yet] Q5; it Q1
  142. merrily] Q1 (merely)

4.2.
  3. Coldfield] Ed.; cophill Q1
  9. lieutenant] Liuetenant Q1
  15. yeomen's] Q2; Yeomans Q1
  18. lief] Ed.; lieue Q1
  32. feazed] Q1 (fazd)
  35. tattered] Q1 (tottered)
  47. Saint] Q1 (S.)
  52. Lord] Q1 (Lo.)
  66. enough] inongh Q1
  83. SD *He exits.*] *Exeunt.* Q1

4.3.
  0. SD *Douglas,*] Q1 (*Doug:*)
  27. horse] Q5; horses Q1
  34. ours] Q6; our Q1
  78. heirs as pages, followed] ~, ~ ~ ˏ ~ Q1;
    Pages followed Q1 Cam., BL;
    Pagesfollowed Q1 Dev.

88. country's] Q5; Countrey Q1

4.4.

18. o'erruled] ouerrulde Q1

33. lord] Q1 (Lo:)

36. not,] ~ ^ Q1

5.1.

0. *Lancaster, Sir*] Ed.; *Lancaster, Earle of Westmerland sir* Q1

10. How] *King.* How Q1

43, 59. Doncaster] Dancaster Q1

89. off] Q1 (of)

121. SD *Falstaff*] Falst. Q1

132. then?] ~ ^ Q1

139. it] Q2; *omit* Q1

5.2.

4. undone] Q5; vnder one Q1

9. Suspicion] Q5; Supposition Q1

14. merrily] Q1 (merely)

28. SD *Enter Hotspur . . . army.*] Ed.; *Enter Percy.* Q1, *1 line earlier.*

95. talking. Only] ~ ^ ~ Q1

98. withal ^ ] ~. Q1

100. Esperance! Percy!] ~ ^ ~ ^ Q1

104. SD *Here . . . sound.*] *run into beginning of 5.3.0 SD in* Q1

5.3.

1. the] Ed.; *omit* Q1

17. won;] ~ ^ Q1

20. This,] ~ ^ Q1

23. A] Ed.; Ah Q1

38. ragamuffins] Q1 (rag of Muffins)

59. SD *him and exits*] this ed.; *him. Exit.* Q1

5.4.

4. SP LANCASTER] Ed.; *P. Iohn* Q1

15. SP LANCASTER] Ed.; *Ioh.* Q1

58. Sir] Q1 (S.)

69. Nor] F; Now Q1

77. SD *who*] F; *he* Q1

83. thoughts,] ~ ^ Q1

89. heart.] ~ ^ Q1

94. thee] Q1 (the)
134. SP LANCASTER] Q1 (*Iohn of Lan*)
158. SP LANCASTER] Q1 (*Iohn.*)
163. The] F; *Prin.* The Q1
163. ours] Q2; our Q1

5.5.        33. SP LANCASTER] Q1 (*Iohn.*)
37. bend˄] ~, Q1

# Historical Background: Sir John Falstaff and Sir John Oldcastle

As we note in "An Introduction to This Text," the character known today as Sir John Falstaff was originally created under the name Sir John Oldcastle. Evidence that Falstaff was once Oldcastle can be found in early printed texts of Parts 1 and 2 of *Henry IV* and in letters and documents from the early seventeenth century. It has long been believed—and there seems little reason to doubt it now—that one of Sir John's descendants, a powerful nobleman in Elizabeth's court, forced the company to rename Hal's companion. This evidence of censorship, along with questions about whether or not Shakespeare was deliberately satirizing Sir John's late-sixteenth-century descendant, have until recently kept scholarly attention focused on the name change rather than on the significance of Shakespeare's having created a comic character bearing the name of a famous proto-Protestant martyr.

While we decided against changing Falstaff's name to Oldcastle in our text (see "An Introduction to This Text"), we agree with Gary Taylor that knowledge about the historical Sir John Oldcastle (known also as Lord Cobham) adds a remarkable complexity to Shakespeare's *Henry IV, Part 1*—a complexity certainly present for Shakespeare's original audience.[1] Oldcastle was a knight who served Henry IV in battles in France and Wales, who was famous for his courage in battle, and who was known to have once been held in high esteem by Prince Hal. At the time Shakespeare was writing his *Henry IV, Part 1*, Sir John's reputation was being hotly debated.[2] Everyone knew that Oldcastle had been put to

235

death in a particularly gruesome manner early in Hal's reign as King Henry V; what was at issue was whether Oldcastle died a martyr as a result of Catholic persecution or whether he was a heretic/traitor whose death was richly deserved.

The story of Hal and Sir John—as told in Holinshed's *Chronicles*, Shakespeare's major source for his English history plays—begins in the *Chronicles'* account of the first year of Hal's kingship.[3] In that year Sir John was accused of heresy against the Roman Catholic church. We know from other records that Oldcastle believed that the Bible should be made available in English for lay people to read, that he did not grant allegiance to the pope, and that he held other religious views that would in later centuries be called "Protestant." At the time, he was called a "Lollard" and a heretic.

When Oldcastle was accused of heresy, the archbishop of Canterbury, knowing Oldcastle "to be highly in the king's favor, declared to his highness the whole accusation. The king first having compassion" for Oldcastle, told the archbishop that Oldcastle could better be returned to the fold of the church through gentleness rather than harshness. The king then sent for Oldcastle "and right earnestly exhorted him, and lovingly admonished him to reconcile himself to God and to his laws."

> The lord Cobham [i.e., Oldcastle] not only thanked him [i.e., the king] for his most favorable clemency, but also declared first to him by mouth and afterwards by writing, the foundation of his faith and the ground of his belief, affirming his Grace to be his supreme head and competent judge, and none other person. . . .

The king at this point sent Oldcastle to the Tower of London—as the *Chronicles* puts it, the king understood and was "persuaded by his council that, by order of the laws of his realm, such accusations touching matters of faith ought to be tried by his spiritual prelates." Soon after, in "solemn sessions" in St. Paul's Cathedral and "in the hall of the Black friars in London," Oldcastle "was examined . . . and fully heard." He was denounced as a heretic by the archbishop of Canterbury and was sent "back again to the Tower of London," from which he escaped.

A few months later Henry was warned that a large assembly of armed men were seeking his life under the captaincy of Lord Cobham.

> [Henry] by proclamation promised a thousand marks to [anyone] that could bring [Oldcastle] forth, with great liberties to the cities or towns that would discover [i.e., reveal] where he was. By this it may appear how greatly he [i.e., Oldcastle] was beloved, that there could not one be found that for so great a reward would bring him to light.

Oldcastle was not captured at this time, but many others were; they were convicted of heresy and treason and put to death by hanging, quartering, and burning. According to the *Chronicles*,

> Some say the occasion of their death was only for the conveying of the Lord Cobham out of prison. Others write that it was both for treason and heresy. . . . Certain affirm that it was for feigned causes surmised by the spirituality [i.e., church officials], more upon displeasure than truth, and that they were assembled [not to kill the king, but] to hear their preacher . . . in that place there, out of the way from resort [i.e., gathering] of people, sith [i.e., since] they might not come together openly

. . . without danger to be apprehended; as the manner is, and hath been ever of the persecuted flock when they are prohibited publicly the exercise of their religion. But howsoever the matter went with these men, apprehended they were, and divers of them executed. . . .

The Hal/Oldcastle story picks up in the *Chronicles* three years later (in 1417), when Oldcastle and his men are sought by 5,000 armed men protecting the lord of Abergavenny against a supposed attack from Oldcastle. Oldcastle's hiding place was discovered and some of his most trusted men captured. Found among his possessions were some religious books

> written in English, and some of those books in times past had been trimly gilt, limned, and beautified with images, the heads whereof had been scraped off, and in the Litany they had blotted forth the name of Our Lady [i.e., the Virgin Mary] and of other saints. . . . Divers writings were found there also, in derogation of such honor as then was thought due Our Lady. The Abbot of Saint Albans sent the book so disfigured with scrapings and blottings out, with other such writings as there were found, unto the King,

who sent the book to the archbishop of Canterbury for the archbishop to exhibit "in his sermons at Paul's Cross in London" so that "the citizens and other people of the realm might understand the purposes of those that then were called Lollards, to bring them further into discredit with the people."

Later in that same year Oldcastle himself was badly wounded and captured; he was charged with heresy and high treason. At that time an assembly was under way in

London "for the levying of money to furnish the king's great charges . . . [for] the maintenance of his wars in France."

> It was therefore determined that the said Sir John Oldcastle should be brought and put to his trial [before] the assembly brake up. [He was] brought to London in a litter, wounded as he was. Herewith, being first laid fast in the Tower, shortly after he was brought before the duke of Bedford, regent of the realm, and the other estates, where in the end he was condemned; and finally was drawn from the Tower unto saint Giles field, and there hanged in a chain by the middle, and after consumed with fire, the gallows and all.

Some editors have argued that Shakespeare chose the name of Oldcastle without thought, taking it from an earlier play about Prince Hal called *The Famous Victories of Henry V*. (In that play Oldcastle, Hal's companion, serves some of the functions of Falstaff in *1 Henry IV*, though he has a much less important role.) Given current awareness of the prominence in Shakespeare's day of the debate about Oldcastle's martyrdom/treachery, it seems unlikely to editors today that Oldcastle was introduced into *Henry IV, Part 1* casually or that the name was chosen carelessly.

While it is impossible to know why Shakespeare chose to portray Oldcastle as a comic figure,[4] it is clear that much of the play has a deeper resonance when one knows Oldcastle's history. In the first place, the play's numerous references to hanging and to the gallows, Sir John's threat to "become a rebel" once Hal is king, his plea that Hal not banish him, and Hal's response "I do, I will," all carry a much more complicated tone. If these moments were present in the Oldcastle version of the play, those in Shakespeare's audience convinced that Oldcastle was a traitor to Christianity and to the king would have found in these moments a special kind of pleasure; for those in the audience who agreed with John Foxe's *Book of Martyrs* that Oldcastle died a courageous if terrible death at his former friend's hand, the moments would have carried instead a somber undertone. Audiences today tend to divide in their responses to Hal and to Falstaff: some see Falstaff as a threat to the kingdom and approve Hal's harsh treatment of the drunken knight in *Henry IV, Part 2* and in *Henry V* (see, e.g., Kenneth Branagh's film of *Henry V*); others find Falstaff human and sympathetic and see Hal as cold and self-serving (see, e.g., the film *My Own Private Idaho*). Awareness of the historical reality of the Hal/Oldcastle relationship can no doubt be used to support either view.

In the second place, awareness of the religious beliefs for which Oldcastle died makes us listen to the language of *Henry IV, Part 1* with new ears. The character we now know as Falstaff is given language heavily dependent on the Bible. In the first scene in which he appears and where his character is established, for example, he echoes Proverbs 1.20 and 1.24 ("Wisdom crieth . . . in the streets . . . and no man regardeth"); he echoes Corinthians 7.20 and Ephesians 4.1 in claiming that "'Tis no sin for a man to labor in his vocation"; he alludes to the hotly debated theological issue of salvation by grace or by good works ("if men were to be saved by merit, what hole in hell were hot enough for him?"); and he exits using the language of prayer found at the close of religious services ("Well, God give thee the spirit of persuasion, and him the ears of profiting, that what thou speakest may move, and what he hears may be believed . . ."). Again, while it is impossible to know how Shakespeare expected his audience to respond if such language issued from the mouth of a character named Sir John Oldcastle, it seems unlikely that the character would have been given biblical and theological language by mere coincidence. At the very least, the language reminds us that swirling around the seemingly timeless comic figure of Falstaff are Reformation controversies still powerfully present in Shakespeare's day.

---

1.   See "The Fortunes of Oldcastle," *Shakespeare Survey* 38 (1985): 85–100.

2.   See Peter Corbin and Douglas Sedge, eds., *The Oldcastle Controversy* (Manchester and New York: Manchester University Press, 1991), pp. 1–33.

3.   The quotations from the *Chronicles* are taken from Raphael Holinshed, *The Third Volume of Chronicles*, 1586, pp. 544, 560, and 561. (These passages are also reprinted in *The Oldcastle Controversy*, pp. 216–22.)

4.   Whatever the changes that may have accompanied the alteration of the name Oldcastle to Falstaff, it seems clear that the Oldcastle character was, in fact, designed to be comic, "a buffoon." In a letter written by Richard James in 1625 and attached to his manuscript edition of *The Legend and defence of ye noble Knight and Martyr Sir Jhon Oldcastle*, we read ". . . in Shakespeare's first show of Harry the fifth [i.e., *Henry IV, Part 1* and/or *Part 2*], the person with which he undertook to play a buffoon was not Falstaff, but Sir John Oldcastle . . ." (printed in *The Oldcastle Controversy*, p. 10; we have modernized the spelling).

# Henry IV, Part 1:
# A Modern Perspective

## Alexander Leggatt

*Henry IV, Part 1* both tells a story and examines a society. The story appears to develop along clear lines to a decisive conclusion. A party of rebels challenges King Henry; his forces defeat them in a single battle at Shrewsbury. Central to this battle is a combat between the rebel leader Hotspur and the king's son Prince Hal, who emerges from the taverns of Eastcheap, where he has apparently been wasting his time, to prove his true worth by killing Hotspur. Various themes come together at the climax, of which the most important is promise-keeping. Sir Walter Blunt warns the king that the rebels are a "mighty and a fearful head . . . /If promises be kept on every hand" (3.2.172–73). Promises, however, are not kept: a number of rebel leaders fail to show up, and the rebel party goes into battle at considerably less than its full strength. Hal, on the other hand, "the Prince of Wales . . . /Who never promiseth but he means to pay" (5.4.42–43), promises his father to redeem his reputation by killing Hotspur, and he does. Seen this way, *Henry IV, Part 1* sounds like a tidy play, a structured action building to a carefully prepared conclusion.

The actual effect is rather different. One large complication is of course Falstaff, the great comic character who dominates the tavern scenes. Falstaff appears at first to fit into the neat story pattern I have been describing: he is the living symbol of what Hal rejects when he leaves the taverns to prove himself in battle. At Shrews-

243

bury there is a telling stage picture as Hal stands over the
bodies of Hotspur and Falstaff, pays a carefully measured tribute to each, and then leaves them lying there,
going off to start his new life having dispatched his great
enemy and seen the last of Eastcheap. Then Falstaff
pops up from the ground; he was not dead at all. It
is a moment that generally gets a startled and ex-
plosive laugh from the audience; it draws on a tradition of comic resurrections in mummers' plays, an
old form of rough popular drama current in England
long before Shakespeare; and it tells us that Falstaff, and what he represents, cannot be disposed of
so easily. When the play was first published in the
quarto of 1598, it was simply *The History of Henry IV*,
with no reference to its being the first part of a two-
part play. But the title page, while advertising the battle of Shrewsbury, also advertised "the humorous
conceits of Sir John Falstaff," and it is Falstaff and his
world, restricted to equal time with the public action
through most of *Part 1*, who break out in a dramatic version of urban sprawl in the sequel, *Henry IV,
Part 2*.

The local effect of some of the political scenes also
works against the general impression of neatness: they
twist and turn. The opening scene seems designed to
get the audience leaning forward, straining to follow.
Henry announces in elaborate and somewhat convo-
luted language the ending of civil strife in England
and the launching of a crusade to the Holy Land.
Then we learn that the crusade will not happen yet
(it never does happen) and that civil strife is still
going on (as Henry evidently knew even while he delivered his speech). On the king's behalf, Mortimer is
fighting Glendower, and Hotspur is fighting Douglas.
But Hotspur is starting to turn against the king, and

before long all these former antagonists will be united in a single rebel front—which will then fall apart. Act 1, Scene 3 takes up Hotspur's refusal to hand over his prisoners to the king. Northumberland claims the prisoners "Were . . . not with such strength denied / As is delivered to your Majesty" (26–27), the implication being that they *were* denied. Hotspur declares flatly, "My liege, I did deny no prisoners" (30), then launches into a vivid and witty set-piece describing the fop who acted as the king's messenger. As the speech develops into a long digression we begin to suspect a cover-up, and our suspicions are confirmed by Hotspur's evasive conclusion that he "Answered neglectingly I know not what— / He should, or he should not" (53–54). In the end Worcester tells Hotspur to free his prisoners. The conflict is taking a more dangerous turn: the real issues have become the king's ingratitude to the Percys, their fear and mistrust of him, and their decision to support Mortimer's claim to the crown. We are also alerted to the fact that the pattern of king versus rebels is not so simple as it looks: Henry was himself a rebel not long ago, taking the crown from Richard II.

The play is full of unreliable narratives: Hotspur's story of the fop, the king's prophecy of the crusade, the Percys' account of themselves as innocent dupes who somehow found themselves supporting Henry's deposition of Richard. Falstaff's tale of the rogues in buckram takes its place among these narratives—except that it is so flagrantly, amusingly dishonest it has a curious kind of integrity. He virtually demands to be challenged by building contradictions into his story: for example, having described what his assailants were wearing, he concludes, "it was so dark, Hal, that thou couldst not see thy hand" (2.4.232–33). When Hal confronts him with the plain facts Falstaff brazens it out with a new and more outrageous lie: "I knew you as well as he that made you" (2.4.278–79). The comic disputes between Falstaff and Hal are partly based on Hal's attempts to confront Falstaff's flow of invention with his own insistence on the facts. Similar disputes occur elsewhere in the play: Hotspur has something like Falstaff's inventiveness, though not Falstaff's control, and Worcester complains, "He apprehends a world of figures here, / But not the form of what he should attend" (1.3.214–15). In his confrontation with Glendower, on the other hand, it is Hotspur who curbs the Welshman's flow, attacking with stubborn literalmindedness his claim of supernatural powers. When the rebels start carving up the map, the tables are turned: Hotspur complains that for his purposes the river Trent is taking the wrong course and proposes to redirect it, while Glendower, pointing to the map, tries to recall him to the plain facts of English geography: "Not wind? It shall, it must. You see it doth" (3.1.110).

The conflict between prolix invention and a terse statement of the facts is acted out in the tavern play, in which Falstaff and Hal, with Falstaff taking the lead, construct their own version of the interview between Hal and his father that will be played quite seriously two scenes later. Part of the fun is a parody of old-fashioned theater: when Falstaff declaims "Weep not, sweet queen, for trickling tears are vain" (2.4.404), the audience would immediately recognize the sort of clunky writing they had heard from an earlier generation of playwrights who allowed themselves to be trapped by the iambic pentameter line Shakespeare himself used with such freedom. But there is also an internal debate between Falstaff's play and Hal's. In Falstaff's, the fat knight is celebrated for his virtue, and whether he is playing the king or Hal, Falstaff invents a future in which Hal banishes everyone but him so that they will have the world to themselves. Hal, on the other hand, takes the opportunity to rehearse in comic terms the devastating attack he will make on Falstaff at the end of *Part 2*, and his reply to Falstaff's request not to banish him is the simple, chilling "I do, I will" (2.4.499).

We might have expected the battle of Shrewsbury to be a test that will show what people really are, no matter how they have presented themselves. Yet it shares some affinities with the tavern play. It is full of impersonation and counterfeiting. Sir Walter Blunt does what Hal and Falstaff do: he impersonates the king. The difference is that he gets killed for it. When Douglas, meeting the real Henry, declares "I fear thou art another counterfeit" (5.4.35), he suggests that the king himself is impersonating the king (as in a way he is, given his dubious claim to the crown). Falstaff briefly impersonates a corpse, fooling both Hal and the audience, and when he goes on to stab Hotspur and then to claim credit for Hotspur's death, he is doing what he did in the tavern play: he is taking over Hal's part. Even the moments in the heat of battle when a character's true nature seems to emerge can be seen as deceptive if we look back from *Part 2*. At Shrewsbury, Hal seems to have shed the Eastcheap world; in *Part 2* he is back in it. Prince John emerges in the battle as a heroic fighter; in *Part 2* he defeats a party of rebels by trickery. Not only does *Henry IV, Part 1* contain some unreliable narratives; at certain points its own narrative is unreliable.

Yet if the battle generates deceptive images, it also

makes us confront that final stubborn reality, death. On the question of honor, Falstaff is a realist. If honor cannot cure wounds or console the dead for being dead, it is worthless. He takes the corpse of Sir Walter Blunt as a practical demonstration of his argument: "There's honor for you" (5.3.35). Hotspur in a way confirms Falstaff's view: no thought of honor consoles him as he dies; death has left him with nothing, robbing not just his own life, but all life, of meaning. One of the play's most eloquent characters, he dies talking; but what he talks of is the failure of his own language—"the earthy and cold hand of death / Lies on my tongue" (5.4.86–87)—and Hal has to finish his last sentence for him.

For Hal, on the other hand, Hotspur's death is the final, decisive evidence of his own emergence as the heroic prince—but once again the play twists. In defiance of what the audience saw with its own eyes, the question is raised, who killed Hotspur? Of course, it is Falstaff who raises it. Before the battle he and Hal argue about who is going to perform this feat, even though we might have thought an encounter with Hotspur would be the last thing on Falstaff's mind. When Falstaff makes his outrageous claim, Hal, as he did with the rogues in buckram, tries to insist on the plain facts, "Why, Percy I killed myself, and saw thee dead," to which Falstaff, speaking (literally) no more than the truth, retorts, "Didst thou? Lord, Lord, how this world is given to lying" (5.4.148–49). What is remarkable is that Hal not only lets Falstaff get away with the lie but promises for once to join him in elaborating it: "For my part, if a lie may do thee grace, / I'll gild it with the happiest terms I have" (5.4.161–62).

What is this play up to? At this point we need to

backtrack to the soliloquy Hal delivers at the end of the first tavern scene, in which he announces his strategy of using his time in Eastcheap to create a misleading impression of his worthlessness so that his emergence as the true prince will be all the more dramatic. The resemblance to image manipulation in modern, media-dominated politics is so uncanny that we need to remind ourselves that Shakespeare is writing from, and about, a political context totally different from ours. The media were by our standards technically primitive, and dealt with contemporary politics at their peril; the kingship of England was not an office depending on popular election. Hal sees himself as playing to an audience, but what audience, and why? There are other plays, notably *Richard II*, *Julius Caesar*, and *Coriolanus*, in which political figures appeal to the common people. This play's focus is somewhat narrower. The clearest representative of Hal's audience is the rebel Vernon, who is surprised and impressed by Hal's appearance at Shrewsbury, falling into just the pattern of response Hal predicted in his soliloquy. Vernon is a member of the governing class. Within that class, as the play shows, people know each other, watch and judge each other. This is the audience Hal needs to manipulate. Hotspur is fooled by the "wild prince" image and fatally underestimates his rival; Vernon is won over even before the battle of Shrewsbury takes place; and King Henry, the key member of this audience, is converted, long before Hal kills Hotspur, by the mere promise that he is going to do it.

Even before the battle begins, then, Hal has won his point with his onstage audience; and when he kills Hotspur no one sees him do it. No one, that is, except the theater audience. Here we touch on a subtle but important difference between Shakespeare's theater and ours. Shakespeare's actors were surrounded by their audience, not stuck in a picture-frame stage. Playing in outdoor theaters in daylight, they were in the same light as the audience; the split produced by the darkened auditorium was an invention of the nineteenth century. This means that in Shakespeare's theater, characters—not just actors, but characters—could have an awareness of the audience and address it directly, as a natural part of the theatrical idiom. When this happens in the modern theater we call it "breaking the fourth wall" and think of it as an experimental technique, a challenge to illusion. In Shakespeare's theater there was no fourth wall to break, no illusion to challenge. When Hal and Falstaff take turns playing the king, Falstaff's "Judge, my masters" (2.4.454) could easily be calling for a verdict from the audience as well as from the onstage characters. The awareness of the audience is more ironic when Falstaff declares, as he stabs the dead Hotspur, "Nothing confutes me but eyes, and nobody sees me" (5.4.129); there are at a rough estimate two or three thousand people who can give him the lie direct. If we think in these terms, then Hal in his soliloquy is not talking to himself or to an undefined space; he is quite simply telling the audience what he is going to do. His onstage audience is satisfied with the mere fact that he has turned up at Shrewsbury; but a theater audience demands action, and it is for our benefit that he kills Hotspur. For this reason he can let Falstaff claim the victory, with an evident sense that he has nothing to lose: the theater audience knows the truth (remembering of course that this "truth" is itself a fabrication, not two heroes in mortal combat but one stage actor pretending to kill another).

There may be more positive reasons why Falstaff is allowed to claim the glory to which he is not literally entitled. I have said that the play does not just tell a story; it examines a society. In story terms, narrowly conceived, Falstaff is a supporting character. In theatrical terms he dominates half the action. In an orderly play, he stands for shapelessness: Hal speculates that if Falstaff's girdle broke, "how would thy guts fall about thy knees" (3.3.161–62). Falstaff's natural environment is Eastcheap, a world mostly untouched by the great events that are tearing apart the governing class of England. If Eastcheap stands for anything, it stands for transgression and inversion: Falstaff's comedy is full of religious parody, Bardolph's nose provokes jests about hellfire. Crime flourishes, mock kings are crowned with cushions, and the regal image of the sun (which Hal in his soliloquy promises to imitate) changes both class and gender, becoming "a fair hot wench in flame-colored taffeta" (1.2.10–11). But Eastcheap is not just a place of parody, for that would ultimately make it dependent on the serious world it mocks; it is also a world in itself, with its own sufficient life. When Falstaff carries off the dead Hotspur, Eastcheap is allowed to claim its own victory.

It is through Eastcheap that we occasionally glimpse a larger England going about its business. The Carriers who open 2.1 complaining about the inn, the stabling, and the fleas are ordinary men doing a job; their modern equivalents would be long-distance truck drivers. Their sheer irrelevance to the political action is the most important point of their scene; there is a whole life going on out there of which the great folks have no inkling.

We cannot say that the court is the center and East-cheap the margin. When we are in Eastcheap the court seems marginal, and vice versa. For us, Eastcheap is a vivid, fully imagined world; the king dismisses it in four words: "barren pleasures, rude society" (3.2.16). Far from trying to harmonize class differences, the play shows a great gulf between one life and another. Nowhere is this clearer than in the depiction of war. Hotspur says of his enemies, whose gorgeous armor Vernon has just described,

> They come like sacrifices in their trim,
> And to the fire-eyed maid of smoky war
> All hot and bleeding will we offer them.
> (4.1.119–21)

Falstaff's recruits, ragged, miserable, half-dead already—"A mad fellow met me on the way and told me I had unloaded all the gibbets and pressed the dead bodies" (4.2.36–38)—show the other face of war. They are not heroic sacrifices but "food for powder, food for powder. They'll fill a pit as well as better" (4.2.66–68).

However, simple dichotomies like court-versus-Eastcheap or Hotspur-versus-Falstaff will not allow us to see the full life of the play. Wales as we glimpse it in 3.1 is a third location, strange and magical, a place of art and enchantment on the borders of the practical daylight world that is England. Admittedly, much of this effect is created by the boasting of Glendower, which is part of his jockeying for dominance over Hotspur, and which Hotspur wittily deflates. Yet when Glendower calls for music, declaring, "those musicians that shall play to you / Hang in the air a thousand leagues from hence" (3.1.231–32), the music actually sounds, and Hotspur comments grudgingly, "Now I perceive the devil understands Welsh" (238). The music is more compelling for being the only nonmilitary music in the play. Equally striking, and more important in the long run, is the simple fact that in this scene, for the only time in this male-dominated play, there are two women onstage. We are allowed (with reservations I will come to shortly) to glimpse yet another sphere of action, the domestic life of the rebels, and the role of women in that life.

One of the key differences between Hal and Hotspur is that Hotspur has such a life and Hal does not. The prince has no home, only the court and the tavern. His one private scene with his father, his "homecoming" in 3.2, is largely given over to the public question of how he is perceived in the political world. Henry allows himself one moment of private feeling, and is ashamed of it, complaining that his eye "now doth that I would not have it do, / Make blind itself with foolish tenderness" (3.2.92–93). Hal presumably had a mother, but we never hear of her. The play's first reference to women is in the opening court scene, Westmoreland's account of the Welshwomen who subject the corpses of dead English soldiers to

> Such beastly shameless transformation
> . . . as may not be
> Without much shame retold or spoken of.
>                         (1.1.44–46)

In the service of antirebel (and anti-Welsh) propaganda, the women are conceived as threatening, demonic fig-

ures, doing (like the witches in *Macbeth*) a deed without
a name. (When we actually see a Welshwoman onstage,
Lady Mortimer, the effect is very different; and the
one character in the play who is shown violating a dead
body is Falstaff.) The only woman in Eastcheap is the
hostess, and she is first introduced as the butt of conventional bawdy jokes about Hal's calling her to
a reckoning; according to Falstaff, "Thou hast paid all
there" (1.2.55–56). The hostess herself, who is trying to
run a business, needs payment of a more practical
kind, and Falstaff puts her off with insulting jokes.
In a comic version of Westmoreland's reduction
of the Welshwomen to monsters, Falstaff says of the
hostess, "she's neither fish nor flesh; a man knows
not where to have her." She walks right into the
trap—"Thou or any man knows where to have me,
thou knave, thou"—and Hal's apparent defense of
her—"Thou sayst true, hostess, and he slanders thee
most grossly" (3.3.135–41)—only compounds the
insult.

Despising the feminine is also part of Hotspur's warri-
or style. Northumberland calls Hotspur's passion "this
woman's mood" (1.3.245), and Hotspur's habitual language seems designed to refute this slur on his manhood. He is offended by the fop's "holiday and lady
terms" (1.3.47) and says of the nameless letter writer
who refuses to join the rebellion, "I could brain him
with his lady's fan" (2.3.23–24). He also works hard to
keep Lady Percy in her place: "when I am a-horseback I
will swear / I love thee infinitely" (2.3.107–8). In the
Glendower scene he makes public jokes about her
sexuality (as Falstaff does with the hostess): "Come,
Kate, thou art perfect in lying down" (3.1.234),
and invites her to what will be their last sexual encounter with the words "An the indentures be drawn,

I'll away within these two hours, and so come in when you will" (3.1.269–71). He is willing to make love, but only after consulting his appointment book. Lady Percy, however, fights back far more effectively than the hostess does, introducing her own distinct perspective on the action. She sees, and cares about, what Hotspur's public life is costing him in terms of sleepless nights and restless dreams, and she speaks to him with a tenderness we hardly ever hear from the men in the play. But she is not sentimental. When Hotspur puts off her demand to know his secrets, she returns insult for insult, calling him "mad-headed ape" and "paraquito" (2.3.82, 90). Knowing he understands "bloody noses and cracked crowns" (2.3.98), she threatens, "I'll break thy little finger, Harry, / An if thou wilt not tell me all things true" (2.3.92–93). In the end he promises to let her follow him a day behind, and asks, "Will this content you, Kate?" Her reply, "It must of force," shows that in the end she has to submit, but she does not have to like it. Her unhistorical name, Kate, recalls the fiery heroine of *The Taming of the Shrew;* but this Kate shows no enthusiasm for being tamed. Her resistance raises at least the possibility of reading her relation with Hotspur as the sort of high-spirited affair that actually thrives on the exchange of ironic insults. Some will find that reading too optimistic; but the point is that the play's depiction of this marriage opens out a range of possible interpretations for both readers and performers, giving it a spontaneity that contrasts sharply with Hal's tight management of his own career.

Lady Mortimer may seem at first to be simply a victim of the male world. She is caught in a political marriage with a man whose language she does not speak. Her own

Welsh speech is a torrent of marvelous-sounding language that neither her husband nor the bulk of the
audience understands; it is her father who relays—and
thereby controls—its meaning. Yet what he conveys
in English, and what she conveys beyond words, in
music and in that language we do not understand,
is an extraordinary range of power and feeling.
Glendower promises that her singing will "on your eyelids crown the god of sleep, / Charming your blood
with pleasing heaviness" (3.1.223–24). She offers,
with a hint of enchantment, the sort of rest Lady Percy
wishes Hotspur could have. She herself is under a spell
of another kind: Glendower declares, "I am afraid
my daughter will run mad, / So much she doteth on
her Mortimer" (3.1.149–50). Passionate, vulnerable,
eloquent yet incomprehensible, able to work enchantment on her husband yet unable to talk to him,
Lady Mortimer is one of the play's most remarkable
creations.

The political action could carry on without the
women; but the play could not. They stand, like
Eastcheap, for the fuller life that cannot be sum-
marized in a narrative or ideological formula. For
the rebels, the England we have seen—lords, com-
moners, women, soldiers, carriers, thieves, men with
red noses—is simply a map to be divided. It is like
watching the realities of war or poverty reduced to
computer graphics. When Hal complains of Francis's
lack of language, we notice that Hal has contrived the
effect himself by playing a trick in which Francis's
attempts to speak for himself are continually interrupted. The play itself does not do this. It lets us listen
to a full range of voices; it fills out the life of England
with an attention to detail we usually think of as novel-
istic. In the tavern, Falstaff calls for "a play extem-

pore" (2.4.291–92)—a play with no script, leaving the actors free to take off on their own. *Henry IV, Part 1* is as carefully contrived a script as Shakespeare ever wrote; yet its most remarkable achievement is to come off sounding like a play extempore.

# Further Reading

## Henry IV, Part 1

Anonymous. *The Famous Victories of Henry the Fifth.* In *Narrative and Dramatic Sources of Shakespeare*, ed. Geoffrey Bullough, vol. 4, pp. 299–343. New York: Columbia University Press, 1975.

One of Shakespeare's sources, this short play is a freewheeling popular treatment of the Prince Hal story that Shakespeare extends across three of his plays, *1 Henry IV*, *2 Henry IV*, and *Henry V*.

Berger, Harry, Jr. "What Did the King Know and When Did He Know It?" *South Atlantic Quarterly* 88 (1989): 811–62.

Berger argues that "speakers should be treated as the effects rather than the causes of their language and our interpretation." He offers a close reading of King Henry's speeches, a reading that emphasizes in the speeches "the pressure of the sinner's discourse and the counterpressure of the victim/revenger's discourse."

Bradley, A. C. "The Rejection of Falstaff." In *Oxford Lectures on Poetry* (1909). New York: St. Martin's Press, 1959.

Bradley considers what an audience is meant to feel at the rejection of Falstaff. Arguing against critical attempts that find Falstaff triumphant or an audience gloating over Falstaff's "just deserts," Bradley reads the event as an insurmountable catastrophe, in terms both of Falstaff's disappointment and of Hal's conduct. Bradley concludes that an audience is at fault if it is surprised by Hal's behavior.

Bristol, Michael D. *Carnival and Theatre: Plebeian Culture and the Structure of Authority in Renaissance England*. London: Methuen, 1985.

Bristol studies the nature and purpose of theater as a social institution, its allocation of authority, and its relation to the plebeian culture of the Renaissance. The burlesque resurrection of Falstaff—a figure of carnival and misrule—engages a persistent plebeian suspicion of authority, one that suspects that it might really be better to be a "live coward than a dead hero."

Burckhardt, Sigurd. " 'Swoll'n with Some Other Grief': Shakespeare's Prince Hal Trilogy." In *Shakespearean Meanings*, pp. 144–205. Princeton: Princeton University Press, 1968.

Burckhardt pursues axes of symmetry in *1 Henry IV* between rebellion and rule, "hot pride and slippery wit, sword-edged honor and fat-bellied self-indulgence." But Burckhardt finds that the play constantly resists neat binaries; just when the play seems about to resolve itself neatly—as Hal stands between the apparent corpse of Falstaff and the corpse of Hotspur—the play reels away toward disorder at the moment of Falstaff's "resurrection."

Campbell, Lily B. "The Unquiet Time of Henry IV." In *Shakespeare's "Histories": Mirrors of Elizabethan Policy*, pp. 213–54. San Marino, Calif.: Huntington Library, 1947.

For Campbell, *1 Henry IV*, in its historical context, is a play about rebellion, but it has become, for us, a play that is memorable mainly for Falstaff and his mockery of honor. Falstaff, with his comic deflation of honor and battlefield conduct, serves as an intruder into the histories, but one who undercuts the workings out of divine justice in the fate of the usurping king.

Greenblatt, Steven. "Invisible Bullets." In *Shakespeare-an Negotiations*, pp. 21–65. Berkeley: University of California Press, 1988.

Greenblatt finds parallels between English incursions into the New World and Hal's course through the taverns of Eastcheap. Like English attempts to subdue native inhabitants of the Americas, Hal cynically relies upon force and fraud to draw his audience toward acceptance of this power. While Shakespeare's Henry plays may confirm this Machiavellian hypothesis about power, Greenblatt questions whether the position of the theater within the state allows drama to raise an alternative voice.

Kastan, David Scott. " 'The King Hath Many Marching in His Coats,' or, What Did You Do in the War, Daddy?" In *Shakespeare Left and Right*, ed. Ivo Kamps, pp. 241–58. New York: Routledge, 1991.

Kastan examines possible relations between the production of power in *1 Henry IV* and in Queen Elizabeth I's England, noting how both monarchs sponsored the ideology of a state unified under their rule. Kastan then goes on to observe how formalist criticism of the play has reproduced this ideology by seeking to unify the play by subordinating its so-called subplot (with Falstaff) while raising to the level of main plot the action featuring the king and, later, the prince—despite the play's resistance to such formalist reading. Thus the play's anarchic organization matches political rebellion, which was such a persistent concomitant to monarchial rule.

Kelly, Henry Ansgar. "*1 Henry IV*." In *Divine Providence in the England of Shakespeare's Histories*, pp. 214–22. Cambridge: Harvard University Press, 1970.

Kelly proposes that if anyone in *1 Henry IV* is presented as receiving divine support, it is Henry IV himself. Therefore, when Henry speaks the *Mirror of Magistrates* maxim, "Thus ever did rebellion find rebuke" (his career being the obvious exception), we are meant to believe that "right has triumphed, and perhaps also to see in it an implicit claim of divine aid."

Mullaney, Steven. "The Rehearsal of Cultures." In *The Place of the Stage,* pp. 60–87. Chicago: University of Chicago Press, 1988.

Tracing Hal's progress through the Eastcheap underworld, Mullaney finds the prince playing at prodigality for the strategic purpose of translating his performance into a profession of power. Similarly, the Elizabethan preoccupation with learning strange tongues and collecting foreign artifacts betrays a culture reformulating itself, as Hal does, through a temporary suspension of cultural limits.

Nye, Robert. *Falstaff.* London: Hamish Hamilton, 1976.

This modern novel presents the memoirs of Sir John Falstaff. Nye's Falstaff's charm is his complete absence of self-consciousness, but only the words of this Falstaff can do him justice: "As for sins and forgiveness of sins—I believe in them both. I'd be a fool if I didn't believe in the former, and I'd be a damned fool if I didn't believe in the latter." Falstaff shares all his sins and commits a gross or two more in the telling.

Porter, Joseph. *"1 Henry IV."* In *The Drama of Speech Acts,* pp. 52–88. Berkeley: University of California Press, 1979.

Applying philosopher J. L. Austin's idea of speech acts (acts performed in speech) to *1 Henry IV,* Porter characterizes the language of the play as lively and active (whether aggressive or playful). Hal's speech acts, in particular, are "directed, communicative, responsible, and consequential." In Hal's language lessons and widely varied manner of speech, Porter discovers a developing mastery of words that assumes greater importance in *2 Henry IV* and *Henry V*.

Saccio, Peter. "Henry IV: The King Embattled." In *Shakespeare's English Kings: History, Chronicle, and Drama*, pp. 37–63. New York: Oxford University Press, 1977.
  Saccio recounts the reign of the historical Henry IV, commenting that Henry's rule came to Shakespeare's hand already possessed of dramatic shape, a shape with a "perceived pattern of historical cause and effect." Although Shakespeare's Henry is forever embattled, attributing all his troubles to his own usurpation of his cousin Richard's crown, the historical Henry's last five years of reign were free of domestic upheaval.

Tillyard, E. M. W. "The Second Tetralogy." In *Shakespeare's History Plays* (1944), pp. 234–314. New York: Barnes & Noble, 1964.
  Tillyard views *1 Henry IV* as part of an epic, a generic classification merited by the play's successful marriage of themes of civil war and high politics to rhythms of local, ordinary life. The coherence of the play's great variety is very different from that of the tragedies but not, for Tillyard, inferior.

Traub, Valerie. "Prince Hal's Falstaff: Positioning Psychoanalysis and the Female Reproductive Body." *Shakespeare Quarterly* 40 (1989): 456–74.
  In a reading of drama through psychoanalysis and psychoanalysis through drama, Traub argues that Shakespeare's drama and modern psychoanalytical theory share in a common estimation of the female reproductive body as a Bakhtinian "grotesque body." Conse-

quently, Shakespeare represses this figure in his narratives of psychic development, although, in *1 Henry IV*, this "grotesque body" is figured in the person of Falstaff, who serves Hal as a sort of surrogate mother.

Van Sant, Gus. *My Own Private Idaho*. Columbia Tristar, 1991.
A modernized film adaptation of *1* and *2 Henry IV*, relocated in the street culture of the contemporary Pacific Northwest. Keanu Reeves plays an updated Prince Hal as the rebel son of Portland's wealthy mayor. He immerses himself in the city's drug- and sex-ridden subculture and keeps company with prostitutes, thieves, and junkies. Chief among his fellow street wanderers are "Bob Pigeon," a translated Falstaff, and a narcoleptic prostitute (River Phoenix) who is searching for a mother figure that Shakespeare's play also lacks.

Welles, Orson. *Falstaff: The Chimes at Midnight*. Internacional Films Española, 1966.
A black-and-white film adaptation of *1* and *2 Henry IV* with fragments of *Richard II*, *The Merry Wives of Windsor*, and *Henry V*. Welles plays Falstaff and stages the story to emphasize and intensify the filial and paternal rivalries that ultimately lead to his character's repudiation by Hal.

# Shakespeare's Language

Abbott, E. A. *A Shakespearian Grammar*. New York: Haskell House, 1972.
This compact reference book, first published in 1870, helps with many difficulties in Shakespeare's language. It systematically accounts for a host of differences between Shakespeare's usage and sentence structure and our own.

Blake, Norman. *Shakespeare's Language: An Introduction.* New York: St. Martin's Press, 1983.
This general introduction to Elizabethan English discusses various aspects of the language of Shakespeare and his contemporaries, offering possible meanings for hundreds of ambiguous constructions.

Dobson, E. J. *English Pronunciation, 1500–1700.* 2 vols. Oxford: Clarendon Press, 1968.
This long and technical work includes chapters on spelling (and its reformation), phonetics, stressed vowels, and consonants in early modern English.

Houston, John. *Shakespearean Sentences: A Study in Style and Syntax.* Baton Rouge: Louisiana State University Press, 1988.
Houston studies Shakespeare's stylistic choices, considering matters such as sentence length and the relative positions of subject, verb, and direct object. Examining plays throughout the canon in a roughly chronological, developmental order, he analyzes how sentence structure is used in setting tone, in characterization, and for other dramatic purposes.

Onions, C. T. *A Shakespeare Glossary.* Oxford: Clarendon Press, 1986.
This revised edition updates Onions's standard, selective glossary of words and phrases in Shakespeare's plays that are now obsolete, archaic, or obscure.

Partridge, Eric. *Shakespeare's Bawdy.* London: Routledge & Kegan Paul, 1955.
After an introductory essay, "The Sexual, the Homosexual, and Non-Sexual Bawdy in Shakespeare," Partridge provides a comprehensive glossary of "bawdy" phrases and words from the plays.

Robinson, Randal. *Unlocking Shakespeare's Language: Help for the Teacher and Student.* Urbana, Ill.: National Council of Teachers of English and the ERIC Clearinghouse on Reading and Communication Skills, 1989.

Specifically designed for the high-school and undergraduate college teacher and student, Robinson's book addresses the problems that most often hinder present-day readers of Shakespeare. Through work with his own students, Robinson found that many readers today are particularly puzzled by such stylistic characteristics as subject-verb inversion, interrupted structures, and compression. He shows how our own colloquial language contains comparable structures, and thus helps students recognize such structures when they find them in Shakespeare's plays. This book supplies worksheets—with examples from major plays—to illuminate and remedy such problems as unusual sequences of words and the separation of related parts of sentences.

# Shakespeare's Life

Baldwin, T. W. *William Shakspere's Petty School.* Urbana: University of Illinois Press, 1943.

Baldwin here investigates the theory and practice of the petty school, the first level of education in Elizabethan England. He focuses on that educational system primarily as it is reflected in Shakespeare's art.

Baldwin, T. W. *William Shakspere's Small Latine and Lesse Greeke.* 2 vols. Urbana: University of Illinois Press, 1944.

Baldwin attacks the view that Shakespeare was an uneducated genius—a view that had been dominant among Shakespeareans since the eighteenth century. Instead, Baldwin shows, the educational system of

Shakespeare's time would have given the playwright a strong background in the classics, and there is much in the plays that shows how Shakespeare benefited from such an education.

Beier, A. L., and Roger Finlay, eds. *London 1500–1700: The Making of the Metropolis.* New York: Longman, 1986.
Focusing on the economic and social history of early modern London, these collected essays probe aspects of metropolitan life, including "Population and Disease," "Commerce and Manufacture," and "Society and Change."

Bentley, G. E. *Shakespeare's Life: A Biographical Handbook.* New Haven: Yale University Press, 1961.
This "just-the-facts" account presents the surviving documents of Shakespeare's life against an Elizabethan background.

Chambers, E. K. *William Shakespeare: A Study of Facts and Problems.* 2 vols. Oxford: Clarendon Press, 1930.
Analyzing in great detail the scant historical data, Chambers's complex, scholarly study considers the nature of the texts in which Shakespeare's work is preserved.

Cressy, David. *Education in Tudor and Stuart England.* London: Edward Arnold, 1975.
This volume collects sixteenth-, seventeenth-, and early-eighteenth-century documents detailing aspects of formal education in England, such as the curriculum, the control and organization of education, and the education of women.

Dutton, Richard. *William Shakespeare: A Literary Life.* New York: St. Martin's Press, 1989.

Not a biography in the traditional sense, Dutton's very readable work nevertheless "follows the contours of Shakespeare's life" as he examines Shakespeare's career as playwright and poet, with consideration of his patrons, theatrical associations, and audience.

Fraser, Russell. *Young Shakespeare.* New York: Columbia University Press, 1988.

Fraser focuses on Shakespeare's first thirty years, paying attention simultaneously to his life and art.

De Grazia, Margreta. *Shakespeare Verbatim: The Reproduction of Authenticity and the Apparatus of 1790.* Oxford: Clarendon Press, 1991.

De Grazia traces and discusses the development of such editorial criteria as authenticity, historical periodization, factual biography, chronological development, and close reading, locating as the point of origin Edmond Malone's 1790 edition of Shakespeare's works. There are interesting chapters on the First Folio and on the "legendary" versus the "documented" Shakespeare.

Schoenbaum, S. *William Shakespeare: A Compact Documentary Life.* New York: Oxford University Press, 1977.

This standard biography economically presents the essential documents from Shakespeare's time in an accessible narrative account of the playwright's life.

## Shakespeare's Theater

Bentley, G. E. *The Profession of Player in Shakespeare's Time, 1590–1642.* Princeton: Princeton University Press, 1984.

Bentley readably sets forth a wealth of evidence about performance in Shakespeare's time, with special attention to the relations between player and company, and the business of casting, managing, and touring.

Berry, Herbert. *Shakespeare's Playhouses*. New York: AMS Press, 1987.
  Berry's six essays collected here discuss (with illustrations) varying aspects of the four playhouses in which Shakespeare had a financial stake: the Theatre in Shoreditch, the Blackfriars, and the first and second Globe.

Cook, Ann Jennalie. *The Privileged Playgoers of Shakespeare's London*. Princeton: Princeton University Press, 1981.
  Cook's work argues, on the basis of sociological, economic, and documentary evidence, that Shakespeare's audience—and the audience for English Renaissance drama generally—consisted mainly of the "privileged."

Greg, W. W. *Dramatic Documents from the Elizabethan Playhouses*. 2 vols. Oxford: Clarendon Press, 1931.
  Greg itemizes and briefly describes almost all the play manuscripts that survive from the period 1590 to around 1660, including, among other things, players' parts. His second volume offers facsimiles of selected manuscripts.

Gurr, Andrew. *Playgoing in Shakespeare's London*. Cambridge: Cambridge University Press, 1987.
  Gurr charts how the theatrical enterprise developed from its modest beginnings in the late 1560s to become a thriving institution in the 1600s. He argues that there were important changes over the period 1567–1644 in the playhouses, the audience, and the plays.

Harbage, Alfred. *Shakespeare's Audience.* New York: Columbia University Press, 1941.

Harbage investigates the fragmentary surviving evidence to interpret the size, composition, and behavior of Shakespeare's audience.

Hattaway, Michael. *Elizabethan Popular Theatre: Plays in Performance.* London: Routledge & Kegan Paul, 1982.

Beginning with a study of the popular drama of the late Elizabethan age—a description of the stages, performance conditions, and acting of the period—this volume concludes with an analysis of five well-known plays of the 1590s, one of them (*Titus Andronicus*) by Shakespeare.

Shapiro, Michael. *Children of the Revels: The Boy Companies of Shakespeare's Time and Their Plays.* New York: Columbia University Press, 1977.

Shapiro chronicles the history of the amateur and quasi-professional child companies that flourished in London at the end of Elizabeth's reign and the beginning of James's.

## The Publication of Shakespeare's Plays

Blayney, Peter. *The First Folio of Shakespeare.* Hanover, Md.: Folger, 1991.

Blayney's accessible account of the printing and later life of the First Folio—an amply illustrated catalog to a 1991 Folger Shakespeare Library exhibition—analyzes the mechanical production of the First Folio, describing how the Folio was made, by whom and for whom, how much it cost, and its ups and downs (or, rather, downs and ups) since its printing in 1623.

Hinman, Charlton. *The Printing and Proof-Reading of the First Folio of Shakespeare.* 2 vols. Oxford: Clarendon Press, 1963.

In the most arduous study of a single book ever undertaken, Hinman attempts to reconstruct how the Shakespeare First Folio of 1623 was set into type and run off the press, sheet by sheet. He also provides almost all the known variations in readings from copy to copy.

Hinman, Charlton. *The Norton Facsimile: The First Folio of Shakespeare.* New York: W. W. Norton, 1968.

This facsimile presents a photographic reproduction of an "ideal" copy of the First Folio of Shakespeare; Hinman attempts to represent each page in its most fully corrected state.

# Key to
# Famous Lines and Phrases

So shaken as we are, so wan with care,
Find we a time for frighted peace to pant
And breathe short-winded accents of new broils
To be commenced in strands afar remote.

*[King*—1.1.1–4]

Before I knew thee, Hal, I knew nothing, and now am
I . . . little better than one of the wicked.

*[Falstaff*—1.2.99–101]

Came there a certain lord, . . . his chin new reaped
Showed like a stubble land at harvest home.

*[Hotspur*—1.3.34–36]

To put down Richard, that sweet lovely rose,
And plant this thorn, this canker, Bolingbroke?

*[Hotspur*—1.3.179–80]

By heaven, methinks it were an easy leap
To pluck bright honor from the pale-faced moon . . .

*[Hotspur*—1.3.206–7]

. . . out of this nettle, danger, we pluck this flower,
safety.                                *[Hotspur*—2.3.9–10]

I am not yet of Percy's mind, the Hotspur of the north,
he that kills me some six or seven dozen of Scots at
a breakfast, washes his hands, and says to his wife
"Fie upon this quiet life! I want work."

*[Prince*—2.4.104–8]

273

Thou seest I have more flesh than another man and
therefore more frailty.        [*Falstaff*—3.3.176–78]

What is honor? A word. . . . Honor is a mere scutcheon.
And so ends my catechism.        [*Falstaff*—5.1.135–42]

But thoughts, the slaves of life, and life, time's fool,
And time, that takes survey of all the world,
Must have a stop.        [*Hotspur*—5.4.83–85]

The better part of valor is discretion . . .
        [*Falstaff*—5.4.122]

# NOW AVAILABLE—THE FOLGER LUMINARY SHAKESPEARE IOS APP

**An interactive reading experience that enriches the Folger Shakespeare edition.** Explore the digital edition of the gold-standard play text.

**AVAILABLE NOW:**

HAMLET  MACBETH  OTHELLO  ROMEO *and* JULIET  *A* MIDSUMMER NIGHT'S DREAM

**Coming soon:** *Richard III* and *Julius Caesar*

## INTERACTIVE FEATURES:

Folger Luminary SHAKESPEARE

### Audio
- Includes a full-length audio recording of the play performed by professional Shakespearean actors.

### Learning Tools
- Richly annotated image galleries, videos, and multimedia enhance the reading experience.

### Commentary
- Includes short, accessible commentaries on key moments in the play written by the world's leading Shakespearean scholars and performers.

### Connect
- Publish private commentaries within the app and on devices of students and colleagues.

- Take and share notes using student groups or social media.

To find out more and see a demonstration of the app.
Visit **Pages.SimonandSchuster.com/FolgerLuminaryApp**

Download on the App Store